# The King's Honor & the King's Cardinal

## *The War of the Polish Succession*

John L. Sutton

THE UNIVERSITY PRESS OF KENTUCKY

To
# JACK E. FREEMAN
*Soldier, scholar, administrator*

**Library of Congress Cataloging in Publication Data**

Sutton, John L   1917–
    The King's honor and the king's Cardinal.

    Bibliography: p.
    Includes index.
    1. Polish Succession, War of, 1733–1738.   I. Title.
DK4326.5.S95      943.8′02      80-51021
ISBN 0-8131-1417-9

Scholarly publisher for the Commonwealth,
serving Berea College, Centre College of Kentucky,
Eastern Kentucky University, The Filson Club,
Georgetown College, Kentucky Historical Society,
Kentucky State University, Morehead State University,
Murray State University, Northern Kentucky University,
Transylvania University, University of Kentucky,
University of Louisville, and Western Kentucky University.

*Editorial and Sales Offices*: Lexington, Kentucky 40506

✠

CONTENTS

✠

# PREFACE

The War of the Polish Succession has long been a part of the furniture of European history courses. It must be mentioned if only
to account for the period from 1715 to 1740 and because it was a
general European war. But one usually gives it a few words of
recognition and then passes on, presumably to bigger and better
things. I was drawn to examine it more closely when it occurred
to me that in a century noted for—sometimes applauded for—
limited warfare, this war was perhaps the best example of all and
yet has been given the least attention by historians. I can find no
work devoted to it in the major languages of Western Europe. I
saw it also as a case where the two superpowers of their day,
France and Austria, had come into conflict once again but, with
unusual care on both sides, had managed the struggle so as to
cause no mortal injury to either. This was accomplished despite
the participation of almost all the continental powers great and
small, including the emerging states of Russia and Prussia. I also
became aware that particularly in English the events of the war
were thinly treated in historical works, perhaps because England
did not participate directly in the conflict. And some of the specific crises of the war—the French attempt to lift the siege of
Danzig, for example—are little known. A European historian of
very wide knowledge admitted that the story of Count Plélo was
unknown to him.

Beyond the broader aspects of the war and its meaning to the
eighteenth-century balance of power, the diplomatic and military conventions of the time were significant, and they were observed with great care in the War of the Polish Succession. These
were restraints which, with some exceptions, kept the war within bounds. The men who exercised these restraints—Cardinal

Fleury, Prince Eugene, Horace Walpole, for example—were interesting individuals and I sought to know what dialogue, official and unofficial, passed among them in the course of the fighting and the negotiations.

In Paris, Vienna, and London (the sequence reflects the amount of time spent in each) the people of the archives, diplomatic and military, were unfailingly helpful. William H. McNeill and Owen Connelly read parts of the manuscript and encouraged me. The University of Pittsburgh at Johnstown granted me a semester's leave to finish the work. My wife and the editor of this volume picked out many inconsistencies and cloudy passages. For those which remain and for the work as a whole I must accept the responsibility.

✣

CHAPTER ONE

# A Problem of Succession

On a day in the last week of August 1733, six horsemen left the
great castle of Chambord in the Loire Valley of France and took
the road to Brittany. Five of the men were obviously an escort for
the sixth, whom they treated with great respect and addressed as
"Your Majesty." The escorting riders understood the sensitivity
and importance of their mission, for they had been told that
they were to accompany Stanislas Leszczynski, the father-in-law
of King Louis XV, from his estate at Chambord to a rendezvous
with the French fleet which would take him to Poland. Stanislas
was addressed as royalty because he was the former king of
Poland, who had been hustled off his throne by the Russians
some years before and replaced by a German prince. But on 1
February that prince had died, and the elective Polish throne
would be vacant until a king was chosen by the Polish nobility
and gentry. All Europe waited to see whether France would back
Stanislas as a candidate against the solemn warnings of the Russians and the Austrians. Frenchmen talked of the honor of the
Bourbon house at stake. The Poles had called a Diet of Election
to convene in late August. Could or would Stanislas present himself in Warsaw?

There were many rumors. According to one, the exiled king
was already secretly in Warsaw; another had it that he was crossing Prussia by permission of the king of Prussia; a third that he
was preparing to arrive at the port of Danzig with a French naval
escort. The Russian ambassador in Warsaw reported the rumors

to his capital and recommended using any justification to arrest Stanislas on the Baltic Sea.[1]

In Paris the British ambassador, Lord Waldegrave, had been watching for any move that might indicate a French fleet moving into the Baltic with Stanislas. He was aware that the ships were ready at Brest, but in June thought it rather "remote" that the French would send Stanislas to Poland.[2] Other observers in France were watching too and were promptly aware of a meeting on 22 August between Stanislas and French Foreign Minister Chauvelin at Versailles. One of these observers noted in his diary that after the meeting Stanislas departed Versailles, dined at the chateau of Meudon nearby, and left for Brest.[3] Some days and hours later Stanislas was seen embarking on the Brittany coast where a French fleet was at anchor. A salvo of cannon was fired. The fleet commander, the marquis de La Luzerne, welcomed him on board and the fleet sailed for the Baltic. The horsemen who had escorted him to Brittany must have felt satisfied that they had accomplished their mission.

But all was not as it seemed. Stanislas did not sail away at high tide with the French fleet. It was not even Stanislas who went to Brittany and was seen boarding a ship. While the five horsemen were galloping westward toward Brittany with their charge, the real Stanislas was rolling rapidly eastward in a German-style vehicle with three trusted companions.

Stanlislas had indeed met with Chauvelin on 22 August and had left for Chambord, possibly dining at Meudon as well. But on the way he was diverted to the estate of a Cardinal Bissi where a Commander Thianges appeared, a man similar in appearance to Stanislas. Thianges put on Stanislas's clothes and continued the trip to Chambord. It was he who, the next day or day after, left for Brittany with an escort who thought he was King Stanislas.[4]

Chauvelin had arranged it all, perhaps with old Cardinal Fleury—the first minister of Louis XV—looking over his shoulder with some misgivings. As early as 22 March, Chauvelin wrote to the governor of Alsace, Marshal Du Bourg, asking that trusted officer and personal friend of Stanislas to look into ways by which Stanislas could leave the country in secret. Money for secret expenses was set aside, and the special German-style vehicle, a *chaise à deux allemande,* was procured by Du Bourg and sent to Paris; Chauvelin queried Du Bourg on the strictness of border inspections in the German states next to France and advised that two passports would be needed under the names of George Baur and Ernst Brauback, German businessmen traveling with two domestics.[5]

Stanislas had lived through enough adventures when he lost his throne many years before and was unhappy about crossing Europe incognito. But there was no way out, and he was driven away acting the part of a private secretary to his traveling companion, the chevalier d'Andlau, an Alsatian who spoke fluent German. Chauvelin was even afraid there might be some backsliding on the part of Stanislas when in cryptic terms he alerted the French ambassador in Warsaw, the marquis de Monti.[6]

The journey began at ten o'clock this evening with one person accompanying and two valets de chambre for the principal traveler. They will avoid Mainz, Frankfurt, and Kassel, and expect to join the main highway from Wesel to Berlin at Münster. At Frankfurt on the Oder they will conform to the arrangements which you have made. The principal traveler seems very hesitant about the possibility of learning at Frankfurt that the Russians may be in Poland. It is for you to determine his progress by the news you will give him.

Stanislas arrived safely in Warsaw, and the secret of Commander Thianges was kept until he reached Copenhagen with the fleet. Here La Luzerne learned that the real Stanislas had reached Warsaw.[7] It was an operatic finish when Stanislas on 10 September revealed himself in Warsaw in the company of Monti, ready to be elected once again as king of Poland.

The German prince whose death as king of Poland brought about the journey of Stanislas to Warsaw was Augustus II, elector of Saxony. The news of his death on 1 February 1733 came to a Europe that had been largely at peace since the Treaty of Utrecht in 1713 and the death of Louix XIV in 1715. The workings of a system based on a balance of power had emerged more clearly during the series of alliances and wars that had prevented Louis XIV from achieving a French hegemony over Europe. Constantly shifting alliances and treaties, with a more limited form of conflict, would keep this balance until the French Revolution at the end of the eighteenth century.

The reaction of the great powers to the news from Poland varied. England was not greatly concerned. She had no candidate, and her ministers had said on more than one occasion that Poland was a faraway place. As the leader of the victorious coalition against France that led up to Utrecht, she had since enjoyed the fruits of trade with the continent and maintained a naval and diplomatic presence from the Mediterranean to the Baltic to stabilize her authority. Two sensitive and possibly vulnerable points remained, however, which suggested caution to the English Whig leadership. First the Stuart Pretender lived on the continent with his court and had contact with Tory supporters in Parliament. He could be thrown into the balance by the French if they wished to gamble on some form of intervention or an invasion of the British Isles. Could he be a candidate for election to the throne of Poland? James Stuart was a Catholic of royal blood with a Polish wife—he could not be ruled out. The second matter of sensitivity was the continental holding of the Hanoverian kings, namely the Electorate of Hanover. As hereditary elector of Hanover, George I had ruled as an autocrat in his German dominions—something he could not do in England—and he spent a large part of his time in Germany. His son, George II, king since 1728, was more reassuringly English. But Parliament had reason for disquiet at the thought of the English monarch and executive head of the government as possessor of a state that was an integral part of the Holy Roman Empire, and potentially hostage to a strong military power on the continent. William Pitt, later in the century, would speak critically of the "Hanover rudder" in British foreign policy. As far as England was concerned, let the Baltic and the German states remain quiet, and the port of Danzig remain open, and the Poles might have any king they desired, excepting of course the Pretender, and if it did not unduly benefit the French.

Austria, imperial Austria, was a more concerned observer of

the Polish scene. Austria had a border with Poland, and information on the various contenders for the throne was carefully collected and analyzed in Vienna. The emperor had reestablished leadership over the German states after Utrecht, although his influence over the larger states, such as Saxony, was diminishing as these took on more the character of modern sovereign states. Augustus II had been too friendly with France; his death promised a chance to bring Saxony back to a more subservient position. It was not to the advantage of the emperor to see any German prince enjoy the additional dignity of a Polish crown, although he had been forced to tolerate it up to this time. His control over even the hereditary lands of the Habsburg family— as opposed to those states which recognized him only as a kind of overlord whose authority emerged during war—was administratively weak. The great nobles tended to live on their estates unmolested by the government in Vienna, a condition which became crucial when the emperor found himself unable to raise funds for his army. And, perhaps not surprisingly in this century of dynastic struggles, Austria too had a succession problem. Emperor Charles VI had no male heir and wished to guarantee the passing of his holdings in undivided form to his eldest daughter, Maria Theresa. There is something strangely naïve in the effort, drawn out over many years, to exact written agreements to what was known as the Pragmatic Sanction from the courts of Europe. Treaties were broken as readily in those days as today. But it was a single-minded policy of the emperor that continued until his death in 1740.

So the emperor watched the Polish situation carefully, partly for fear of marauding bands entering his lands during the chaos of an interregnum, and partly because he wished to control, or at least approve, the succession. He must be assured that it did not favor his ancient enemy the house of Bourbon in France, and he had a tentative agreement with the Russians on a successor prince. He wanted a foreign prince, a non-Pole, who would not provide too much leadership for the various Polish factions.

Even faraway Spain and Portugal were not indifferent to the Polish succession. Spain resented the loss of her Italian appanages in the settlement of Utrecht and was probably the most dissatisfied of the major powers. To an extraordinary extent this discontent was centered in a single person, Elisabeth Farnese, queen of Spain as the second wife of Philip V. From the ruling house of Parma, Elisabeth had come to Spain in 1714 and soon had three sons for whom she sought kingdoms. Philip's son by his first marriage was expected to succeed to the throne of Spain, and Elisabeth set out with great energy to reverse the dictate of Utrecht and recover the Italian provinces for her sons. So at this time the appearance of a vacant throne could not be overlooked as a possibility for the Spanish princes, and Spanish representatives were ready to test the diplomatic waters in eastern Europe when the moment came.

In Portugal there waited a prince who believed himself chosen by the major powers in the East to be the next king of Poland. The emperor had convinced the Russians during the previous year that a Portuguese prince was the best answer to the expected Polish succession problem, and the tentative agreement was in effect as Augustus II lay dying. Prince Emmanuel of Portugal was ready to make his money contribution to the Polish magnates and accept the crown.

Other states in Europe had played lesser roles in the active diplomacy of the first part of the eighteenth century, but they were alert as to how they might profit from the succession in Poland. Saxony would hope to keep the Polish throne in the hands of its ruling house and possibly make it hereditary. Prussia, on the other hand, had no desire to see a rival German state increase itself and would block this as far as possible.

Sweden had seen her client king of Poland, Stanislas Leszczynski, driven from the throne by the Russians and replaced by Augustus II before the end of the Great Northern War in 1721. Sweden hoped for a restoration of influence in Poland but no longer had the will or resources to counter the growth of Russia, which was seeking, physically and spiritually, a way to the West. In the southeast, the Turkish Ottoman Empire, not yet the sick man of Europe, still held the Balkans and had a border with Poland. The Turks acted as a counterweight to policies the Austrians undertook in the West, a fact that French diplomacy frequently exploited. At this time, however, the Turks were beset by the Persians and would be unable to act against either Russia or Austria.

France had been keeping the closest watch on events in Poland, although seeking—not very successfully—to conceal her attention. Stanislas, living comfortably as the father-in-law of the king of France, had insisted more than once that he was content to forget his former kingship. But there were many in high positions in France who felt that his eventual restoration was necessary for the honor and glory of his daughter and for the house of Bourbon. It was assumed by all that France would make some move when the succession was open.

France had emerged from the wars of Louis XIV somewhat chastened although not truly diminished in power. But the death of the Sun King had left a void in leadership, for he had acted as his own first minister, and his successor had been a five-year old child. His son, grandson, and one great-grandson in line for the throne had all died within a four-year period. The second great-grandson, the infant Louis XV, survived, although he was destined to remain an indifferent executive. This lack of strong political leadership was to be a mark of French policies for most of the century while the country went on to assume the unquestioned intellectual leadership of Europe.

Since 1725 France had been allied with England against a strong Spanish-Austrian plan to reduce vastly her place in Europe. But Spain was shifting back toward an understanding with France. Cardinal Fleury, the young king's tutor, came to power in 1726 and carefully avoided antagonizing either England or Spain. Already over seventy years old, patient and pacific by nature, he nevertheless possessed the shrewdness to cling to his position until his death in 1743.

The beginning of 1733 had seen a relatively quiet Europe. Dissatisfaction in Spain had been given some relief by provision for Spanish succession in several Italian duchies; British trade was unhampered; Cardinal Fleury and his counterpart in Britain, Robert Walpole, seemed to understand that neither sought war. But the death of Augustus would set some of the old tensions in play once again. There were no heated exchanges, no appeals to the masses, no patriotic statements, no undue haste; but the machinery of the sovereign states of Europe was in motion and some adjustments must be made. Eventually military action would ensue.

When military force was applied to effect or hasten these adjustments, it tended to be a stylized and limited form of conflict. Scholars have commented on the decline of military violence after the religious wars of the seventeenth century and the reemergence of large-scale sanguinary conflicts in the French Revolution. It can be argued that since the French Revolution, national wars on a great scale have become the standard. The unpleasantness of their ferocity and destruction has been balanced by a more appealing justification of their objectives. Contrariwise, if one considers the limited conflicts of the eighteenth century, the terms "mercenary forces" and "dynastic wars" come to mind with mildly distasteful overtones. Neither the instruments nor the objectives of such wars were truly admirable by nineteenth- or twentieth-century standards. War in these latter centuries became a matter too serious for mercenaries; everyone could and must participate in it. Nor was it fought for capricious sentiments of dynastic pride, but for reasons that governments tied closely to the national well-being and the interests of every citizen.

The War of the Polish Succession may have been the most typical of eighteenth-century wars, a kind of model for the cautious and restricted warfare of the time. It cannot be termed insignificant, because it was a struggle among the great powers of Europe, with actions in Poland, the Rhineland, and Italy, and it resulted in significant changes in the political map of Europe. But military historians of recent decades have found it, by their standards, a spiritless conflict and have given it scant attention. Delbrück, for example, in his multivolume history of warfare, apparently found in it little relevance to his theory of military history and barely mentioned it.[8]

The mass citizen army is indeed the great military manifestation of the national state. The citizen of today is expected to approve it in principle and to feel a proprietary participation. It was not so in the first part of the eighteenth century. The army was still the king's army, and an army commander writing to his sovereign did not speak of the victory or defeat of *my* army, nor of *our* army, but of *your* army, sire! This would change. Lee Kennett, in his study of the French army in the Seven Years' War (1756–1763), noted that from the mid-eighteenth century, officers spoke of service to "the state" or to "the nation."[9]

The War of the Polish Succession may have a meaning as a turning point, a kind of nadir of military activity, where an old formal system of warfare dominated aging players, who moved with increasing slowness, like gladiators in slow motion.[10] At the same time one could see in the background that new players were preparing for a more zealous exploitation of military conflict for the future. The War of the Austrian Succession, which began in 1740, and the Seven Years' War were taken far more seriously and were appropriate forerunners to the military explosion of the French Revolution and Napoleon.

✠

CHAPTER TWO

# The Commitment to War

The interest of France in the Polish throne was both dynastic and strategic; in addition it reflected a somewhat curious emotional preoccupation for France during a period of more than a hundred years. At the end of the Jagellon dynasty in the sixteenth century the kingship of Poland became elective, and its first elected king was a Frenchman, Henry of Valois, younger brother of King Charles IX of France, acclaimed by the Polish nobility and gentry in a mass electoral meeting in 1573. Henry stayed in Poland only a few uncertain months before he fled back to France to succeed his brother as Henry III. But a precedent had been set, a sympathetic tie established. Whether this elective kingship (in contrast to the hereditary divine-right monarchies of most European states) and the representative machinery associated with it held any real attraction for the French is questionable, although one German historian asserts that the guarantee of a free election was an eternal bond with France.[1] Whatever the cause, there does seem to have been a bond, for in 1697 a serious attempt was made to place another Frenchman on the throne of Poland. The prince de Conti, supported by France and by a goodly outlay of money, sought success in an election, but this election went to the elector of Saxony, the same Augustus II of Poland whose death in 1733 set the diplomatic gears of Europe in accelerated motion.

The strategic implications in the possession of the Polish crown by France may be more obvious now than in the eighteenth century. The geopolitical aspect, reinforced with accurate maps, is very persuasive today, whereas the dynastic aspect is less easy to credit as a real motivation. The possibility of securing a sphere of influence geographically behind or above the core of Habsburg power in central Europe was well worth careful consideration. In their long conflict with the emperors of the Holy Roman Empire the kings of France were continually attempting to build power and influence among the German states between Paris and Vienna. If the Austrians could be occupied with matters farther east, so much the better for the French. The emperor would then have less time to give to his affairs in the Austrian Netherlands, in Italy, or even in the German states of the Empire. (By the "Empire" is meant the Holy Roman Empire; in effect the empire of the German people in the German states, then numbering some three hundred, *das heilige römische Reich deutscher Nation*.) To press the Habsburgs back to the east was a conscious objective of French strategy. French statesmen in 1733 could hardly forget that Charles VI a few years earlier had thought of himself as the rightful king of Spain, a potential successor to the rule of Charles V whose lands had encircled France on three sides. The War of the Spanish Succession was on the whole a check to French aspirations, but it forced Charles to give up the title of king of Spain. For whatever meaning one chooses to give it, the Spanish ceremonial customs prevailed at the court in Vienna despite the acceptance of German and French as the working languages, and a so-called Spanish party was identified in court circles.[2]

Moreover, while French officials did not provide a clear view of long-term strategy in their statements, they must have regarded the growth of Russia with uneasiness. It has been suggested that French diplomacy at this time sought to construct a barrier against Russia, consisting of Sweden, Poland, and Turkey.[3] Of course these countries, especially Turkey, could also be used and had been used as weights, active or inactive, in the balance of power against the Habsburgs. To a great extent it depended upon the amount of money that could be spared to secure their tenuous support at any given moment.

Finally, whatever the positive value of staking out a distant sphere of influence, it could also impose a danger. The support of a distant friend, particularly one unable to master his own

affairs, could be expensive and onerous and require commitments of power in areas far from home. The French government would soon have occasion to reflect on this point.

But there were other than strategic considerations involved.
The dynastic element must be accepted with all seriousness in
the statecraft of the eighteenth century. The king of France had
quite obviously married beneath himself. It was probably the
best that could be arranged at the time by a court that trembled
over the possible extinction of the direct Bourbon line. The
young king must be married as quickly as possible. A painful crisis with Spain had occurred in 1725 when the little Spanish princess selected as the bride of Louis was sent back to Spain, but she
was too young and the matter of heirs to the throne was pressing. Marie Leszczynska was the daughter of a king, although a
deposed one, and she appeared fecund. Her father, Stanislas,
had been king of Poland from 1705 to 1709 under the strong
protection of Charles XII of Sweden. When that Scandinavian
warrior-king was defeated, Stanislas lost his throne to Augustus
II, from whom he had taken it to begin with. After the marriage
of his daughter to the king of France he had shown little desire
to return to Poland. But the French had contingency plans.

At this time foreign-policy decisions of the French government were taken by a Council of State dominated by Cardinal
Fleury.[4] Marshal Villars, the old soldier of the War of the Spanish Succession, reported most of the meetings of 1733 in his
memoirs. The discussions reflected the eagerness of the old ser-
vitors of the Bourbon house to recover the glory of the Bourbon
court they had known under Louis XIV. Accordingly, they
wished to correct the mésalliance of their king by restoring his
father-in-law to active kingship. But Cardinal Fleury intuitively
sought peace with France's normal rivals and was less than eager
to leap into the adventure of securing a throne for Stanislas. In
the first council meeting after the death of Augustus was known,
that of 11 February, the cardinal approached the problem gin-
gerly, asking whether Stanislas had abdicated this throne in
1709. Others, including of course Villars, assured him that there
was no abdication. In the meeting of 18 February Villars advised

that Stanislas should go to Danzig immediately and the Poles should be informed that his confirmation would be worth money to them. Fleury's more cautious attitude prevailed, however, and Stanislas remained, for the time being, in France.[5]

Whatever Fleury's reactions at the time, the French had already spent considerable time and effort preparing for the vacancy on the Polish throne. Detailed instructions were given in 1729 to the new French ambassador to Saxony and Poland, the marquis de Monti. He was advised how to proceed in sounding out future support for the exiled Stanislas and told that he should have a plan ready.

The Austrians were aware that there was a "French party" in Warsaw among the Poles and they could not remain neutral to it. The question was how far Vienna would go in opposing Stanislas. Once the French saw their candidate actively opposed, they had to assess the spirit and strength of this opposition and either withdraw gracefully or bring pressure upon the emperor. They had not long to wait for a clue to the emperor's determination. In the council meeting of 1 March, Villars noted that the dispatches from Vienna showed that the emperor was doing all that he could to block Stanislas and to reach an understanding with Tsarina Anna on this question. The French were not in a mood to yield, however, and by May their determination was demonstrated by a council decision to make some preparations for war. The secretary of state for war was charged with preparing memoranda on provisions and artillery depots. As Villars put it, war was decided upon in spite of the cardinal.[6] Actually, war was not a foregone conclusion; first there would be a busy period of diplomacy for the French as they sought allies.

It is not easy to allocate motives among the French leaders as they moved closer to war. Villars seems to have thought in dynastic terms. Fleury probably would have abandoned the entire project had he dared. The marquis d'Argenson, an observer close to the court who would himself become the foreign minister in a few years, felt that the situation allowed France to use it as a pretext for a bold attack upon the emperor and his holdings. In particular it would permit France to "pulverize the Pragmatic Sanction," that agreement by which Charles VI sought to secure for his daughter's inheritance of his Habsburg lands.[7] But the national existence of France was not at stake, the strategic benefits to be gained were speculative, and France made no claim to additional territory. Only the dynastic factor was clear.

André Hercule de Fleury, bishop of Fréjus, had been brought to the court at Versailles as the boy-king's tutor and there won his cardinal's red hat. He also won the king's confidence, which he never lost, for after the failure of the ministry of the duke of Bourbon in 1726, Fleury was entrusted with the powers of a first minister for the remainder of his life. The brilliance and aggressiveness of the marquis de Chauvelin—effectively the minister for foreign affairs, although generally known by his title of keeper of the seals—sometimes led one to believe that he was managing the old cardinal, in 1733 in his eightieth year, but this is simplifying the relationship. It may be that at times Chauvelin seemed to have the upper hand over the cardinal, yet the ultimate resolution of this rivalry—if it was a rivalry—showed the strength of the cardinal. He dismissed Chauvelin in 1737.

Argenson during the early thirties spoke of "our two first ministers," meaning Fleury and Chauvelin.[8] The nineteenth-century historian Driault acknowledged the power of the cardinal to dispose of Chauvelin, whom he believed to have been greatly wronged, and seemed to agree with Argenson that the crime of Chauvelin was to have made the cardinal jealous. But Driault saw Chauvelin as the active aggressive spirit in French foreign affairs and Fleury as a timid old man who was forced to surrender his powers temporarily to Chauvelin in order to surmount crises. In his memoirs, Count Maurepas, secretary of state for the navy in 1733, speaks in one place of Fleury as being ruled by his counselors and in another of his making decisions despotically. Chauvelin's influence over the cardinal was assessed as considerable by the English and as basically anti-English. Horatio Walpole, a brother of Robert and ambassador to France from 1723 to 1730, spoke of Chauvelin as a "most treacherous, false and ambitious spirit, but at the same time, of an assiduous, supple, dissembling and sinuating disposition, where it was his interest to please."[9]

Dangervilliers, the secretary of state for war, was in a secondary class as minister, along with Maurepas. Maurepas maintained that Dangervilliers was only a kind of secretary to Fleury and Chauvelin. On another occasion he referred to Dangervilliers as a clairvoyant blind man ("aveugle clairvoyant").[10] Few personalities come off well in the Maurepas memoirs—Berwick is an exception—but it is probably true that Dangervilliers made few policy decisions even though his hand is often seen in the drafting of dispatches and in marginal notes on incoming messages. The envoy from the court of Lorraine in France wrote to his duke on 25 January 1734 that Chauvelin had taken one of the secretaries from the military department and was occupying himself with all the military affairs. "This makes M. Dangervilliers very unhappy and it is believed that he may well resign."[11]

It is not entirely clear how Chauvelin felt about the Stanislas candidacy as such, but there is no doubt of his bitter and aggressive attitude toward both Austria and England. There are some indications that Chauvelin at first favored the candidacy of the elector of Saxony in order to maintain the French treaty with that court, which represented a German state that had not yet seen fit to sign the emperor's all-important Pragmatic Sanction.[12] But he doubtless saw very quickly the impossibility of standing against the dynastic factor involving the king's immediate family, and his active support of Stanislas appears in council meetings shortly after the news of the death of Augustus II. Evidently neither Chauvelin nor the cardinal liked the "forced situation" of February 1733, but Chauvelin's energy in pursuing the war tends to discount any reports that he ever seriously considered another course of action.[13] It is only that what we know of him suggests that he was the official in France most likely to question the values behind the support of Stanislas for what were demonstrably reasons of family pride. Probably, like Argenson, he accepted the Stanislas candidacy as a pretext for action that could later be directed elsewhere.

Chauvelin's personal papers have not been found, and without them our view of him as a policymaker and as a man is partly obscured.[14] Argenson, in his journal, seems to have despised him, admired him, disliked him, and considered him his best friend—at different times. And Argenson's wry comment has clung to him: "He travels underground, like a mole." Driault, in his article praising Chauvelin, observes: "There are few examples in our history of such an active campaign as that which filled the last months of 1733; one detects a plan rigorously and energetically pursued."[15] The searching memoirs, the drumfire of messages to the ministers abroad, all support this conclusion. Chauvelin represented the national statesman of the future rather than the dynastic servitor of the Bourbons, whatever his relation to the cardinal.[16]

England was an ally, and had been one since France had perceived the menace of the 1725 Madrid-Vienna alliance in the First Treaty of Vienna. But France had less and less need for her ally, and the forced friendship was wearing thin. In retrospect it is an odd little moment of peace between two long-term rivals. The War of the Polish Succession would be a step toward terminating this alliance.

As France moved toward an active policy on the Polish candidacy, her ministers sought to know the attitude of the London government without giving away too much of their own intentions. Behind all the French dealings with England was the cherished belief that sooner or later England would be seriously weakened by internal strife arising from the reluctance of many Englishmen to accept the Hanoverian dynasty and its Whig government. In January 1733, Chavigny, French ambassador in London, reported the low esteem in which the king of England was held. "The hate and scorn which pursue him have no limits."[17] Chauvelin evidently was somewhat of the same mind when he confided to Chavigny his opinion that a war for England would mean internal revolution. They are trying, said the French minister, to prevent any breakdown of relations with Austria and Spain, and they are in the position of compromising either the states of Hanover or the commerce of the nation. "It may be the moment to strike decisive blows." [18] Despite this confident statement from Versailles, Chavigny's initial instructions from Chauvelin following the death of the king of Poland advised caution. Chavigny was reminded that when the French "union" with England was formed, the English had indicated that they would be agreeable to a restoration of King Stanislas and would even participate in the expenses of a Polish election. But, he admits, this good will may have been effaced. Make no *démarche*, said Chauvelin, we do not yet wish to declare what we will do. [19]

For about a month there was polite diplomatic sparring, the English murmuring that Poland was a very distant area for them to worry about and the French content to talk of other matters. Chavigny said he had to be dragged to the subject. After a conversation with Lord Harrington he wrote, "the more I back away the more he pursues me." [20] This changed in mid-March when a declaration of Louis XV was sent to the courts of Europe committing France to the protection of a free election in Poland. When Harrington was read the declaration by Chavigny, he noted the affirmative quality of the wording and admitted that the "play might become more serious than he had thought." When he asked whether, in case France acted offensively, she would move in the Lowlands or in Germany, Chavigny replied that he did not know, but "for every man the emperor moves on the borders of Poland we will move ten where they are needed." After a few additional remarks the dialogue ended, obviously on a strained note. [21]

But Chavigny had gone too far. In a 2 April message Chauvelin pointed out his errors in unmistakable terms ending with the remark that it does not become a great power to threaten. Paul Vaucher expresses the opinion that Chauvelin himself thought the English could be intimidated; the sudden change of tone, Vaucher believes, represented the old cardinal entering the scene and modifying the French attitude. [22] In any event a penitent response came back from Chavigny. It was less a threat than a confidence that Harrington had drawn ("extorqué") from him, he said. [23]

Chavigny's opposite number in Paris, the English ambassador Lord Waldegrave, showed far less concern. On 23 February he sent his superior the duke of Newcastle half a dozen pounds of truffles with the possibly ambiguous remark that "it is all that can be found in Paris fit to be sent." On 11 March he briefly noted that there was stirring on the Polish election matter and that a visitor had come from Poland to see Stanislas. But Waldegrave continued unflappable, directing most of his messages to Delafaye in the Foreign Office with the observation that there was nothing worth troubling the duke about. Regarding naval preparations, he wrote in June: "I know of none besides those often mentioned, of the four men of war to go to the Levant and the three at Brest which some day are to carry King Stanislas if he is chosen."[24]

By midyear the French must have felt the English gravitating toward the Austrian side and became more insistent about an understanding. Chauvelin directed Chavigny to seek specific answers from the king and sent a set of questions to put to the monarch. Newcastle told Chavigny that George II would see him with pleasure and on 6 July the audience took place. The king denied that England had agreed to support the emperor at all costs but took refuge behind such observations as his certainty that the emperor would not force an election in Poland, that Poland was a distant place for England to make decisions on possibilities, that the whole affair was not worth a war, and that, in any case, he could not speak for the tsarina.[25]

After reading the report of the 6 July meeting, Chauvelin concluded that the English would not take a position but that France must consider the courts of Russia, Austria, and Saxony as solidly against her.[26] It was not the best reaction from the English, which would have been a strict neutrality, but it was not the worst, which would have been outspoken support of the emperor.

In Paris, as the attitude of the French became firmer, Waldegrave still did not believe that it would come to war. On 12 August he dined at the cardinal's with Marshal Berwick before the latter left to take command of the French Army of the Rhine. "From the looks of both I cannot think they are yet in earnest. What may come from the acts of others, is not to be penetrated, but from appearances it is hitherto but a sham fight. . . . If they do anything at all it will be in the way of insults to the Emperor, bombard Luxembourg, and block it up for the winter."[27]

The events that were to take place in Poland, dramatic as they would be, and essential as they were to set the larger scene in motion, constituted only a kind of sideshow or operatic scene. The truly important events must occur in the West. The armed clash between the two major powers of Europe—France and Austria—could not take place in Warsaw or Danzig. Impoverished though he was by a lack of administrative control of his realm, the emperor had too many advantages in eastern Europe. France must challenge him in the West.

But the emperor could not be attacked directly across the Rhine except in a few imperial fortresses, such as Breisach, Kehl, and Philippsburg, or the fortress city of Luxembourg. An invasion across the Rhine into what is today the Federal Republic of Germany would have been an attack, or at least an occupation, of several independent principalities, and the French would become willy-nilly the bully to drive them individually and collectively to seek the protection of their emperor. At first glance the emperor appeared vulnerable in his possession of the lower half of the Netherlands, but a French attack there could not be tolerated by the English or the Dutch, the so-called sea powers.

The long-term opposition of the French to Habsburg pretensions is reflected in a French memoir entitled, "Means to Use against the Emperor." It is basically a French effort to find the best means to pick and pry at the rickety framework of the Holy Roman Empire. It is dated November 1733, when the war had already begun but before its course and extent were clear.[28] First the memoir considers the case of Prussia.

It is certain that the king of Prussia is now very displeased with the emperor and the tsarina and that he is incensed by the treaty which has been concluded at Vienna with the elector of Saxony. We think that it may be possible to engage the king of Prussia in a neutrality agreement and have him agree to hold all the troops he can on the borders of Brandenburg and Magdeburg. By this troop disposition the king of England

would be obliged to keep his state of Hanover armed, the elector of Saxony likewise, and the emperor would not be able to release some of his
troops in Silesia.

The French have found a sensitive spot here. The English
ambassador in Vienna believed the aggressive attitude of the
king of Prussia toward the state of Hanover was mainly due to
the intrigues of Count Seckendorff, the Viennese representative
in Berlin. "That odious man," wrote Robinson from Vienna, and
set about trying to effect Seckendorff's removal, in which, incidentally, he had a limited success.[29] To continue with the French
memoir:

The animosity awakening now between the house of Hanover and Prussia on the subject of the administration of the Duchy of Mecklenburg, to
which the house of Prussia has the right of succession by family pacts, is
known to be well founded. We may profit from this by a treaty of neutrality in assuring the king of Prussia that he need not worry about some
suitable arrangement for the states of Berg and Jülich. We can also let
him hope that, in the case that France achieves complete superiority, we
may consider accommodating him with two bailliages in Silesia. . . . In
case we can bring this prince into the war it appears that the king of
Poland might try to get the senate to cede him Thorn, Elbing, and Mar-
ienburg, provided that he would engage on his side to procure for the
crown of Poland the reunion of the provinces of Smolensk, the Ukraine,
and Courland, which the Russians have taken from Poland.

It was an interesting attempt to find sensitive pressure points
involving the growing Prussian power. Unfortunately for the
French, the king of Prussia would finally support his emperor
more firmly than the French had hoped and make his contribution of troops to the army arrayed against France. But the memoir goes on:

The Swedes may also join this alliance to retake Livonia, Ingria, and Es-
thonia. We do not believe that the elector of Saxony, the Russians, and
the emperor can oppose them considering the strong diversion we will
make against the emperor in Italy and on the Rhine.
    The house of Hesse has always been attached to France but appears

now closer to England. However, if we present to Prince William of Hesse an objective that flatters his ambitions, and if he may hope to become king of Sweden, or even to place his son on that throne, we believe that he may be swayed. . . .

We do not doubt that France is assured of the neutrality of some electors, including Palatine and Cologne and much more so the elector of Bavaria, in case events furnish him the means to act without exposing him to the loss of his states.

The memoir goes on to list some of the lands that could be given to Bavaria and notes that when the other princes of the empire see the above states allied with France or neutral they will not make a great effort for the emperor. Finally, the memoir suggests that by means of presents the grand visier of Turkey may be brought to hold a greater proportion of his troops on the frontiers of the empire, thus causing the emperor to put fifteen or twenty thousand additional men in Hungary. The Turks probably will not attack the empire at this time but, concluded the memoir hopefully, they might well attack the Muscovites, whom they scorn.

So much for a French memoir seeking alternative actions against the emperor on the east. It was somewhat inventive but not very practical as things turned out. But if the French could not easily get at the emperor in central Europe or in the Lowlands, the emperor was definitely vulnerable in the South.

In Italy the emperor enjoyed possession of the city of Milan and the rich province around it, the Milanese, as well as the kingdoms of Naples and Sicily. Tuscany, Parma, and Piacenza were held by Spain. The only native power in Italy, apart from the Papal states, was the kingdom of Sardinia, which occupied the Piedmont and Savoy. With its capital at Turin, it was governed by the dukes of Savoy, who had recently upgraded themselves to kings by acquisition of the island kingdom of Sardinia. If the French were to damage the emperor they must do it in Italy, and, since the Piedmont separated the French from the emperor's lands, an alliance with Sardinia was the one the French must have before beginning any serious military operations.

France also counted on Spain, but there was almost no doubt of Spanish support. The Spanish, after all, could not go over to the Habsburg side, because they could only be gratified in their desire for recovery of lands in Italy by despoiling the emperor. The king of Sardinia, on the other hand, was less obviously tied to a single course of action. He had reasons to fear the Spanish as much as the Austrians, and he might suddenly find a solution in Vienna if he were not properly satisfied by Versailles. He was also the head of the family of which Prince Eugene of Savoy, the leading official and soldier of the Habsburg regime, was a member. Charles Emmanuel, king of Sardinia, must take a deep breath before signing a treaty with the French.

So the French were at a significant disadvantage negotiating with the court in Turin, particularly because they were eager to engage in military operations in northern Italy during the latter part of 1733. As time slipped by during the summer they became increasingly impatient. But the kingdom of Sardinia, as a small power located at that point where the interests of three major powers converged, had a great deal to win and possibly more to lose. Sardinia hoped to expand into the Milanese. The French, in their original negotiating position, used a proposal that would be copied more than a hundred years later by Napoleon III—namely, to offer the Milanese to the king of Sardinia who, in turn, would surrender Savoy to France. Both times, of course, the French were offering something which they did not possess and would have to take by force.

In order that the French ambassador in Spain should appreciate the problems of his colleague in Turin he was sent a message on 23 June 1733 which outlined them briefly. The memoir of Ambassador Vaulgrenant in Turin to Ambassador Rottembourg in Spain was roughly as follows: at first the king of Sardinia wanted only the Milanese and we asked for several states for the Infant (Don Carlos, eldest son of Philip V of Spain and Elizabeth Farnese, and since 1731 ruler of Parma). We were finally reduced to not insisting on Savoy and asking only the Lodisan and the Cremonese for the Infant. However, the king has shown that he is sensitive to the emperor's continued possession of the fortress of Mantua. This may be used to bargain for Savoy and for additional territory for the Infant. The king does not want the emperor in that area. On the other hand he is fearful for the growth of the house of Bourbon in Italy and knows that the power of the emperor there can restrain it.[30]

As the summer wore on, the French found the king and his minister Ormea content to move with exasperating slowness. In June, Ormea complained to Vaulgrenant that the queen of Spain was deceiving them both and negotiating with the emperor to put one of her sons on the throne of Poland.[31] This accusation was probably intended to elicit information or to divert attention for no negotiations are known to have taken place. But Rottembourg had reported in March that the Duke of Liria suggested the crown of Poland for the Infant and that a negotiator had left the court in Seville for Poland.[32] Doubtless all possibilities, even the more remote, were examined to find employment for the queen of Spain's offspring.

On 6 July more urgent instructions arrived from Versailles. Chauvelin suggests reminding the king that he has nothing to fear from the emperor's dispersed armies. Then, in language more conversational in tone, he adds: "He wants the Milanese, well, we will separate it from our just claim to Savoy." It was a considerable concession. But at least try to get them to yield on the Cremonese, begs the minister. "Faites le traité au plus simple," goes on the instruction, ticking off the points: establish an alliance, promise the king the Milanese, promise to act in concert, work out the aid the king desires.[33]

But it was not as easy as the ministry seemed to believe. Ormea explained to Vaulgrenant that Sardinia was not ready to act as rapidly as France would prefer. It is your concern with Poland that presses you, said Ormea. But he wondered whether the advantages that would accure to the son of the queen of Spain would be sufficient to engage the king of Spain and the Spanish nation to observe the treaty. Amid the coming changes in the Spanish monarchy, "What are our guarantees?"[34]

Ormea had reason to wonder. The Spanish monarchy was dominated by a termagant queen and a neurotic king who for days and weeks would refuse to communicate, or bathe, or even cut his fingernails, and who had once abdicated in favor of a son who later died. The possibility of another abdication was ever present at the Spanish court. Moreover, the agreement sought by the French would not be a triple alliance; Sardinia would have an agreement only with France.

And there was the question of money. On 2 August the French council discussed the demands of the Sardinians—namely, a 4-million-livre loan and 500,000 livres per month in subsidies. One million livres was to be paid immediately.[35] Vaulgrenant was told in a 3 August message that the king would be paid the one million if he would be ready to enter the campaign, although the ministry observed that the subsidies were much higher than those paid in 1696 and 1701.[36]

The French were now showing more impatience and the Sardinians were coolly aware of it. On 8 August, Vaulgrenant complained that he had been unable to see Ormea for fifteen days.[37] Perhaps the king and Ormea knew that on 28 June the French council had discussed which projects could be carried out against the emperor without the alliance of Sardinia and found it an unsatisfactory list.[38]

Vaulgrenant was pessimistic in his 12 August communication with the ministry, but the Sardinians must have felt that they had pushed the French as far as they could and that it was time to come to terms, for as of 15 August things began to move.[39] In effect the king of Sardinia was willing to accept the French loan and subsidy amounts and agreed to contribute 12,000 men. These articles came out in the 23 August draft treaty, which also stipulated that Sardinia would get all the Milanese, that there would be no separate peace, and that the combined army would be under the command of the king of Sardinia. In secret articles it was agreed to attack the emperor in Sicily and Tuscany as well as in the Po Valley.

Although it was necessary to "conciliate" several points in the treaty, and this dragged on for another month, the Sardinian court seemed to expect the French to perform instantly after the agreement in substance. The French were moving as rapidly as they could, and it must have been not a little exasperating to be first delayed by Sardinian tactics and then prodded to hasten by the same people. Dilatory tactics of the king of Sardinia delayed the signing until 27 September, yet on 30 September, at a public function, Ormea whispered to Vaulgrenant that he was disappointed at the slowness of the French plan for introducing troops into Italy.[40]

The agreement with Sardinia was the last major requirement for French plans for the action against the emperor with military force and the French did not commit themselves, in Italy or Germany, until it was achieved. Cardinal Fleury was a cautious man.

The Habsburg court was disappointed if not shocked to learn of the French-Sardinian treaty. The English were likewise surprised and disappointed to see Italy once again open to a French army. Perhaps, as has been suggested, England was badly served in Turin by the eccentric Lord Essex.[41]

As previously noted the French were less worried about the support of Spain. As early as June 1732 the queen of Spain had told the French ambassador, "If you begin the war we give you our word that we will follow with all our forces."[42] In the spring of 1733 the French ambassador in Seville was duly assuring his government that there was no sign of a treaty by Spain with Vienna or London.[43] But it probably was not reassuring to the systematic French to recall that a great part of the diplomatic reporting from Spain was, and had been for years, concerned with the state of the king's health and his unstable behavior. Negotiations with Spain lasted until nearly the middle of 1733. On 31 May the king of Spain wrote his nephew the king of France that he had empowered his ambassador in France to sign the treaty.[44] Presumably this was the message that was read before the French council on 28 June, after which, according to Villars, they were able to proceed with preparations for war.[45] From this time onward Spain, and especially the queen, pressed for war, while at the same time showing fear that the emperor might lay hands on the relatively unprotected state of Parma and the Infant Carlos. Doubtless the Spanish court felt that an early attack by France provided greater security for Parma than a long-drawn-out period of negotiations. The French answered the queen that they were resolved on war, and indeed they were.

In all, what has happened? The French have taken the initiative to precipitate a war, is the simple answer. Only ripples would have appeared on the surface of European political waters had the French government made only a pro forma claim for Stanislas. But France made alliances and other preparations for war and, in effect, dared the emperor to oppose Stanislas in Poland. France at the outset of the war sought no territorial gains and apparently foresaw none. The immediate cause of the conflict was dynastic.

Of course one may believe that the real motivation behind French actions was a master plan in the mind of Chauvelin to reduce the power of the Habsburgs, the case of Stanislas serving only as a pretext. The later treatment of Stanislas admittedly supports this view. Driault saw it all as an effort to rework the balance of power in southern Europe—to drive the Austrians out of Italy and set up a tier of states between France and Austria. These states were to include Bavaria, Sardinia, and probably new creations in Italy that would be dependent upon France for their existence. Given French moderation, he argued that this would remove the great danger of Austria.[46]

Whether one wishes to advance the strategic or the dynastic factors as paramount, there were reasons for moderation. Two important reasons were Cardinal Fleury and Robert Walpole, neither of whom wanted war. In the nineteenth century nationalist historians of their respective countries found them sadly wanting in zeal. Nevertheless, in the fall of 1733 the potentialities for a long and bitter general war were present. And yet *this* war did not get out of hand. With military operations in three areas quite distant from one another, and with most of the powers of Europe involved in one way or another, the war would still remain a limited struggle—a king's war, not a people's war.

✠

CHAPTER THREE

# The Habsburg Position

The fact that Augustus II, as king of Poland, held a throne from which he had deposed a ruler who subsequently became the father-in-law of the king of France did not automatically mean that his relations with France were strained. Nor did the fact that Augustus, in his role as elector of Saxony, was an integral part of the Holy Roman Empire mean that his relations with his emperor were particularly close. The Saxon prince, in his capital at Dresden, was one of the stronger members of the Empire, and he had maintained as much independence from the Habsburg court as he dared. This independence could be achieved only with French support. Further, Augustus as king of Poland was also concerned with the treaty of 1726 between Austria and Russia, which weighed heavily upon the courts of eastern Europe until the French Revolution. The government of Poland, despite its Saxon monarch, has been described as a kind of Russian-Austrian condominium against the national party in Poland.[1] But the idea of a dismemberment of Poland was already current in the first half of the eighteenth century, and the nations that were to carve up the failing state were already eyeing their respective portions in advance. One countermove that had been considered by Augustus was a Saxony-Bavaria accord with France. This had been discussed with French Ambassador Monti in Dresden.[2] Another effort, apparently an initiative of Augustus, was a November 1732 proposal to Berlin that the constitution of Poland be overthrown and Poland be made a monarchy under his house—elective still, but with the understanding that it re-

main in the Saxon house of Wettin. Under this arrangement
both Prussia and Austria were to acquire parts of Poland.[3] This
was never agreed upon, however, and the death of Augustus
changed matters. Prussia and Austria did not wish to drive the
new elector of Saxony into the arms of the French. He had in-
herited the electorate of Saxony but it was probable that he
would need Austrian support to gain the elective throne of Poland. It was a situation that might well permit Vienna to rein in
an overindependent German sovereign and bring him to what it
considered a proper relation to his emperor.

This is why only a week after the death of Augustus II,
Bussy, French chargé in Vienna, reported that the Habsburg
court saw the death of the king as a favorable event and that they
believed the house of Saxe would break all engagements with
France. Further, he reported that Austria would oppose the
Stanislas party in Poland with the help of Prussia and Russia, although imperial troops would not be sent into the border area of
Silesia until contact had been made with Berlin and Saint Petersburg.[4] Bussy's quick estimates of the situation were generally
correct, but the development of the Habsburg position on the
matter of the Polish succession was not a foregone conclusion,
nor was it achieved overnight.

In Vienna the affairs of state were still mainly in the hands of
the great field commander Prince Eugene of Savoy. As chairman
of the Privy Council (*Geheime Conferenz*) and of the War Council
(*Hofkriegsrat*) he had exercised both military and civil authority
since the Treaty of Utrecht with, however, some ups and downs
in the extent of confidence bestowed upon him by his emperor,
Charles VI. He had enormous influence throughout Europe, especially among the princes of the empire, and his carefully chosen ambassadors reported back to him from the courts of Europe.
These were often men who had served in military campaigns with
him and owed him their personal allegiance.

But "der edle Ritter" as he was affectionately called, was in
failing health. Diplomats began to comment on his increasing in-
ability to shake off coughs and "catarrh" and had even begun to
question his powers of concentration. He continued to chair the

councils, to receive the intimate notes in the emperor's hand, and to send the emperor his considered opinion on decisions of state, but there was increasing evidence that his reliance upon his secretary Ignaz Koch was extreme. More important still, in terms of the shifting of influence at the Habsburg court, was the increasing reliance the emperor placed upon the young state secretary, Johann Christoph Bartenstein. This very able Strasbourg native had risen rapidly in the imperial service in Vienna and had been since 1727 the secretary of the Privy Council (*Protokollsführer*). He would be the last challenger of the influence of Prince Eugene upon his sovereign, and ultimately his challenge would succeed. Bartenstein's preparation of briefings and dispatches placed him, along with Ignaz Koch, at the apex of the Habsburg decision-making machinery.[5]

The early months of 1733 following the death of Augustus II required unusual activity on the part of the government in Vienna. Bartenstein's briefings with their marginal notes in the emperor's hand, the notes of the secretaries taken during council meetings, and the diplomatic correspondence, both Austrian and foreign, emanating from Vienna reflect a mood of caution and indecision at the Habsburg court.

The detailed briefing of 5 February 1733, which Bartenstein prepared for the emperor and the Privy Council, suggests that he was prepared for the death of the king of Poland and had his material well in hand. He began by stating that the news of the death of the king arrived early that same day from the minister in Warsaw, Count Wilczek. Luckily, he added, Wilczek understood what had been agreed upon with Russia and Prussia and had guidance for the moment.[6]

It is true that the succession question had been threshed out among the three powers during the previous year and a treaty signed in Berlin was in process of ratification when the king of Poland died. It provided for the exclusion of the French party in Poland and for the stationing of troops on the border to "protect the freedom of the Polish election from foreign influence." A secret article provided for 36,000 ducats to be used to further the election of the Infant Emmanuel of Portugal, and in a second secret article Russia agreed to see that the second son of the king of Prussia was chosen duke of Courland when the reigning duke died.[7]

Bartenstein's briefing continued, noting that Stanislas was, of course, among the "excludeds." There was some concern that he might be chosen immediately by acclamation but it was hoped that jealousy among the Polish factions would prevent this. The new elector of Saxony, the son of Augustus II and the man who would eventually become king of Poland with Russian and Austrian help, was also at this time among the excludeds, if unofficially. "He has spoken against Your Majesty and your house in such a way that it is not possible to trust him." He had been poorly prepared by his father, added Bartenstein, but it was better not to bring out a specific exclusion against him, for this would only turn him toward France and Bavaria. The court should speak only of excluding Stanislas and preserving the free election and not outwardly acknowledge opposition to the elector of Saxony. The emperor's hand appears in a short marginal note approving this attitude.

Then the "includeds" are considered, beginning with the Infant of Portugal, who has been the presumptive choice of the emperor in recent months. Bartenstein advised caution here and to be prepared to accept another candidate in case the Infant were not successful. He then listed the possible candidates: the two princes Wiesnowicki, Crown Grand Marshal Mnischek, Prince Sangusko, Prince Lubomirski, and the palatin of Kiev, Joseph Potocky. He found none of these candidates worthy of strong support and then turned to the means to be used. What he called the "media prima classis" consisted of the 36,000 ducats which were to be drawn from the bank and sent to Wilczek immediately. Secondly, troops were to be sent to the Silesian border, and thirdly, a precise understanding between Austria and Russia must be maintained—a matter in which there were some unsatisfactory items. The proposed instructions to the ministers in Warsaw, Berlin, and Saint Petersburg were attached as rescripts, noted Bartenstein, and he asked for his emperor's approval. The emperor had made approving marginal notes throughout the document and at the end he gave his approval once more and directed Bartenstein to forward all, along with the money, as rapidly as possible.

England's ambassador in Vienna, Thomas Robinson, seems to have been very promptly informed of the decision and he reported to London the departure of the courier with instructions and money for Warsaw. He also noted the departure of couriers to Berlin and Saint Petersburg to ask the Prussian and Russian governments to advance troops to the Polish borders.[8]

The agenda notes taken during the meeting of the Privy Council on 22 February do not reflect any actions taken, although Prince Eugene, and counts Sinzendorff, Starhemberg, and Königsegg were in attendance. But the French chargé in Vienna had already reported on 11 February that the first order to nine imperial cavalry regiments had gone out and they were to be ready to march to the borders of Poland and Silesia. On 14 February he reported that the War Council had sent the second order to the troops, along with 600,000 florins needed to put them in condition to march on the third order.[9]

On 23 February Bartenstein gave Charles VI another long and detailed briefing on the Polish situation.[10] He noted that new information had come from Warsaw and began with the problem of estimating the support Stanislas might have and the means available to frustrate his candidacy. According to Bartenstein there was no longer a danger of a declared succession based on the original election of Stanislas in 1705, but a no less dangerous situation was developing in that the approaching Polish Diet meeting, the so-called Convocation Diet, called for 27 April 1733, would not be the usual assembly of nobles on horseback (*Reichstag zu Pferd*) but would include a great number of lesser landowners (*Landbotten*), who were generally favorable to Stanislas. There were also reports of a secret design by which they might proceed to the election of a new king at that time.

The policy Bartenstein proposed was a difficult one to carry out as he and the emperor must have realized. In essence they called for a free election, while at the same time seeking to prevent one, for a truly free election would obviously go to Stanislas. It was not as logically contradictory as it appears at first glance, because the imperial position was that Stanislas was constitutionally disqualified by the solemn proceedings attending his loss of the throne in 1709. But it was a difficult position to explain.

Yet it does not seem to have been too difficult to explain to their English allies. The English did not blink at the Austrian concept of free elections. Harrington told Robinson: "You need make no scruple of assuring the imperial court that His Majesty approves most entirely their resolution promoting a new and free election and endeavoring to make the choice fall on such a person who may be unexceptionable both to the Polanders and to neighboring powers." Harrington added that the English resident in Warsaw had "the most positive orders to act in perfect concert with the ministers of the Empire," and went further to state that England did not wish to displease the French by open opposition to Stanislas and would thus confine the resident in Warsaw "to a secret and underhand opposition."[11]

But to go back to Bartenstein's briefing, he declared that it was not yet time to settle upon a candidate, nor to disclose intentions toward the Infant of Portugal or the elector of Saxony. A proposal by Prince Lubomirski, the palatin of Cracow, to form a confederation in greater Poland, he saw as a favorable development, although Lubomirski's desire to use 900 imperial troops to assist him was to be rejected. The possibility of James Stuart's becoming a serious candidate did not seem either in the English or Habsburg interests but, he asked, should we bring it up humorously with the English ambassador just to be sure there is nothing in the idea?[12] (Harrington's message of 20 March and other messages from the English court made it clear that support of the Pretender would have been considered a slap in the face of the English sovereign.) The emperor approved the briefing.

His Imperial Majesty in Vienna then received a message on 16 March signed by His Christian Majesty, the king of France, declaring that France would overlook the movement of troops already made by the emperor but that France would support the liberty of election in Poland. A similar message was sent to French embassies in other countries for communication to these governments.[13] The importance of this declaration must not be underestimated. It was a statement declaring support by the strongest power in Europe for a principle, and it involved the king's own family. The implication that military force would be applied if necessary was inescapable, and it undoubtedly raised the hopes of supporters of Stanislas in Poland, perhaps more than was justified. The declaration brought forth from the emperor a reply that by virtue of the *pacta conventa* Austria had for two centuries maintained the freedoms of Poland. Further, the emperor noted that he was not obliged to give an accounting of his troops in Silesia, a hereditary state.[14]

The declaration of Louis XV had no noticeable effect upon the Austrian court. But rumors moved rapidly, and in Warsaw the Russian minister heard that the imperial court was in a "terreur panique" over a report that a 12,000-man Swedish army in French pay was ready to be used in support of Stanislas.[15]

The difficulties for the Habsburg court in the Polish question continued to be reflected in the meetings of the Privy Council. The notes taken in the meeting of 23 March give us a view of Prince Eugene as chairman listening to the views of his three colleagues, Sinzendorff, Starhemberg, and Königsegg. All of them find it difficult to accept the elector of Saxony but realize that they are gravitating in this direction for lack of a better position. Starhemberg and Königsegg are willing to accept the elector but want his acceptance of the Pragmatic Sanction and a binding alliance as conditions. Sinzendorff seems to have had the greatest difficulty in accepting even the notion of another elector becoming a king. But he also wondered whether, if the elector succeeded without the emperor's help, this would not be even worse.[16]

On 6 April a meeting of the same participants found them still baffled. They were now aware, and somewhat reassured by the knowledge, that the members of the Polish Diet had decided not to try to proclaim Stanislas king at the Convocation Diet in April, but they were frustrated by the need to respond to the diverging position of their allies Russia, Prussia, and England.

Meanwhile the Saxon court was active. In March the elector sent two ministers to Vienna with a personal letter to Charles VI requesting his assistance in attaining the Polish throne and promising loyalty in the strongest terms. The Habsburg historian

Arneth suggests that the acceptability of the Saxon approach was greatly improved by the fact that the new elector appeared to be a much weaker man than his father and would not understand how to use the crown of Poland to attack the hereditary lands of the emperor.[17] But apparently the court in Vienna was not immediately convinced of this, and on 23 April the Privy Council was still discussing the position to be taken toward the Saxon ministers.[18] The hatred of the king of Prussia for his rival the elector of Saxony and some delay in communications with the Russians had put the Austrian court in an embarrassing situation. Bussy, the French chargé in Vienna, reported this mixup with an obvious satisfaction, noting that as late as 1 April the Saxon ministers had had no conference with the imperial ministry.[19]

It was in the meeting of 23 April that the members of the Privy Council mentioned an item that would be of great importance in the outcome of the war, yet one that occasioned relatively little discussion in the diplomatic correspondence of the major powers involved. This was the matter of Lorraine. Although the transfer of Lorraine to France would represent the last sizable addition of territory to the French royal house, and would represent a mortifying loss to the duke of Lorraine, this matter was seldom mentioned until the peace negotiations began to take form in 1735. Did the Habsburgs fully realize that when the duke married the Habsburg heiress Maria Theresa and became emperor of the Holy Roman Empire they could not incorporate the territory of Lorraine into a Habsburg-Lorraine dynasty? Britain and Holland would frown and French territory almost completely surrounded the area. Were the Austrians resigned to this unpleasant fact and did they for this reason simply push it to the background of their discussions?[20] In this meeting, however, during a discussion of relations with Holland, it was advanced, presumably by Prince Eugene, that Lorraine was of great importance for France and that France would probably bring out new conditions involving the duchy. Some weeks later, on 8 August, the French chargé in Vienna reported that Count Starhemberg was convinced that France wanted war regardless of Poland and that the real reason was the impending marriage of the duke of Lorraine.[21] These statements are the exceptions. Still, in spite of the limited direct references it must be assumed that all sides were aware of the importance of this exposed province.

So much for the reaction of the government in Vienna to the immediate succession problem—that is, how to deal with the elector of Saxony and the other candidates for the Polish throne. Now, while the French sought new allies with some success, the Austrians were forced to examine their standing alliances, and with less success.

The Habsburg formulation of a diplomatic position was demonstrably more difficult than that of the French. The latter decided what they wished to do and simultaneously sought allies. The court in Vienna found that it could not take a position without the concurrence and support of its allies and was forced to reconsider its policies continuously. Although the extensive Habsburg holdings and the Holy Roman Empire, laid out on a map, suggest a great power dominating Italy and central Europe, the emperor's hereditary lands actually constituted a beleaguered dynastic state with uncertain allies, faithless imperial liegemen, and inadequate preparation for conflict with the strongest power on the continent.

The English alliance was the most important for the emperor. But the days when Marlborough and Eugene were comrades-in-arms against the French may have led the Habsburg court to expect too much of England. Although there was strong sentiment at the English court to support Austria, the government of England was firmly in the hands of Robert Walpole, a man who was as willing to restrain the hawks on his side of the Channel as the cardinal was in France, and, for the time being at least, was meeting with more success.[22] Even the obvious readiness of George II, king of England and elector of Hanover, to offer himself as a field commander did not shake Walpole's determination to stay out of the war—indeed it may have reinforced it. The English design, in which they would be successful, was to defeat the French plan as thoroughly as they could but without a true commitment to war.

The Austrian minister in London, Count Philip Kinsky, wrote on 14 April 1733 that in a written response the English ministers were very cautious but that in conferences they did not hesitate to say that they would regard an attack by France as a *casus foederis*. He wrote again on 17 April to note that in spite of French preparations for war, in London it was believed that it would all end in only "campmens."[23] This suggests that the English assurances were those diplomatic statements that are maintained so long as they do not have to be acted upon.

The English ambassador in Vienna was told to state that England hoped force would not be used in Poland and to warn that if it were used England might not feel that its treaty obliged support of Austria. The instructions to Robinson made it quite clear that England would be very difficult to draw into a war as an ally of the emperor over the Polish question. Harrington observed that only in a case involving the very letter of the treaty would England be obliged to act. "You have already had assurances . . . that in case of war upon account of Polish affairs nothing of that kind would be expected from His Majesty."[24] The English had already established a similar freedom of diplomatic movement regarding France in the talks between George II and Chavigny.[25] The emperor promised that his troops would not cross the frontier and even began to withdraw some troops from Silesia in July.[26]

All this was quite clear to Bussy in Vienna. The English were forcing the emperor to come to terms with the Saxons. On 6 May he reported that the English were in all the negotiations with Count Lützelburg, the Saxon special emissary.[27] The Austrian agenda notes of Privy Council meetings are sprinkled with the names of Robinson and Dieden, the British and Hanoverian ministers in Vienna. In the notes for the 23 April meeting, which considered the proposals of the Saxon ministers, a marginal addition indicates that England advised bringing in the Saxons.[28]

On 16 July 1733 the emperor acquired, somewhat reluctantly, a new ally when the treaty was signed between Austria and Saxony. The text, available in the French archives, specifies the emperor's help with 12,000 men—8,000 infantry and 4,000 cavalry—to assist the elector in his candidacy for the Polish throne.

The elector was to furnish 6,000 troops with a similar proportion of infantry and cavalry. The elector also agreed that after
his election he would not seek to reduce the "liberties of Poland"
and would ask for ratification of his election by the Polish Diet.[29]
The "liberties of Poland" at this time meant the rights of medium-sized and large landowners to be unmolested by a central
government authority. In addition the Pragmatic Sanction was
accepted by the elector and the emperor gave up any claim he
may have had to the bishoprics of Naumburg, Merseburg, and
Meissen.

This was a first step down a diplomatic road which the Viennese court entered with unwillingness. They did not wish to be
tied to the active support of the Saxon candidacy. As late as July
there was a chance that just the threat of a Saxon invasion might
cause the Poles to abandon their support of Stanislas. But it did
not, and the next step was the threat of a Russian invasion. The
final step would be the actual invasion by Russian and Saxon
forces. The important part of the emperor's plan was that imperial troops would not be committed. In such a case the emperor
would be able to move some of his forces toward the West to face
the French, while at the same time claiming that his hands were
clean in Poland and that the French had insufficient cause to attack him.

After the agreement with Saxony the emperor needed an
agreement with the Poles—that is, with those Poles who would
support a Saxon candidacy. It was not difficult to achieve. On 22
August a treaty was signed in Warsaw between the palatin of
Cracow (Prince Lubomirski) and the representatives of Austria,
Russia, and Saxony. The treaty was required, so states the text,
by the palatin's consideration of the "imminent misfortunes
which menace his country if Stanislas comes to the throne of Poland, by which the torch of war could be lighted over all Europe,
especially in the North, and in which Poland would become the
principal theater by the entry of the Turks and Tatars."[30] The
threat from the infidel East was still worth mention in any appeal to the Austrians, even though it would be the Turks from
this time on who were threatened.

The specific provisions of the treaty recognized that Lubo-

mirski was to head a confederation that would do all in its power
to put the elector of Saxony on the throne of Poland and would
be reimbursed for its efforts. The reimbursement, and any in-
demnity for damages resulting from these efforts, would be
guaranteed by the three signatory powers. With regard to Stanislas, all the signatories promised not to lay down their arms until Stanislas was expelled from the country and the elector was in
peaceful possession of the crown of Poland.

From the emperor's point of view all this sounded very fine.
But there was a missing signatory to the treaty. The treaty of
1732 determining the succession in Poland, which was in process
of ratification when the death of Augustus II occurred and was
never in force, included Prussia. The new treaty mentioned that
the elector of Saxony was acceptable to the emperor and the sovereigns of Russia and Prussia, but there was no Prussian signature to the treaty nor any specific Prussian obligations.

The understanding between Austria and Russia would become the basic reason why the party of Stanislas would ultimately be defeated. The emperor had hoped, however, to have the
full agreement of the king of Prussia as well.

Frederick William I of Prussia is remembered as the father
who forced his young son, who later became Frederick the Great,
to assist at the execution of the son's companion in a juvenile esca-
pade. In the middle of 1733 he was in a sustained fury against the
government of Holland, which had executed an overeager Prussian recruiting officer who had sought to subvert the Maastricht
garrison. The king had imprisoned Dutch officers and men in
Prussian territory and threatened to execute them. A detailed
briefing on the Prussian-Dutch matter was given the emperor on
14 April 1733.[31] The king was in the wrong, and his high-handed
recruiting methods had alienated his neighbors; still he expected his emperor to support him, and the emperor well knew that
he competed with the French for the affections of the imperial
princes great and small.

Prince Eugene wrote a personal letter to the king in February
1733, and correspondence between the two courts through
Count Seckendorff, imperial minister in Berlin, continued

throughout most of the year. The king swung between declarations of loyalty to the emperor and expressions of obvious mistrust. Probably the real trouble was the elevation of a hated rival house and the danger that the Saxon kingship in Poland would become hereditary. While Prussia would carry out her military obligations to the emperor when the war began, the king's attitude toward Saxony became steadily more bitter.[32]

A fourth ally of the emperor—after England, Saxony, and Prussia—was Holland, usually referred to at the time as the States General. The Dutch states in this period had no true central executive, or stadtholder, but were represented diplomatically by an official at the Hague known as the high pensionary.

On 13 July 1733 the emperor called the ministers of England, Prussia, Denmark, and Holland to a meeting to discuss whether they were ready to carry out their treaty commitments in case of war. All declared that in general their governments were ready to fulfill their obligations. However, the Dutch minister hoped the imperial troops would not enter Poland and that the emperor would seek to restrain the tsarina from sending troops into Poland. Further, he stated that the States General did not expect to enter the war unless they were themselves attacked by France.[33]

The English were disturbed by the emperor's stripping the barrier fortresses between France and Holland of 10,000 men, a part of the 16,000 he was obliged by the Peace of Utrecht to maintain there in peacetime. These troops had been moved into Luxembourg and the maritime powers, England and Holland, had been given to understand that they must take upon themselves the care of the barrier. The important fortresses of Mons, Ath, and Charleroi, which should have been garrisoned by imperial troops, were entirely defenseless. This exposed situation made the States General feel obliged, for their immediate security, to enter into negotiations with the French minister at the Hague for a neutrality agreement by which they would not concern themselves with the Polish election and France would agree not to carry the war into the Netherlands. This surprised the English, who sent Horatio Walpole to the Hague with instructions to divert if possible the States General from concluding what he termed a precarious neutrality with France.[34] But Walpole found that matters had already gone too far before his arrival. In August a Dutch proposal was submitted to French minister Fénelon on the neutrality of the Austrian Netherlands, according to which, if the French would not attack the Austrian Netherlands, which constituted the barrier, the States General would continue their good offices to achieve a peaceful solution. If they were unable to do this they would seek to dispose the emperor not to attack France from the Netherlands, or in case such an attack were made, they would not supply him with troops.[35]

A Dutch document in the French Foreign Office files indicates that the French accepted the proposal. However, there was not a complete meeting of minds. Fénelon had received instructions from his government which dealt only with the barrier area, whereas the States General were speaking of all the Netherlands, or Lowlands. The difference was, of course, Luxembourg, an imperial fortress city which the French did not wish to include in the area they agreed not to attack.[36] As the Prussian foreign minister observed: "Voilà une neutralité sans neutralité!"[37]

A fifth important ally for the emperor was Russia. Here the difficulties and delays in communication seemed more important than possible differences. The death of Augustus II, according to prior agreement, should have led to the candidacy of the prince of Portugal. As the emperor fell away from this position, he had to communicate the fact to his Russian allies. Already on 7 March Bussy had heard that Vienna had proposed to the tsarina to annul the article of the treaty which stipulated opposition to the elector of Saxony as a candidate. Then on 1 April Bussy reported that an express had come from Russia and that he was aware of the contents. The tsarina supported the emperor in his favoring the prince of Portugal, or any other, but she did not want the elector of Saxony or Stanislas. The court was embarrassed.[38]

A further indication of the confusion came in a 27 March message from Count Wilczek in Warsaw stating that the Russian minister was pressing for an understanding on what the tsarina should communicate to the Polish primate in writing.[39] The ministers of the two powers were obviously working closely together: Löwenwolde, the acting Russian minister in Warsaw, reported to his government on 3 March that the Habsburg minister had shown him his instructions from Vienna.[40] But they were not necessarily in agreement. In the emperor's briefing of 3 June we find that the two Löwenwolde brothers (the senior had returned to Warsaw to resume his duties as minister) can hardly conceal their distaste for the elector of Saxony, and the emperor's resident in Saint Petersburg reported that the Russian court wanted a more definitive support for the elector from the emperor. By 18 July they had it in the Austrian-Saxon treaty mentioned above. The emperor had little choice if he wished to deny the French a clear reason to attack him. Bussy understood this too and so reported to Versailles.[41]

It was the best the emperor could do with the diplomatic and military resources at his disposal. He had not achieved either understanding or support in sufficient measure from his allies. Within the empire he did not know precisely how neutral many of the German states would be, but he could be sure that he would have no help at all—and conceivably active opposition— from Bavaria, Cologne, and the Palatinate. Bavaria had not agreed to the Pragmatic Sanction and its monarch fancied himself a candidate for election, not for the throne of Poland, but, at an appropriate time, for the imperial crown. There was no male successor in the Habsburg line to succeed Charles VI and the choice of Habsburgs by the imperial electors was, after all, only a matter of custom. The remainder of the states hoped to remain neutral if there was any chance they would be in the area of military operations.

Braubach says flatly that the emperor allowed himself to be diplomatically isolated.[42] The evidence supports this conclusion. After the emperor received an unmistakable warning of imminent hostilities from France in August, he seemed to show some misgivings. The warning came from the French minister in Mainz to the elector there, who sent it next day to the emperor.[43]

A few days later the emperor wrote to Seckendorff in Berlin. "If Stanislas were not excluded by law and the nation was unanimously for him in a free election, we would place no obstacles in his path in spite of the prevailing considerations against his person."[44] But it was too late to turn back.

✠

## CHAPTER FOUR

# The Road to Danzig

The diplomatic and military preparations of the French and Austrian governments had made the Polish election a matter affecting the balance of power in Europe. But it was, after all, in Warsaw and Saint Petersburg that the definitive steps were taken which set the war in motion.

Augustus II, Augustus the Strong, of the Saxon house of Wettin, had come to Warsaw for the convening of the Polish Diet. But the king had a gangrenous foot, and during the last days of January 1733 his Saxon court awaited his death. There was talk and rumor in the dying king's antechambers. One Polish magnate offered the Kalmuk chamberlain—who was himself a gift from Peter the Great, incidentally—1,800 Spanish ducats to gain the king's ear. But the king refused an audience and demanded the right to die in peace. Augustus had lived a lusty and profligate life, siring several hundred progeny, and there was now a pious story that he had repented all and had described his life as one great sin. But the Russian chargé, Löwenwolde, heard only that the king in his delirium had cried out several times "oh coquins" (rascals) with no indication of what was meant.

The king died early in the morning of 1 February and the messages went out from Warsaw to the capitals of Europe. Löwenwolde found himself somewhat inconvenienced by the event, for he had prepared a reception and dinner for the day honoring a date in the reign of his sovereign, the tsarina. His guests excused themselves and Löwenwolde wrote a somewhat petulant account to Saint Petersburg. Since the king's death had not been publicly announced they might well have ignored it for the moment, thought the chargé. In any case he told his guests when they excused themselves, "A live monarch is worth more than a dead king."[1]

Privy Councillor Brühl accepted the heart of the king, which was to be taken to Saxony and, on 19 February the Saxon court that had come to Warsaw with the king, numbering some 1,200 persons, left for Dresden. The primate observed to Löwenwolde on this occasion: "At last we shall be rid of all those Saxons."[2] He was badly mistaken.

The death of Augustus II made the primate of Poland, Theodore Potocky, bishop of Gnesen, the interrex. To the extent that there was any central government in this land of great magnates possessing tens of thousands of acres, the primate and a small senate of aristocrats and bishops held the executive power. A "Colloquio" of the senate on 6 and 7 February called for a Diet of Convocation to be held beginning 27 April. This meeting would be only to establish guidelines for the election and set an election date. But it would make the Austrian and Russian courts nervous since they feared it might abruptly resolve itself into a Diet of Election and elect a king, probably Stanislas, by acclamation. Assuming that it did not attempt an election (and in fact it did not), a Diet of Election would be called, made up of representatives selected by the regional diets. These would come to Warsaw and elect a new king.[3] Although the story of the election is marked by violence and extraordinary corruption, nevertheless certain constitutional provisions were carefully carried out.

Primate Potocky, as noted earlier in the Bartenstein briefings, was counted as pro-Stanislas, although he did not immediately reveal his position publicly. Bartenstein also described him as money-hungry, while Löwenwolde referred to him as crafty ("listig"), at the same time observing that he was an old man, not very competent in the morning and much less so after midday. The whole Potocky family, thought Löwenwolde, was trying to stand between the two camps, while secretly favoring Stanislas.[4]

Quite as important for the fortunes of Stanislas Leszczynski was the French ambassador in Warsaw, the marquis de Monti. A man of Italian origin, Monti had fought in the French army in

Italy under Vendôme and had left the service with the rank of brigadier. The instructions given him when he took his post in 1729 as representative in Dresden and Warsaw consisted mainly of guidance related to the possibility of Stanislas succeeding to the Polish throne. The instructions were specific and showed long-range planning and intentions. One may wonder, however, whether the personal character of Monti was not as important in the final outcome as any other single factor. Had Monti been less energetic or less zealous in his efforts, things might have gone otherwise. But Monti was a soldier serving his king.

Monti's 1729 instructions were to make contact with the primate, but to do so cautiously. The primate, he was told, was for Stanislas, but Monti must think in terms of what might happen in case of a vacancy on the throne. By custom the Poles will sell their support to several candidates and it will not be possible to avoid some payment in advance, although this must be undertaken very sparingly. For several reasons this election should not cost as much as the effort to elect the prince de Conti in 1697. And it will be necessary to have an election; it will not suffice to assume that Stanislas is still legally king. If the primate will agree to an election by acclamation—that is, one in which the members of the Diet of Election will have the authority to choose a king without referring the decision back to their provinces—this could be accomplished before the Saxons would have time to form a party. And remember, while it may be thought that France will support Stanislas, it is another thing so to state. These instructions should be kept very close. Among the members of the diplomatic corps only the Swedish minister may be confided in. Remain with the king of Poland in Dresden and go into Poland only when with him. Thus the burden of the instructions given to Monti.[5]

Monti had accompanied the king and court to Poland for the meeting of the Diet and was therefore ready to begin the execution of his instructions without delay. Had he been in Dresden his appearance on the scene in Warsaw would certainly have been delayed and perhaps not even possible had the Saxons wished to prevent it.

Monti's message after the death of the king was dated that

same day, 1 February 1733. It reflects the strange and chaotic situation in Warsaw.

> The confusion is going to be very great in the kingdom, especially during a time of the Diet, and the animosity among the families goes beyond any description. Everyone wants to be the general; everyone will seek to detach troops from the army and everything will be in disorder.
>
> Already the primate, hungry for money, said that he was astonished that the ambassador of France had not spoken to him since the ministers of other powers here had already made proposals to him.

Monti went on to say that he had as yet no orders. He did not believe that Stanislas could be accepted by acclamation. It was not necessary to act immediately on money questions since the one who gives last is right. Because of the great luxury that reigns in Warsaw, however, large sums of money would be needed. Monti then went on to discuss the candidates, much as Bartenstein would do in a few days in Vienna.[6]

The English representative, George Woodward, reported that it was impossible to "make any judgment how the Poles are inclined as to an election, for all the wise people keep their thoughts very private and will have good reasons before they declare themselves." A few days later he reported that the general bent of the nation was for Stanislas, but this must be encouraged by goodly sums of money. His reports did not seem to excite much interest in London except that he was told to make a strong representation against the Pretender as a candidate.[7]

Among the interested observers of the situation developing in Warsaw were the principal officials of the Russian court at Saint Petersburg—at that time several Germans who enjoyed the confidence of the tsarina. The first was Count Biron, a Livonian of low birth who was the Tsarina Anna's paramour. The British resident at Saint Petersburg, after nearly three years there, stated that the tsarina was absolutely governed by her favorite, Count Biron, the two counts Löwenwolde, and Baron Osterman.[8] The resident seemed to find Löwenwolde the elder an agreeable contact, mentioning him as his "particular friend." He described this count as a former chamberlain to the king of

Prussia and noted that he governed Biron as Biron governed the tsarina.[9] Osterman he found less agreeable, describing him as a Westphalian who was taken into the service of a Dutch admiral as a valet de chambre and became his secretary by reason of proficiency in languages. "He is full of finesse and artifice, false and treacherous in his deportment, submissive and insinuating with low cringings and bowings which is reckoned the best policy among the Russians wherein he outdoes all the natives."[10]

The French resident in Saint Petersburg observed as early as 28 February that the Polish problem completely absorbed the attention of the ministry.[11] It must have been the same, or nearly so, in most of the other capitals. In the meantime, Poland was uneasy. Acts of violence began to occur. Wilczek reported a skirmish in Sandomir and another in Grodno in March.[12] But the Poles insisted on the observance of certain constitutional functions despite the obvious fact that they were not truly masters of their own destiny. Indeed, it may have been the very realization of this which impelled them to stress the juridical character of their actions in the midst of chaotic rule and foreign intrigue.

The primate had been given some assurance by the declaration of the king of France on 16 March 1733. On 14 April the emperor addressed a message to the primate in Latin, the language of official acts in Poland at that time, reminding him that during the past year when the liberty of Poland was in peril the primate himself and others had asked the emperor to defend it. He had always been a good neighbor and a faithful ally, protested the emperor, and he wished to gain no advantages. He too supported the free election, he said, but he was in agreement with his allies who had troops on the Polish borders. There was no mention of Stanislas by name.[13]

The primate did not answer immediately. He was doubtless sufficiently occupied with the Diet of Convocation which convened on 27 April and continued through twenty-seven sessions until 23 May, at which time it resolved itself into a general confederation, a constitutionally recognized creature. The "Confederation of the States of Poland and Lithuania" on 23 May swore to elect a Pole, one having no territories outside Poland, and to use all its force against a foreign prince.[14] The primate assumed credit for this in his publication of the "universals" which announced the Diet of Election to be held in September: "I succeeded in ending this Diet with a confederation to ban from future elections the intrigues and machinations of foreign powers."[15] He added another hopeful statement: "I was the first to swear the oath, in order to give an example to others, in the belief that the nobility and all those to whom it pertained, would have no difficulty in swearing a similar oath which excluded any foreigner from the throne."

On 13 June the primate responded to the emperor's warning. "The Republic should not imagine that it had anything to fear on the part of its neighbors; it does not believe that it has offended any." Your reign, he told the emperor, will be more glorious for having kept the liberties of the kingdom and universal peace.[16]

This polite fencing continued with another letter from the emperor on 13 July. There was still no mention of Stanislas by name, but there was no mistaking the growing concern in the emperor's tone. He warned again of those who sought disorder under the pretext of valid counsels.[17]

In the meantime the primate was writing to other nations for support as well as carrying on a written dialogue with the Austrian representative in Warsaw similar to that which passed between him and the emperor. He wrote also to Ali Pasha, grand vizier at Constantinople, and received the desired reply that the Porte would never consent to the suppression of Polish liberty.[18]

There was less fencing in the letter from the tsarina to the primate. She noted the violence that had taken place at the Diet of Convocation in April. Although she emphasized freedom of election, she also noted that Stanislas was excluded in perpetuity by law and was a declared enemy of the country, recognized as constitutionally incapable by the "oath of the whole nation and of your own in particular." Efforts to place Stanislas on the Polish throne were described as an effort to break the peace between Poland and Russia and thus Russia might use the force necessary to sustain the laws and liberty of the Polish Republic.[19]

There was also no mistaking the meaning of the declaration made by Monti on 4 September, during the Diet of Election, but as we shall see, he was unable to bring his country to carry it out. Monti promised a great deal to the not-yet-elected king of Poland. "The king, my master, promises to support him, not only effectively and with all the forces which God has confided to him but, beyond this, if the neighboring powers of the republic wish to attack him by reason of this election, the king, my master, promises to place in my hands, from the sums drawn from his own coffers, what will be needed to augment the army of the republic."[20]

Monti had not gone beyond his guidance; similar assurances were being made and would be made in the future. But this was to be another in the series of assurances that would not be carried out.

The many reports of money paid to influence the Polish election give alternately the impression that what is known is only the tip of the iceberg or that enormous exaggerations are the rule. Doubtless we can never know the complete story of the money payments. But there are enough reports to assure that Poland became a kind of sink for money during the preelection period and that the interested powers were well aware that the Polish magnates accepted money freely from all sides.

The French paid their money through Monti. Although Cardinal Fleury was famous for his economies, the Council of State as early as 25 February agreed to send 1.6 million livres in what Villars called the "voie la plus sûre avec les Polonais." The news of the payment apparently did not take long to reach Vienna, for Bussy reported in March that the court there had heard that a million écus had been sent to Monti to put Stanislas on the Polish throne. If one accepts the usual rate of three écus to the livre, it was a figure not too far from that determined in the council. This was not all, of course, and we are told that by April the French had sent 3 million livres.[21]

The French were also ready to use money rather directly in the Russian court. During the first part of 1733, or possibly even earlier, French resident Magnan in Saint Petersburg was attempting to negotiate with the court on contingencies that would follow a vacancy on the Polish throne. A present of 100,000 écus was offered to Biron. Osterman, the foreign minister, objected on the grounds that it would compromise his relations with Vienna.[22] Perhaps Osterman thought Biron was doing too well, for there is evidence the latter acquired considerable wealth in his service to the tsarina.[23]

Further evidence of French money in Poland is noted in the 11 April report of Magnan. Field Marshal Burkhard Muennich, the assistant to Osterman, had complained to Magnan that the sums of money the French had put into Warsaw and Danzig tended to contradict the principle of a free election. Magnan did not say that he protested the statement.[24]

Money was a painful problem for the Habsburgs. The French and English, great trading nations, were able to use subsidies throughout Europe to further their diplomacy. Spain had known great wealth in earlier days and still drew funds from her colonies, although not in a measure to support an aggressive foreign policy. But the Habsburgs and their inland empire were always hard put to find money. The Austrian possessions in Italy were under pressure from the Spanish, and the English had forced the Austrian-supported Ostend trading company in the Netherlands to be closed. The emperor was thrown back upon his own resources—the Habsburg family lands, with their income largely in the hands of the great magnates who guarded their rights and estates against his encroachment, and the states of the empire from whom he could only beg money and troops. Of course there was borrowing, and the Habsburgs had done a great deal of it. The failure of the Habsburgs in the time of Philip II to repay the Fuggers brought that great house into its decline.

The impressive boundaries of the Holy Roman Empire and the lands of the house of Habsburg emcompassed most of the population of central Europe. But the emperor was financially strained to put even a few thousand troops in the field—that is, to field an army in addition to maintaining his garrison troops throughout his lands and the fortresses of the empire. It was reported to require 600,000 florins to prepare the troops for action in accordance with the decision of the War Council in February. In July, French chargé Bussy learned that 600,000 florins had been borrowed in Silesia at 9 percent.[25]

By September it was obvious that urgent preparations were necessary and that greater sums must be considered. It was reported that the emperor was forced to send a million florins to Saint Petersburg to reimburse the tsarina for the troops he did not furnish. The payment was to be the equivalent.[26] By October the war had begun and the emperor found that although the states of the empire would vote to support him by a majority vote in the Diet at Regensburg, they looked to him to furnish the money to set their forces in motion to join with his own. Throughout the fall he struggled with the question. The king of Prussia, who had an alliance with the emperor, did not furnish money, and the smaller German states took the lead from his behavior. The emperor was able to draw considerable sums from the Church and from various rich nobles, all in the inner Habsburg lands, who came forth to pay additional taxes. But it was not enough and eventually a property tax was needed.[27] In the meantime loans were sought. The French chargé in Vienna heard in October that the court had settled on a figure of 15 million florins required and intended to raise this by contributions of 5 million from Bohemia, 2.5 million from Moravia, 3 million from the silver mines in Silesia, 2 million from Naples, 1 million from the Bank of Vienna, and 1.5 million from cutting pensions in half.[28] And in what sounds like a sequel to the problems of Philip II, it was reported that the "famous" Jew Wersheim declared bankruptcy. The court in Vienna owed him 1.8 million florins, Count Sinzendorff 90,000, the electors of Bavaria and Cologne 3 million. The bankruptcy was for 6 million. The Chamber of Finance denied the debt, but Wersheim was to be given safe conduct![29]

As for the Russians, the younger Löwenwolde wrote from Warsaw on 13 February that there were only three means at hand to be used in the Polish situation—money, force, or both together, and in full measure. He lost no time in telling his sovereign that money would be needed before the opening of the Diet of Convocation and thought it wise to have 100,000 thaler on hand by that time. Because of the lack of security on the roads he suggested that it be sent to Warsaw with a troops of 20 to 30 dragoons who might come on the pretext of being a guard for the minister.[30]

Others at the Russian court also seemed ready to accept money from the emperor—that money which was so hard for him to find. Bartenstein proposed in his briefing of 18 September that the brother of Count Osterman be given the title of imperial councillor and a yearly pension of 2,000 florins.[31] At least this type of payment would not require immediate heavy outlays.

So, with the money flowing from Paris and Vienna into Warsaw and Saint Petersburg, the Poles act out the drama of the election.

There was initially some hope by the French that Stanislas could be acclaimed king at the Diet of Convocation. Monti was asked by Chauvelin to "do the impossible" and have it occur at that time since things would become uncertain if it were dragged out.[32] When this could not be accomplished the French looked forward to winning the election as the alternative.

The role of Monti is so prominent it sometimes appears that the later difficulties were due in great part to his overzealous actions. But the evidence suggests that Monti was only reflecting the attitude of his superiors, and he may have represented a relatively cautious element. For example, in May he suggested that if Stanislas came to Poland it should be by entry into a port near Danzig to see how things would turn out. This, he pointed out, would preclude the possibility of his being in Poland without assistance—an eventuality that actually occurred. But Monti left it to the French court to decide whether Stanislas should come by land or by a naval squadron. It is uncertain when the final decision was made, but a clue is the strong approach made to the English in late June. Chauvelin asked Chavigny to demand an unequivocal statement of friendship. It was apparently a last attempt to allow the English to change their effective but unstated opposition. "We will regard any equivocal response as a proof of the information we have received."[33] Of course the English made no such commitment and the French thus could not consider the Baltic a safe area. Stanislas would travel by land.

Stanislas had warmed quickly to the idea of becoming king of Poland once again. In letters to Marshal Du Bourg he revealed that he had information from Poland which led him to great expectations. He then began to write letters to Poland, to the great annoyance of Monti, who wrote to him: "I beg Your Majesty to write no further letters and let me act." Stanislas answered that he would not comply with this "unless required by the cardinal or the keeper of the seals" (Chauvelin). Monti also complained to Chauvelin: "It is desirable that King Stanislas does not write at all but one may not hope for this. Poland is awash with his letters."[34]

Despite this aggressiveness on the part of Stanislas while he lived at Chambord, Boyé notes that he became suddenly quiet when he was told that he would travel alone to Poland.[35] Had he expected to arrive at the head of a French army?

It appeared logical that Stanislas would not attempt to cross Europe through Prussian or Saxon territory but would try to enter through the port of Danzig, a semiautonomous city in Poland. The French did nothing to correct this notion but set about devising the scheme described in chapter 1.

One of the more incredible footnotes to this journey was the apparently careless manner in which Cardinal Fleury passed on the information of Stanislas's voyage to the king of Sardinia in a letter written only two days after the secret departure. "King Stanislas left the day before yesterday in the night, disguised and accompanied by three trusted men, to go by land to Warsaw, where we hope he will arrive within two weeks. . . . His departure is an absolute secret from everyone, even from members of the king's council."[36]

The interception of diplomatic and military communications was a fairly frequent occurrence. Such behavior on the part of the cardinal supports the story of his lack of enthusiasm for the whole project. Did the cardinal have a plan to put into action had Stanislas fallen into enemy hands—possibly a plan to avert the approaching war?

The Diet of Election had convened in Warsaw on 25 August. Its constitutional life, according to customary law, was six weeks, after which it would automatically dissolve. Stanislas was in Warsaw by 10 September and on the next day the primate took definitive action on the electoral plain at Wola. He got on his horse and made a tour of the field in a driving rain, passing before the representatives of the palatinates, then among the 60,000 nobles. Of each he demanded the choice of a king. Several opposed Stanislas. He stopped for the night and began again the next day with the throng becoming more violent. Finally the marshal of the Diet, Radzewski, called for a vote on the spot. A noble named Kaminski uttered the fatal word "Veto" but on questioning revealed that he was not against Stanislas but simply wished the election deferred and retracted his veto. Then, three times, at quarter-hour intervals, the marshal of the Diet asked if the members would accept Stanislas as king. He was elected by acclamation.[37]

It was very probably, as Boyé said, "an irreparable imprudence." The nobles thought in terms of national pride and were challenging both Russia and Austria. The election was only an appearance of strength; the primate had appealed to them on a higher plane: "The Republic has only to invoke the assistance of heaven by a unanimous decision and I assure you that it will not permit a hair of our heads to be harmed. It is not the first time that threats have been made to the homeland but thanks to the grace of God, they have never been carried out." He went on to say the nation was assured of being under the protection of the "roi des rois."[38]

In fact the nobles would all return to their estates after the election. The few regular troops would be mostly on the frontiers under one or another of the greater magnates. There would be no one to fight for the republic. The adversaries of Stanislas had been more or less outshouted at Wola, but even earlier, on 8 and 9 September, one of the princes Wiesnowicki had given the signal for revolt. A group under the leadership of Prince Lubomirski left the electoral camp and went to the other side of the Vistula. Count Wilczek wrote that following the election of Stanislas, which involved violence against foreign ministers and against "well-intentioned" Poles, "many thousands" left the electoral camp to join Lubomirski, including the Wiesnowicki brothers and the bishop of Posnan.[39]

The Russians, who had already begun their invasion of Lithuania, thus had a confederation in Warsaw, one which had asked for their protection. Doubtless they would have invaded without this, but there was a case for constitutionality in the formation of a confederation during an interregnum. The theory was that the powers given the elected king were returned to the Polish nation upon his death. Until a new king was elected, the formation of a party by leading citizens was regarded as constitutionally legal. Osterman placed some importance on the notion when he wrote in August: "A confederation, however large or small it may be at first, will give the affair a great deal of weight, and will grow stronger after the intervention of the troops."[40]

Bartenstein, preparing his presentation for the emperor on 18 September for a Privy Council meeting on the nineteenth, wondered whether the leaders of the rump confederation in Warsaw would proclaim the elector of Saxony king of Poland as they had indicated they wished to do. He also brought several other problems forward. It was possible that the French would use the nonrecognition of Stanislas as a pretext for a break in relations with Vienna. Another problem was that the elector might wish to enter Poland with more than 6,000 Saxon troops. There were 6,000 imperial troops in Gross-Glogau near the Polish border, and the elector might insist that the emperor provide as many men as the elector was prepared to commit. Bartenstein hoped the imperial troops would not be needed at all and could be used to strengthen the camp at Pilsen. But, he admitted, if the elector did not invade at all it might be up to the emperor to send in his own troops. This might come about if there were no proclamation in favor of the elector by the Lubomirski confederation.[41]

It is clear that the Austrian position was militarily unsound. The Pilsen camp was a kind of halfway camp between Poland and the Rhine, but it was still a very great distance from the Rhine and an attack by the French from that quarter was every day more threatening. The emperor was probably not yet fully aware that he was to be diplomatically isolated in a few weeks or months, nor that he was well on the way toward having his only field forces north of the Alps misplaced at the outset of hostilities.

Therefore the Austrians were dependent upon the Russian invasion and found themselves in the strange and uncomfortable position of chafing at the slowness of the Russian army ap-

proaching Poland. In the 25 September briefing of the Privy
Council it was suggested that Field Marshal Muennich might secretly have placed obstacles in the way of more rapid movement,
or even that the Russian court was playing false. They were
probably relieved by the message of 3 October from the Austrian chargé in Saint Petersburg, who wrote that the Russian
army had been held up by bad weather and a bad road.[42]

What were the French doing in Saint Petersburg to prevent
this slow but certain movement of Russian forces toward the dis-
organized forces of the Republic of Poland? In fact they had
been busy during all of 1733. Magnan had been given full powers
even before the death of Augustus II to conclude an alliance. His
instructions after the death of the king were "to engage the
tsarina indirectly to take no part in the Polish election and particularly to prevent her from using Russian troops."[43] But it was
not an agreeable task in a court where he found that all the foreign representatives were pro-Russian or pro-Austrian, with the
possible exception of the Swedish representative. Despite the fact
that Magnan's negotiations were principally through the sympathetic Field Marshal Muennich, who had served in French armies, he made little headway. He believed that Muennich had tried
to change the views of the tsarina but that Osterman and Biron
had much greater influence. It even appeared that Muennich's
known friendly attitude toward France was causing him difficulties. By April, Magnan heard rumors that Muennich was being
paid by France and that his disgrace was expected. He also heard
that the ministers about the tsarina had given her the impression
that the election of Stanislas would plunge Russia into war.[44]

Sweden was a cautious ally for France, by this time too weak to
be useful to France but still strong enough to be disliked by Russia. Magnan found that the Russian court would oppose by force
the election of anyone who was friendly to France or Sweden. The
Swedish resident kept his distance from Magnan, telling him that
he had no instructions and making the unlikely statement that he
was not following the Polish affair closely.[45]

The Russian position became clearer each day. Magnan called
attention in Versailles to the movements of Russian troops to em-

phasize the firmness of their stance. On the surface the amenities were still observed. A letter passed from the tsarina to the king of France on 21 June congratulating him on the birth of a child. On the other hand, the ministry at Versailles during this same month ordered Magnan to return to France and he left on 4 July. His successor, Villardeau, continued the representation but, in keeping with the custom of the Russian court, could not act as a chargé d'affaires and had no right to correspond with the Russian ministers. He observed that he was no more than a consul. He continued to report the preparations for war, however. He heard that incoming and outgoing communications were being examined, and that Marshal Muennich was no longer in the war councils and had been sent off to visit fortifications.[46]

The French diplomatic effort then switched out of the normal channels, forfeited by the departure of Magnan, and was directed by Monti through a Polish representative. The primate in his statement to the Diet of Election announced that he had sent Rudomina, the chamberlain of Bracklaw, to Saint Petersburg. The chamberlain's reputed skill, good intentions, and credit with the Russian court made the primate hope that the mission would succeed and that he would return with peace. The British representative on 4 July noted the presence of a Polish envoy in Saint Petersburg named Rudomina whose mission was to persuade the tsarina not to send troops into Poland.[47]

Villardeau was puzzled by Rudomina, the more so when he found him apprehensive for his own safety. So we may assume that Villardeau was not aware of all that was taking place.[48] The envoy who *was* kept informed was the British minister, who was told by Osterman that the French had offered Russia an alliance which would also involve the allies of France, and that Monti would come to Saint Petersburg as ambassador if there were any chance of its success. The proposals made through Rudomina were the following, according to the British representative: 1) the French and Poles would, after the election of Stanislas, persuade the Turks and Swedes to conclude a defensive alliance with Russia; 2) Courland would be allowed to elect another duke following the death of the current sovereign; 3) Poland would give up its pretensions to Livonia; 4) the frontiers between Russia and Poland would be "wasted" for a space of 30 to 40 miles; 5) a considerable sum of money would be paid Count Biron.[49] The French proposals reflect, beyond the requirement to satisfy Count Biron, the concern of the Russians and Austrians over their uneasy border with the Ottoman Empire. In past confrontations France had not overlooked this area as a means of placing pressure on both Austria and Russia, and the War of the Polish Succession would mark another attempt, this one unsuccessful. As early as October 1730 Chauvelin had alerted French Ambassador Villeneuve in Constantinople that the French government would do all possible for Stanislas when the Polish throne became vacant.[50] Villeneuve set about organizing support among the Tatar tribes in the Black Sea area. In the spring of 1733 he attempted to raise a Tatar army through subsidies and was told by the end of August that two Tatar forces, one to move against the Ukraine, the other against the Caucasus, were ready to take his orders. At the same time he had solicited a strong statement from the Turks regarding the Polish election, as the primate had done. It was all too good to be true. Villeneuve was unable to bring the Tatars to action and found that the Turks had turned cold on the Tatar plan, with the sultan ordering the Tatars not to attack. It may be that the French had oversold the menace of a Russian threat to the Turks. They had pointed out that Russia had dismembered Sweden, would dismember Poland, and then do the same to the Ottoman Empire. In response the Turks began to talk of a grand alliance with France. Alas, a major alliance with an infidel nation was not acceptable to the cardinal. In addition, the Turks were at war with Persia and experienced a setback in the fall of 1733.[51] Thus the attempt of the French to bring a live force against the Russian rear was a failure.

A successful Tatar expedition against the Russian frontiers might have embarrassed the Russian court and given some additional negotiating leverage to France. The failure of the plan made Magnan's efforts to reach an understanding in Saint Petersburg quite impossible. The Russians noted with suspicion the movement of a Turkish diplomat through Poland in March, his two- or three-hour conference with Monti, and his passage on to Sweden by way of Danzig.[52] The Austrians too were suspicious that Stanislas and the French were ready to use the Turks against Christian countries, an item pointed out in Bartenstein's 23 February briefing. In Saint Petersburg the French representatives picked up what information they could of the Turkish-Persian struggle, realizing that Turkish success was to French advantage. Villardeau heard of a Turkish success in October, adding that Russian generals had been sent to Persia in an attempt to prevent a Persian-Turkish peace.[53] But despite a considerable volume of reporting and what must have been an expensive long-term effort by the French, the Turkish presence and Turkish actions do not seem to have affected materially the decisions in Saint Petersburg or Vienna in 1733.

The critical decision of the Russians to enter troops into Poland was evidently made in a lively meeting on 10 July with the tsarina and all the former councillors of state in attendance. The question was whether the Russian intervention was to wait until the election of Stanislas occurred, not whether the intervention should take place. The group proposing premature movement carried the day, but Villardeau, reporting the meeting, was not convinced that they would move quickly. This information he passed on to Monti on 14 July.[54]

The Russians—Muscovites, as many called them—moved slowly, as we have seen, but by 5 October an army under Irish-born General Peter Lacy was across the Vistula from Warsaw. Shortly before their arrival they had been joined by those Poles who were Saxon sympathizers, and when they reached the plain of Praga, near the village of Kamien, and near where Henry of Valois was elected in 1573, an election was held. The election could not be put off, because the constitutional period of six weeks for a Diet of Election was about to expire. The Russians, according to one account, withdrew a certain distance to give the appearance of a free election. Prince Lubomirski harangued the assembly. After the name of Augustus III had been applauded, the bishop of Posnan declared him king of Poland and duke of Lithuania. From the city of Warsaw, Woodward heard the firing and bell ringing that attended the proclamation.[55]

On the west side of the Vistula it was called an election under duress. A letter purportedly from Lacy to Osterman described the method used to bring about unity among the Polish magnates. "The Polish nobles being divided among themselves on the choice of a candidate, I persuaded them by promises, and still more by threats, to confer the crown on the elector of Saxony." Perhaps this is what Prince Lubomirski meant when he wrote to the tsarina on that same day stating that in a free election "under the auspices of your army" we chose the elector of Saxony to be king of Poland.[56]

General Lacy then crossed into Warsaw. A great many had left the city, and there had been a general breakdown of order with scattered violence amid efforts to raise troops. An attack had been made on the home of the Saxon minister, and the Russian and imperial ministers were under siege in their homes.[57] The bridges had been destroyed, and Lacy was forced to build boat bridges and cross under artillery fire from the palatin of Kiev, who had mustered a force of 8,000 men. The Russians reportedly lost 600 men who fell on the spot, with a larger number drowned and 400 taken prisoner. Nevertheless the Russian force crossed the Vistula and entered Warsaw on 10 October.[58]

Stanislas had departed on 22 September for Danzig, arriving on 2 October.[59] The primate and Monti were in his party. Lacy levied contributions on the city of Warsaw and notified Danzig that if Stanislas were not expelled he would bombard and besiege the city with 30,000 men.[60] Lacy did not have the 30,000 men, however, as he came into Warsaw. The imperial minister, Count Wilczek, appears to have been counting the Russian troops carefully as they entered. On 2 November he noted that the Smolensk corps was approaching, although most of its infantry had been left behind on orders of Löwenwolde to garrison Lithuanian cities. The troops that had already arrived, Wilczek noted, were being reequipped, and as soon as the rest arrived a decision was to be made as to which would remain in Warsaw and which go to Cracow or Danzig. Wilczek also heard that the corps had skirmished with a party of Polish irregulars, about 2,000 of whom had remained on the other side of the river.[61] As the Smolensk corps came into Warsaw on 11 November he reported a total of 6,850 men, having counted them himself, and noted that supplies were moving slowly. Although the men had passed through in several hours, the supplies were still moving for two days in the two-wheeled "moscowitschen Wagerln." Further movements of the army may be delayed, wrote Wilczek.[62]

The Russian troops had been dispersed in Poland as an occupying force and it was many weeks before Lacy was able to assemble a force of from 12,000 to 15,000 and appear before the city of Thorn on 16 January 1734. Thorn opened its gates and received a Russian garrison. But it was not until February that the Russians approached the city of Danzig. The French would soon be faced with the problem of whether they should try to relieve a besieged city.

After one of the longest peaceful periods among the nations of western Europe the flame of war was once again ignited. The intervention of the Russian army in Poland and the departure of Stanislas for Danzig signaled a new situation, although not one to be regarded as profoundly affecting the existence of the nations involved or their societies. Preparations had been made by the several courts and the diplomatic play carefully completed. An unmistakable final warning had been given by the king of France. When it became obvious that the Russians intended to use force to overthrow the election, the French decision was made. The king wrote to Monti that he intended to support at any price the free election and to show that his promise of a powerful protection to the Poles was not in vain. The same courier who carried the dispatch to him in Warsaw, he told Monti, also carried the orders to Marshal Berwick in Strasbourg to attack the fortress at Kehl and establish bridges over the Rhine.[63] There were no real surprises; the formalities complete, the war, at some undetermined level of violence, would follow. Limiting factors arose either from the nature of the societies of eighteenth-century Europe or from tacitly agreed upon conventions.

The war was, of course, among courts rather than among or between peoples, and the diplomatic correspondence reflects this clearly. The diplomatic conversations and the meetings of the highest councils show an attempt to justify their positions,

and sometimes an indignation at the moves of an opponent. But
the indignation lacks the ferocious righteousness and certitude
that attended the religious wars of a century before—and would
attend the great struggles of the twentieth century. The old notion of just war in the Middle Ages had not survived the religious wars of the sixteenth and seventeenth centuries, if indeed
it could be said to have been present at that time. Moral indignation had taken on a juridic tone. Chauvelin protested to Villars
in a council meeting against a suggested course of action: "But
you declare yourself the aggressor!"

Yet the broader notion of aggressive warfare, as developed in
the twentieth century, had not emerged. The nation was not at
war, but rather the court, and the dynastic claims that evolved,
various and complex as they were, provided only a basis for
juridic anger and legal abomination. The interlocking family situations of the princely houses of Europe permitted almost any
claim to be made, and the dynastic rivalry fell neatly into this le-
galistic pattern.

A major power then was less concerned about the possible
capture of its capital or the overthrow of its society. Its army
might be defeated, but neither the army nor the state would
likely be destroyed. Except for a temporary seizure of Berlin by
Russian forces in the Seven Years' War, no major capitals were
taken in the eighteenth century before the French Revolution.
Clausewitz's famous remark that war is a continuation of politics
by other means, written in the nineteenth century and reflecting
the effect of the Napoleonic wars, is a far more reasonable observation for the eighteenth century.

In this period the danger of a war based on moral justification, or crusade, and of the excesses that might be expected to
follow, was unlikely. Further, the mobilization of a large proportion of the population in support of war in any state was still
technologically impossible for lack of physical communications
and food supply. Consequently the war would acquire a professional, sometimes tedious, quality that was the mark of commanders seeking suitable conventions to achieve limited success
rather than pitched battles to destroy the opponent's forces.

✠

CHAPTER FIVE

# Military Operations North of the Alps in 1733

It was a little late in the season to turn things over to the military and ask for notable results, as the French government was doing in October 1733. True, preparations had been made, but eighteenth century armies normally went into the field in late spring and were preparing for winter quarters when autumn came. But as the summer waned, the French were frustrated by two undeniable facts: first, they had no allies—the treaties with Spain and Sardinia were not yet signed—and second, until the entry of Russian troops into Poland in October, no overt hostile act had been committed by either the emperor or his allies. Even the Russian move, which allowed the French to maintain that the emperor was using Russia to carry out his measures against France by an invasion of Poland, was not a completely satisfactory casus belli for the French to use as an explanation in the various courts of Europe. Despite the preparations, the fact is that they did wait until the Sardinian treaty was in hand and until the Russian troops had crossed the border of Poland before ordering a military move against the emperor.

We are privileged to know in some detail what military actions were considered in the highest council of the French government. Marshal Villars sat on the Council of State and attended most of the meetings during the spring and summer of 1733. His memoirs, which reveal a somewhat pompous and bombastic old man, nevertheless square generally with other information, and they indicate that the meetings were in great part concerned with the negotiations with Spain and Sardinia. The dispatches from the ambassadors were read, and the answers and instructions to be sent back were read and discussed. Chauvelin, as secretary of state for foreign affairs, read the incoming and outgoing messages.[1] As to what extent the young king was a participant in the discussions we have no direct documentary sources and must rely on Marshal Villars's memoirs. During 1733 Villars sometimes mentions the presence of the king in council meetings but gives little indication that he took an active part in the give-and-take of the discussion. Respect or discretion may have inhibited Villars from quoting the king or even noting his attitude toward a given question. But what we know of Louis XV in later years—his shyness and his carrying out a secret diplomacy behind the backs of his ministers, for example—suggests that the young king at this time was probably a silent observer at the Council of State meetings and willing to accept the positions of his former tutor, the cardinal. Lee Kennett described him as more a spectator than an active participant in the councils a quarter of a century later during the Seven Years' War.[2]

The question of how and where to attack the emperor came up repeatedly in the discussions. It seemed an accepted matter that the emperor must be shorn of some of his holdings in Italy. But what of the Empire? In the meeting of 28 June, when the matter of examining a method of attack upon the emperor without Sardinian help was before them, the council considered attacks upon the imperial fortresses of Breisach, Philippsburg, Luxembourg, and Mons.

On 12 July, Cardinal Fleury advanced the suggestion that Luxembourg be bombarded but not attacked. Villars was greatly irritated. He had already taken the position that the empire must be attacked—that is, strong points or areas must be seized. (After the 20 May meeting Villars had observed that war was decided upon in spite of the cardinal, "but there are still many ways by which he can prevent it.") In this case Villars declared that they must act seriously or not at all. At the 12 July meeting Chauvelin proposed an attack on the imperial fortress at Kehl, across the Rhine from French-held Strasbourg, but the meeting ended with no agreement. By the 23 July meeting the cardinal was ready with a proposal to besiege Breisach or bombard Luxembourg. To besiege Kehl, thought the cardinal, would involve the Empire in the war. Villars objected that Breisach and Luxembourg were less important as fortresses than the others but would draw the Empire into war just as surely.[3]

A short memoir in the French military archives discusses the basic problem before the council—namely, how to make war on the emperor and not on his Empire. It includes two important considerations peculiar to war in this era in the German Empire: that one must always be aware of which princely domain of the several hundred German sovereignties would be affected by a given military act, and that the question of forage for the cavalry must be ever present in the military planner's thoughts. The memoir pointed out that only Luxembourg, Breisach, and Freiburg were to be considered imperial cities. Perhaps the decision to contain Luxembourg without an attack had already been made before the writing of the memoir, for it discusses attacks only on Breisach and Freiburg. To besiege Breisach, it goes on, you need a bridge at Hüningen, near Basel. However, after crossing this bridge you enter the lands of Baden, then those of the duke of Württemberg and other princes of the empire before arriving in the lands of the emperor, which extend between Breisach and Freiburg. The army must forage and eat. Are contributions to be imposed upon the lands of the princes? Further, when the enemy forms an army, he will advance toward Strasbourg and Kehl and will establish lines to the mountains which will prevent a siege of Kehl unless the lines are broken.[4]

By the meeting of 20 September it appeared that the council had agreed upon Kehl as the best objective. Meanwhile a hitch had developed in the treaty negotiations with Sardinia. Although the agreement was very close to signing, the king of Sardinia asked for a stipulation that the French would not attack anywhere in the empire—obviously an impossible condition. Doubtless the king of Sardinia wished assurance that the French would place the bulk of their forces in Italy and not commit armies in the north which might draw strength away from the

Italian front. The French could not agree to this, of course, but the treaty finally was signed on 26 September. Even so, we find that in the meeting of 4 October the decision had not been made beyond the possibility of recall, and the orders to cross the Rhine were held up until the word from Turin was sufficiently reassuring.[5]

Most of these discussions have been concerned with the French view across the Rhine. What other military opportunities were open to the French north of the Alps? The Austrian Netherlands was a second area, but one of great sensitivity for the British. We have previously noted the neutrality agreement, over British protests, between France and Holland which followed the withdrawal of imperial troops from the barrier fortresses. This tended to cut both ways for the French as they sought opportunities around their perimeter. The neutrality agreement and a reluctance to anger the British had closed the Austrian Netherlands proper to them as a theater of operations. But the emperor was in solid and bold possession of the fortress city of Luxembourg at the edge of this forbidden zone, a city that frequently was considered a part of it and had drawn the greater part of its garrison from the men in the barrier fortresses. To the extent that France admitted the inviolability of Luxembourg the emperor was relieved of the danger of an attack; but the emperor might very well make a diversionary attack himself into northern France from this strong point. In any event, the presence of a strong imperial garrison there immobilized a considerable force of French troops. That is why the subject came up repeatedly in French reviews of the situation. As late as 25 August the designated commander for the area, Lieutenant General Count de Belle Isle, complained that Marshal Berwick seemed determined to bombard Luxembourg after the siege of a Rhine fortress.[6] Dangervilliers, obviously sympathizing with Belle Isle, wrote to the latter saying that a bombardment of Luxembourg had not been decided, and he surmised that the principal stores were underground in the rock and safe from the shells then available. A few days later, however, the same minister wrote to Berwick assuring the marshal that he had explained to the king the reasons favoring a bombardment of Luxembourg.[7]

But the order to attack or bombard Luxembourg never came. The French elected to be satisfied on this front with Dutch neutrality and British inaction.

A third area for scrutiny was Lorraine. What was usually referred to as Lorraine was at this time the combined duchies of Lorraine and Bar which comprised an irregular island in the midst of French territory. The annexation of the three bishoprics of Metz, Toul, and Verdun by the French in 1648 and the annexation of Alsace on the east had left Lorraine surrounded by France. Moreover, its independence had been an on-and-off thing with a temporary annexation to France during the seventeenth century and a French occupation as late as 1715. Yet it was still an independent duchy and it had a sovereign who proposed to link himself in marriage with the powerful house of Habsburg.

Since 1729 the sovereign of Lorraine had been the young Duke Francis III, a man whose limited competence would be established in time. What was intolerable for the French was that Francis had been educated from the age of fourteen at the Viennese court and was betrothed to the eldest daughter of the emperor, Maria Theresa, the daughter to whom the emperor sought to bequeath all the possessions of the house of Habsburg. The alliance of the houses of Habsburg and Lorraine, with the continued possession of Lorraine, would press the power of an ancient enemy far too close to Paris. Nor would it be satisfactory to the British, whose policies had been to keep the Austrian power at a modest level in this area and especially to prevent it from breaking out in strength on the Atlantic coast. Britain had as recently as 1729 secured the agreement of the emperor to terminate his Ostend trading company in the Austrian Netherlands.

Although the Austrians had observed that the French were quietly seeking to acquire Lorraine, the French records offer little evidence of the fact. There is little discussion of the need to invade Lorraine in wartime—the need is assumed. As Marshal Berwick wrote a few days before the beginning of hostilities in his matter-of-fact way: "I have sent you the plan on Lorraine. It will be executed on the first order."[8] But did this mean a retention of Lorraine? It was not to be retained as an automatic result of an occupation; that would be a political matter to be dealt with later. Whether the cardinal and Chauvelin saw Lorraine as the last block to be fitted into a map of France and quietly worked in this direction as a priority matter is easy to believe but difficult to demonstrate. Proprietary rights arose from dynastic rights, and the rights of the sovereign of Lorraine would not disappear with a French invasion. The sovereign of every small and medium-sized state in the empire must have watched this carefully. And it seems appropriate that the king of France was personally interested as well. Although we must assume that most initiatives from the king at this time were directly inspired by the cardinal, the reassurance Marshal Berwick had to give the king for occupying Lorraine may well have been in answer to a direct question from that hereditary monarch. It must be done to keep the enemy moving and to keep the Lorrainers from making war on us themselves, said Berwick. Dangervilliers said that he had read the letter to the king, who understood.[9]

So much for the aggressive strategy of the French north of the Alps. The decision not to engage the Austrian forces in the northern part of this area required some defensive measures for the French. In August, Marshal Berwick, on his way to Strasbourg to take command of the French forces facing the empire, passed through Metz, where he wrote to the ministry that he had worked out with his subordinate commander, Belle Isle, the measures to be taken to prevent the enemy from operating in French territory and to assure French communications. He proposed fifteen battalions of infantry and thirty-four squadrons of cavalry as an army of observation to watch the fortress of Luxembourg and cover the country between the Moselle and the Meuse. From the Moselle to Alsace he proposed to deploy six additional battalions and fourteen squadrons, not counting garrisons. Counting garrison troops and reserves it all amounted to forty-four battalions and fifty-eight squadrons, or, assuming a reasonable unit strength, between 20,000 and 25,000 foot soldiers and between 7,000 and 8,000 riders. Belle Isle wrote the minister the next day noting his discussion with Berwick and stated that for the moment he would occupy himself with reestablishing the most essential fortress on the Moselle, that of Sierck, halfway between Metz and Trier.[10]

Thus the French were concerned with the plans for offensive warfare in Italy and along the Rhine, and with neutrality and defensive measures along the northern and northeastern borders of France. When we turn to the Austrians, we find that they saw their problem as primarily defensive. If there was a strategy it seems to have been completed, in a negative sense, when the emperor's plan to avoid a clash with the French by using Russian forces in Poland was demonstrated a failure. The Austrians had no real strategy except to defend the various fortresses and cities they held with whatever forces they could muster.

Along the Rhine the defenses of the Holy Roman Empire had not held up well against the ravages of eighteen years of peace. Starting with the upper Rhine, the imperial fortress at Breisach presented some problems for French planners in devising an attack, as we have seen, but the Austrians saw it as a potential disaster for the defender. Prince Eugene wrote to the commander in July 1733 promising a strengthening of the garrison as soon as possible, adding, however, that if the reinforcements could not be made in time he trusted the commander would defend the honor of imperial arms. In September he tried to reassure the commander of forthcoming reinforcements but admitted that they would be a part of those which had not yet arrived in Freiburg. Again the prince was satisfied, he told the commander, that the honor of the imperial arms was in good hands if the French should overrun the area.[11] It was not a very cheerful assurance for a commander in the forward area awaiting an enemy attack. The attack did not come, but even as late as the first part of 1734, the Duke of Württemberg complained that the status of the fort was such that it simply was not capable of resistance.[12]

Farther north, in the imperial city of Freiburg, the commander received instructions in midsummer 1733 to prepare for a blockade or siege.[13] His situation on 1 October found him with about 1,200 regular troops. Militia and armed peasants made up several hundred more, although a considerable part were without weapons and hundreds of all categories were sick. The repair of fortifications was also slowed by disagreement between the Austrian officials and the military administration as well as the general shortage of funds.[14]

At Kehl similar difficulties emerged. In January 1733 the commander, Baron Phull, complained to the imperial representative at Regensburg that the funds allocated by the diet had not yet been received. As the threat of French attack grew, the emperor sought more action and the imperial representative at Regensburg on 18 September demanded approval of funds for the repair of both Kehl and Philippsburg. This was duly granted in December, by which time Kehl had already fallen to a French siege.[15]

Farther downstream, Philippsburg was the most formidable of the imperial fortresses along the Rhine, possibly the strongest in Europe at that time. In June the Franconian Circle was ordered to strengthen the 500-man garrison with circle troops. But by November there were only slightly over 1,500 troops capable of duty instead of the 7,000 needed for a thorough defense, and there was a great shortage of artillerymen. New works in the fort were either incomplete or had not been started.[16]

In Hesse, along the left bank of the Rhine below Bingen, was Schloss Rheinfels, also in a sad state of repair. The emperor in August 1733 asked the king of Sweden, as landgrave of Hesse, to repair the fortress, with no reported results. In early 1734 troops of the Rhine Circle were sent to Rheinfels.[17]

Across from Coblenz, high above the right bank, is the great fort of Ehrenbreitstein, then part of the territory of the elector of Trier. The elector had asked Prince Eugene to equip his fortress, which had neither troops nor an effective commander, with imperial troops and an imperial commandant.[18]

The fortified city of Luxembourg seems to have fared better. The Villars memoirs indicate that the French had been carefully watching the efforts of the Austrians to improve the fortifications and increase the garrison as the year 1733 progressed.[19]

The correspondence of Prince Eugene with the imperial commanders of strong points, and with the leading German

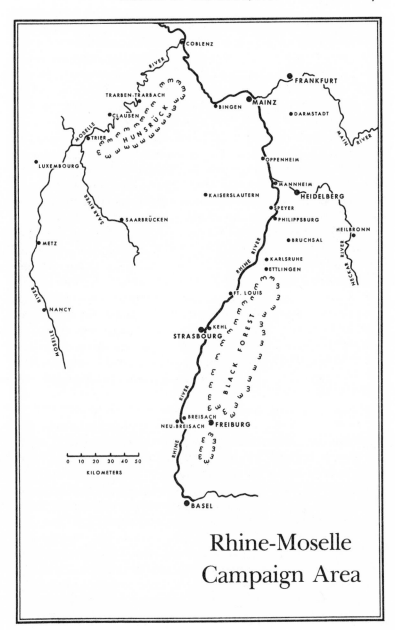

# Rhine-Moselle Campaign Area

princes in the West, is a sad compilation of commanders' complaints coming to Eugene and the tireless but often futile efforts of Eugene to squeeze money or troops from the imperial princes and to cheer the unhappy commanders.

French military preparations, meanwhile, had been quickening during the late summer months. Colonels were to be with the troops by the end of August. More important was the selection of commanders for the two principal theaters of operations, Italy and the Rhine-Moselle. The veteran Villars, in spite of his work with the minister in the formation of the armies, found that the top command, that of the Rhine-Moselle, was destined for Marshal Berwick and that he was to be made commander in Italy. This was taken badly by the public, according to Villars— meaning we assume, by his friends at court. Chauvelin, to relieve the old warrior's embarrassment, put it out that Villars had refused the other command, but Villars was not mollified. When told that the king wished him to command in Italy, however, he was forced to accept. Before leaving France he demanded an honor; he wished to be made a constable of France, a rank last held by the great Turenne, and he asked Chauvelin to obtain it for him. But on 19 October the war minister came from the king to tell Villars that he would not be made constable but would be a marshal general with precedence over all other marshals. On 26 October Villars left for Italy to take over his command, and his journal came to an end.[20]

The selection of Berwick for the Rhine-Moselle theater was a wise one. He was a commander who could be expected not to exceed his orders, and it was in this theater where restraint must be exercised if France were not to have the empire of German princely states grouping defensively about their emperor. Berwick has been criticized as overcautious and unimaginative in his actions in this war. He probably was, but that was undoubtedly the performance desired by the cardinal. The struggle Berwick had with Belle Isle over the deployment of his forces was an example of the conservative commander seeking to hold back an enthusiastic subordinate.

The northern wing of Berwick's command would prove to be the least active of the war areas, but its commander, Belle Isle, was an ambitious young general who was able to formulate extensive and daring projects. The general and his brother, the chevalier de Belle Isle, were both active in the Moselle area and aggressively seeking fame and recognition.

During the month of September 1733 a considerable amount of time was spent on the study of two projects proposed by Belle Isle in a memoir dated 29 July.[21] On 7 September a document which might be called a short staff study appears in the records. Entitled *Reflections on the Memoir of M. de Belle Isle of 29 July*, it examined the requirements of the first of Belle Isle's projects. This was a manned defense line that would stretch troops from the Meuse at Mezières south to Verdun, then east to Toul, then north along the Moselle to Sierck, then farther east along the Saar to Wissembourg in Alsace, using sixty-three battalions and fifty-three squadrons. The study concluded that the proposal, besides greatly increasing the work corvées and putting local inhabitants in a state of armed alert more onerous than contributions, would require more troops than the king had at that time.[22]

The second project of Belle Isle, that of creating a defensive barrier by inundations and felled trees from Sédan to the Moselle at Sierck and thence to the Rhine, is treated less summarily and it is suggested that the memoir be forwarded to the king. On 8 September a message from Dangervilliers to Berwick revealed that the memoir had been studied by the minister and by generals Puységur and d'Asfeld. The second project, which they described as a containment of the garrison at Luxembourg, was considered a possibility. Questions were raised, however, as to whether it would suffice as a defense of Lorraine, whether it would require fewer troops than the first project, and how much damage would be done by the tree cutting and inundations.[23]

On 10 September a further letter from the war minister to Berwick advised that the project was favored by d'Asfeld and Puységur. Of course, admits the minister, it is true that the emperor has made no assembly of troops against us. Still, it seems from the map to be a simple way to protect a large part of the area. But, he adds finally, of course nothing will be done without your opinion. D'Asfeld then traveled to Strasbourg to talk to

Berwick about the lines, and on 14 September Berwick wrote the minister that he had listened to all the arguments but had not changed his mind. It would be impossible to have armies elsewhere if so many men were committed to a line.[24]

Apparently Belle Isle continued to press his case, for a letter from the war minister to Belle Isle on 21 September revealed that the decision had not yet been made. When Berwick gives his position, the king will take a position, said the minister. But a final judgment came from the marshal on 10 October, only a few days before the beginning of operations, and by this time he must have been extremely impatient with the whole matter. He speaks of the lines as a useless expense; the measures should be those he had outlined before.[25]

So much for Belle Isle's plan; but he will have others. On the face of it we may call it a rather unashamed attempt to preempt a large part of Berwick's army for his own ideas. With his plan rejected he must content himself with the prospect of occupying Lorraine.

The time approached for military action and as late as 7 September Berwick indicated that he thought Breisach to be his probable objective. The important question was whether the emperor could assemble a large army. On 16 September Dangervilliers wrote to Berwick that the king wanted an attack somewhere on the Rhine during the fall. The war minister pointed out in the letter that an attack on Philippsburg would be a long siege but that Kehl was an immediate target that could be handled easily from Strasbourg. Berwick found this agreeable and stated that he would be ready within two days after the king's order to place two bridges over the Rhine, one above and one below Kehl. On 8 October, in a message to the king, Berwick was more specific: "I consider that I can cross the Rhine with a large detachment on the thirteenth and establish a boat bridge below Kehl." After this, he added, he would establish another bridge above Kehl and that he would pay great attention to keeping strict discipline among his troops in their attitude toward the German states. A letter from the minister of war in this same period to an unknown recipient asserts that Marshal Berwick was correct in forbidding acts of hostility against the princes of the empire. Of course, he added, we do not carry this so far that we cannot defend ourselves.[26]

The king's order to Berwick to cross the Rhine—always a momentous occasion for a French commander—went out on 6 October.[27] The crossing began on the night of 12–13 October with a detachment of twenty companies of grenadiers who landed near the village of Augenheim north of Kehl and worked all night putting a bridge across the river. By the fifteenth Berwick was able to report that on the day before "toute l'armée passa le Rhin," although they were not yet well established in the swampy, stream-covered area.[28]

The problem of the German princes emerged immediately. Berwick was visited on the fourteenth by the court marshal of his majesty the duke of Württemberg with a letter from his master asking for a passport and security—which was accorded. The count of Baden had already asked for safe passage for two companies of circle troops and his own personal guard. This also was accorded. Berwick's letter to the duke was extremely polite and spoke of protecting the princes of the empire as a guarantee of the Treaty of Westphalia.[29]

Berwick had every reason to mean what he said. The Treaty of Westphalia confirmed the sovereignties of the German princes. Or, if one perceives the guarantees from the point of view of a German nationalist, it effectively prevented the emergence of a German national state. The individual rights of the German princes represented a long-term security guarantee for France —one that ended with the formation of the German Empire under a Prussian monarch in 1871.

Behind the courtesies, however, the hard facts were that the French army would forage and levy contributions. The burning of several villages, along with severely forced deliveries of hay and grain, caused Berwick to promise repayment and drew from him the statement that the French came as friends, not enemies. But Baden was levied with a contributions total of 40,000 florins, and other nearby areas negotiated as best they could when faced with French threats. The duke of Württemberg, an ardent supporter of the emperor, made a contributions agreement with the French as the lesser evil.[30]

How large was Berwick's army and what was it to do? Were the Austrians aware of the size of his forces? If his army was up to establishment strength in its units—and at the outset of a campaign we might expect it to be at least approaching full strength—it would have had about 38,000 foot troops in its fifty-six battalions and about 10,000 riders in its sixty-three squadrons of cavalry.[31]

On the Austrian side, Count Ferdinand of Fürstenberg, the imperial commissario at Regensburg, who was then at his own capital at Messkirch near the Swiss border, was sending Eugene in Vienna daily reports of French preparations. He had reported on 13 October the French construction of a boat bridge and on the fifteenth he wrote that he had a completely reliable report that the French had crossed the river with 50,000 men.[32]

The attack on Kehl was an attack on an isolated garrison and it alarmed the Austrians, who then saw that their field forces, such as they had, were too far to the east if the French intended a drive into the empire toward the Habsburg hereditary lands. They would have been relieved had they been able to read the communication from the minister of war to Berwick on 28 October, which revealed that there were no such plans at all. There is no precise news about the Austrian camp at Pilsen, wrote Dangervilliers, but the Prussians will not march this year. "I think you will have a quiet siege." Regarding what Berwick was to do after the siege, the minister suggested that he restrict himself to repairing the bridge at Fort Louis and to reducing his troops to the smallest number possible for the winter. It is possible, he added, that there will be peace on the frontiers.[33]

In the meantime Berwick had a siege to perform and he wrote that the trenches were opened on the nineteenth. This announcement was a key statement for those days and sufficiently important for Berwick to enclose a special note to bring it to the king's personal attention.[34]

The detailed report of the French army positions drawn up

for 21 October showed Berwick's forces deployed about Kehl, with a special Trench Command under a lieutenant general composed of six companies of grenadiers, three battalions of infantry, and 2,000 workers.[35] The French also found that the enemy commander was either unwilling or unable to mount an active defense. General Noailles, commander of the French right wing, reported that he went down into the trenches on the night of the twenty-first. "The night passed in quiet. We have nothing to worry about except colds and chest congestion." Berwick on 22 October also noted that the enemy had not fired a shot during the preceding two nights.[36]

Doubtless the fortress commander knew how unlikely was the possibility of relief. He chose a brief defense—about as brief as was permissible under the conventions of his time. By the twenty-ninth he had agreed to articles of capitulation, of which the following were crucial: "Il est convenu que demain 30, la garnison sortira armes et bagage, tambour battant, enseigne deployé, avec deux pièces de canon." Thus they would march out, drums beating, flags flying, to join their forces elsewhere, and the commander's honor would be intact.[37]

On the Austrian side the reports of the commander at Kehl show that he had 1,200 Swabian Circle troops and 250 imperials, but a serious lack of artillerymen. When he saw the French crossing the Rhine in boats, he destroyed the pontoon bridge linking Kehl with Strasbourg and burned houses in the town that were too close to his walls. The attack was initially directed against the hornwork, which unfortunately had been razed and was in process of being rebuilt. (A hornwork was one of several fortified constructions used as forward defenses to a fortress.)

The commander on 18 October issued a list of instructions that directed his troops in how they should fall back toward the central fort as they were driven from the forward works. As the French moved their sappers and their batteries closer, there was little the garrison could do with the meager artillery at hand. On the twenty-fifth they made a sortie against the positions between the Rhine and the hornwork, which was repulsed by the French grenadiers. By the twenty-seventh the French were bombarding steadily. A fire in the hornwork drove out the Austrian troops

there, and after a council of war among his officers Phull decided to ask for terms. He had hardly 500 effectives and did not
wish to have the fortress taken by storm. Fourteen canon were
surrendered along with a large supply of munitions which had
been destined for Breisach and sent to Kehl by mistake. They
did not fit the caliber of the guns and mortars used at Kehl.

On the thirty-first the garrison marched out with sixty wagons, between the ranks of the French, who presented arms and
continued a drum roll until the evacuation was completed. The
garrison had not lost more than 40 men killed and wounded and
numbered about 1,200. (The discrepancy with the garrison figures mentioned before probably represents desertions during
the siege.) The French escorted the garrison as far as Ettlingen
where the Swabian troops were turned over to local authorities
and the imperials set out to join the imperial garrison at Freiburg.[38]

This lackluster defense hardly came up to the accepted requirements for siege defense in the eighteenth century. There
were more or less specific rules as to how long a fort must be
held after the artillery and digging operations against it are
in motion. One professional observer, the count of Bavaria, a
French general commanding one of the units in the siege, wrote
in his diary that the garrison marched out with honors, "except
that of having made a good defense, for I don't think there has
ever been such a miserable one."[39]

The French lost 16 soldiers killed, 46 wounded, 2 officers
killed, 7 wounded, and had 179 deserters.[40] The last figure tells
us why eighteenth-century armies invariably fought in close
ranks and why they dared not fight at night if they expected to
have very many troops present in the morning.

The siege terminated, the marshal announced that he would
proceed to Fort Louis with the bulk of his army and construct a
bridge. The siege of Kehl was about as much campaign as the
French desired to have on the Rhine in 1733. There is even a
letter from Marshal Du Bourg, the governor of Alsace, to Prince
Eugene, assuring him that there would be no further operations
along the Rhine. We want to destroy the rumor that we will lay
siege to Philippsburg, wrote the marshal. The artillery is going

back into the magazines at Strasbourg and you may negotiate at leisure during the winter. We wish to show good intentions to the circles and all the empire.[41] It is a friendly letter of one gentleman to another and probably in good faith. Of course Du Bourg did not necessarily speak for Italy, where more lively operations were taking place.

While Marshal Berwick, with the larger part of his command, crossed the Rhine near Kehl, a smaller part of his army, under Belle Isle, simultaneously began operations to the northwest. As Berwick had already pointed out in earlier messages, the requirements in that area were to oppose Luxembourg, cover the Meuse Valley, invade Lorraine, and maintain communications with Alsace.[42]

On 13 October Belle Isle's troops entered Lorraine unopposed and he presented himself personally at the gate of the city of Nancy where he was hastily given the keys to the city. He then passed on to the ducal residence in nearby Lunéville where he had an audience of one hour with the duchess, the mother of the absent sovereign. The command of troops in Nancy was given to General Lutteaux who began to concern himself with repairs to the citadel.[43]

It was obvious that the French made strenuous efforts to keep the goodwill of the ruling house of Lorraine and of its citizens. Forage was to be paid for as it was under Louis XIV, for example. But it was not long before misunderstandings arose. General Lutteaux found himself asking for the traditional "lit, bois, et chandelle" for his troops and being confronted by a duchess who stated that she was quite surprised by this, that it did not accord with what she had been told in a letter from Louis XV, and that she intended to write to Louis. The unhappy general found that he must delay his actions and wrote to his minister. The response of the minister a few days later does not seem to give him clear authority. The general was probably more unhappy still to receive a copy of a letter sent to the duchess by Cardinal Fleury on 25 October according to which Lorraine was not to bear any expenses even for its own security. The general then wrote to the minister saying that because of the cardinal's letter the city of Nancy would not give him the wagons and other articles needed to repair the fortifications unless they were paid for. The duchess, said General Lutteaux, stands on the letter from the cardinal and the Treaty of 1702. I await further orders, said the frustrated general. Poor Lutteaux even wrote to the minister showing in opposing columns what he had been ordered to do and what had been done. We have not advanced beyond the first day, he admitted.[44]

By January 1734 Lutteaux would write that he was still having troubles but that things were getting better. It was difficult to occupy a country and enjoy the friendship of its citizens and its hereditary rulers, although in this case the French bent over backwards. The duchess was offered the choice of remaining securely in Lunéville or coming to any city she wished in France. She finally elected to go to Luxembourg.[45]

Lorraine would remain a quiet area throughout the war, although there were rumors from time to time that the Habsburgs were planning an attack along the Meuse. The French kept an army of observation south of Luxembourg without making any attempt to initiate hostilities.

The immediate concern of the Austrian emperor and his government on learning of the death of the king of Poland was to maintain the border security with Poland. It was believed that in the confusion of the Polish electoral period some of the Polish nobility and their forces would venture over the border and plunder villages in neighboring states. Therefore in March the emperor ordered the movement of imperial forces to the border in Silesia. The orginal camp site was Oppeln, about fifty kilometers from the border. A strength of 10,000 men was assembled there. In June a part of the force was moved to the northwest to Gross-Glogau while the others were moved back southward into Bohemia to Pilsen. By September there were 20,000 men available in Pilsen, some 13,000 infantry and nearly 7,000 cavalry. Some of the infantry had even been brought there over the passes from Italy.[46]

The available evidence indicates that the aging and failing Prince Eugene must bear some responsibility for the misplacement of Austrian forces and also for misjudging French and Sardinian intentions. On 7 October 1733, in a letter to Prince Friedrich von Württemberg, who then shared the command of imperial forces in Italy with Marshal Daun, Eugene noted that there was probably little to fear for 1733 this late in the season and that he found it difficult to believe that the king of Sardinia would expose his states by permitting the passage of a French army. Finally, he concluded, the "fire" may well spread to Italy in the next year and "I will consider therefore the sending of timely reinforcement troops in proportion to the need which we shall have for them."[47]

It was a weak and complacent statement. The French would attack in less than a week after this message, and the French-Sardinian treaty had already been signed on 26 September, although the Austrians were not aware of it until 8 October.[48] It was a bitter surprise for Prince Eugene of Savoy to find that the head of the house of Savoy, King Charles Emmanuel, had turned to his old enemy, France. On 14 October the imperial minister in Turin was given the declaration of war. By the twenty-fourth Eugene would write to another of the Württemberg princes that this was the beginning of a hard and bloody war.[49]

Thus, in mid-October, with the unpleasant fact of an active war with France already under way, the first thing to do was to move the forces in Pilsen into a more useful position. Obviously the Austrian leaders had relied on hopes rather than judgment in leaving the Rhine unprotected.

In a long written presentation of 27 October, Prince Eugene reviewed the entire military situation and informed his emperor that the Pilsen corps had broken camp on the twenty-first and was provided with hard money for the purchase of supplies and with the necessary vehicles. Field Marshal Duke Ferdinand Albrecht of Braunschweig-Bevern was in command, and he had been advised by special messenger to expedite the movement westward by direct march and should do all possible short of ruining the troops to secure the city of Ulm. Eugene noted that the distance from Pilsen to Ulm was twice that from Strasbourg to Ulm and that if the French seriously intended to make a juncture with the Bavarians then Bevern might not be able to reach Ulm in time and might have to retreat towards Regensburg in order to keep the Danube bridges there under his control. The possibility of an understanding between France and Bavaria might mean that France would move toward Ulm or Donauwörth to maintain communications with the Bavarian lands. Bevern should further secure the depot at Ulm by sending a supply officer ahead to load the grain there on boats or rafts if the French should approach. It could then be moved to Regensburg or wherever the duke desired.

Eugene went on to discuss other force movements. He thought there was no further question of the imperial forces entering Poland and that some of the Gross-Glogau troops might be moved to guard the Tirol passes or to Upper Austria to keep watch on the Bavarians. In Hungary he noted the need for cavalry to secure this large area. Admitting the bad effect on the Turkish frontier of withdrawing troops, he still recommended the movement of regiments to inner Austria or to the Tirol.

Eugene left no doubt that he spoke for the War Council and as its president, and that he was greatly concerned about the attitude of the elector of Bavaria. Bevern had not only been told to use his intelligence to observe all Bavarian movements and to report anything suspicious, but had been given the authority to act with prudence in circumstances in which it might be impossible to secure a sufficiently rapid approval from Vienna.

Finally, these immediate matters covered, Eugene went on to discuss more fundamental military measures with the emperor. He considered that little could be done this late in the season but believed that a great deal must be accomplished before the next spring.[50]

First he summed up the emperor's military forces in rough totals: Netherlands, 20,000; Naples and Sicily, 21,000; Lombardy, 18,000; forward Austrian bases, 9,000; hereditary lands, 7,000; Hungary and bordering provinces, 30,000; field forces, 45,000. This made a total of 150,000 men.

He qualified these figures by noting that Hungary, because of its local population and the Turkish threat, needed reinforcement, and that the hereditary lands must be reinforced because of the proximity of Bavaria. Further, the forces in Lombardy were below strength from desertion and sickness. He then warned that if the emperor did not send an army into Italy against the 40,000 enemy forces, one position after another would be lost, and if the French succeeded in occupying the Adige Valley they might well force the Austrian army back across the Alps as they did in 1701.

North of the Alps Eugene noted that France and Bavaria would have the Danube to their advantage if they could join forces. The emperor must not rely on fortresses in this area; only an enlarged field army could protect the hereditary lands from a break-in by enemy forces. The imperial force must be one that could either prevent the juncture of French and Bavarian forces, drive back the enemy forces, or bring them to a decisive battle. This army must be ready by the end of February or the enemy would be able to break into the hereditary lands. The need was to be ready to hold off the enemy long enough for allied forces to join and launch an attack.

Eugene's old bitterness against the house of Bourbon, as well as his hope for active allies, comes out toward the end of his presentation: "The danger cannot be too strongly represented; the house of Habsburg has never been in such a crisis. The Polish affair was simply a pretext and the intrigues which have been glowing under the ashes for so long a time have now broken out into a great fire. It is fortunate that it did not occur later and now the entire empire and the sea powers can see their too great indolence towards the house of Bourbon and have their eyes opened once again."

It is a resolute document and probably represents, for a moment at least, the resurgence of the Eugene of former times. But it was very late. It would be the inaction of the French rather than Austrian efforts that would save the hereditary lands from invasion.

On 31 October Eugene wrote again to the emperor stating that he had once more urged the duke of Bevern to hasten toward Ulm. But it was a race without an opponent. The French had no intention of occupying the Swabian Circle lands and soon would retreat back across the Rhine, holding only the fortress at Kehl. Berwick understood perfectly the urgent movements of the Austrians and on 9 November reported that the

Pilsen corps had been sent to the Ulm area to prevent a French juncture with Bavaria.[51]

Eugene had reason to be suspicious of Bavarian intentions and to sense the existence of a solid agreement between Bavaria and France. Negotiations had taken place between the two during the summer of 1733. The treaty that was finally approved committed the elector of Bavaria to work against anything contrary to French interests in the empire. The elector also repeated his refusal to sign the Pragmatic Sanction. The king of France agreed to support the elector in the assemblies and courts of Europe, to support the elector's protest against the Pragmatic Sanction, and to protect him, if necessary, by force. In two secret articles France agreed to provide two million livres annually for Bavarian forces of no less than 26,000 men and to maintain these forces for five years. The treaty was signed on 15 November 1733.[52] Despite these arrangements the position of the elector between the two great houses of Europe was a perilous one. We find in the French archives a letter from the duke of Bevern, dated 24 November, from a town in Bavaria near Ulm, stating that he would pass through several Bavarian locations on the shortest route to Ulm.[53] The elector could not, according to the imperial constitution, refuse passage of the troops of the emperor nor those of any other state of the empire. The direct road to Ulm lay across Bavaria.

So much for the Austrian military reaction. They must now do all possible to organize the empire against the French. Not only would the individual states be asked to supply their contingents of men, but the central organ of the empire, the Diet at Regensburg, must be urged to declare war, although it was well known that several of the larger members were sympathetic to the French, and the attitude of the Prussians was ambiguous.

There is in the Austrian Kriegsarchiv a large printed poster, a rectangle a meter long on the longer side, which is the imperial declaration of war. Dated 4 November 1733, it calls attention to the "Decret" against the breaking of the peace by France, Spain, and Sardinia, and it appeals for help from all parts of the empire.[54] However, this is only one step toward a declaration by the empire itself. The emperor would have to wait several months before a *Reichskrieg* would be declared.

The imperial court laid great importance on the war declaration and sent representatives to each of the German princes whose vote was questionable. Field Marshal Count Königsegg went to the elector of Bavaria and to Cologne, Count Ferdinand Küfstein to the Palatinate. But in vain. The three princes in these states, and the bishop of Regensburg, were the only German princes who would not approve the declaration of war.[55] Count Fürstenberg wrote that there were representatives at Regensburg with devotion and fidelity but that Baron von Plettenburg of Bavaria in hate and recrimination opposed the declaration and influenced Cologne. Braunschweig and Hanover, he observed, had more "patriotic" instructions.[56]

It was not until 9 April 1734 the *Reichskrieg* was declared, over the objections of the dissenters noted above. By this time the armies were in motion and the effect of the decision on the war for that critical campaign season was problematical.

During the winter of 1733–1734 the emperor sought to increase his forces. The 150,000 troops Eugene mentioned in his presentation represented the units of the imperial army on a war footing. The army was not on a war footing when the French attack came, however, but on a peacetime footing, which was roughly 15 percent less. Moreover, the units were seldom up to their full peacetime strength, some falling as much as a third below. All this was touched upon by Eugene as he sought a way to draw units together to form a field force while not jeopardizing the borders of the Habsburg Empire. This would include, of course, bringing all units up to wartime strength. In addition he urgently requested the formation of six new infantry regiments plus the recruiting of Swiss regiments and battalions.[57]

Fritz Redlich, in his study of the German military enterpriser, finds that the Austrian recruiting of "five" new regiments in 1733 of special interest as a turning point in recruiting. The practice in which noblemen raised regiments on their own account was giving way to financing by the state. In this case the cost of raising five of the ten companies in each regiment 'was paid by the treasury and the other five by the colonel-designate of the regiment in question.[58]

In spite of the standing Turkish threat some troops were taken from the Croatian border region. According to Rothenberg the use of *Grenzer* for the first time outside the border area was a complete fiasco. "The departure of the *Grenzer* for Italy, in December 1734, led to tumult and disturbances. At first the troops refused to depart at all and insisted on submitting a lengthy memorandum of their grievances to the emperor." Later, in Italy, when they heard reports of religious persecution by the Austrians in their homeland, they mutinied.[59]

There were also other sources of troop strength. The first category was "troops in imperial pay" ("Truppen im kaiserlichen Sold"). Already thirteen regiments were promised, of which some were already in imperial service. They came from the states of Würzburg, Saxony-Weimar, Saxony-Eisenach, Saxony-Gotha, Braunschweig-Lüneberg, Württemberg, Mainz, and Waldeck. Auxiliary troops ("Hilfs-truppen") were another category. These were the expected forces from Austria's allies, including Prussia, Holland, Denmark, and England. (England's contribution would include troops from Hanover, of course.) Here the Austrians would be disappointed. They would eventually receive contingents from Hanover, Prussia, and Denmark, but there would be no help from the sea powers—England proper, or Holland. From all these sources the Austrian forces might have been increased by 100,000 men during the course of 1734, bringing the total Austrian forces up to 250,000. But the special interests of the German sovereigns and the poor execution of their agreements as well as poor cooperation from the allies thwarted the mobilization from the beginning.

The Pilsen corps, on the march since 20 October, placed its vanguard in Ulm on 11 November. Eugene wrote to Bevern to take care, that even so late in the season the French might undertake an operation, particularly if they had Bavarian help.[60] But the French were already crossing back over the Rhine into Alsace, holding Kehl as a guarantee for a Rhine crossing for the next year. Bevern's corps then moved forward to position itself as a thin line of forces along the Rhine from the Neckar River to

Freiburg, establishing communication with Philippsburg and strengthening its garrison with 2,000 men. The positions for the winter would to some extent reflect the threat from the elector of Bavaria, whose armies could move against the thin flanks of Bevern's command. But in general the Austrian positions were intended to occupy as much of the territory as possible. "The more areas on this side of the Rhine that we occupy the more difficult it will be for the French to draw subsistence from the German states, and the easier for the troops of Your Majesty," wrote Eugene to the emperor in November.[61]

The war along the Rhine was over for the year. Berwick went back to Paris in November, leaving Du Bourg in charge. Both sides would plan their strategies for the spring campaign that both knew would occur.

CHAPTER SIX

# The War in Italy to May 1734

The war in Italy would prove disappointing to all concerned, and the available evidence suggests that each party merited at least a good part of the frustration all shared. The mobilization of the resources of the allies—France, Spain, and Sardinia—in coalition warfare was limited by conflicting objectives. On the imperial side lack of resources, indecision, and uncooperative German princes plagued the emperor's efforts.

The Po Valley was a cockpit in which French armies had fought for several centuries. The French strategy, given a weak Austrian army in northern Italy, was compellingly simple. Villars said it all in a few words when a meeting of the Council of State in June 1733 discussed the advisability of scattered attacks in northern Italy. "No," said Villars, "the king's army must reach Turin, march straight to Milan; the country is fresh and filled with food. From there, with the same dispatch, it must march to the foot of the Alps and prevent entry of the emperor's troops into Italy. You have behind you the state of Parma and Piacenza; you are positioned on the Po, and you carry out the siege of the citadel in Milan at your leisure" ("en pantoufles").[1] But Villars would find that putting this strategy into deeds was a difficult matter.

The French appeared to be moving with considerable dispatch as an army was assembled in the Dauphiné and prepared to cross the mountains into Italy. Message traffic with Fontanieu, the intendant in the Dauphiné, became lively in September. (The intendant was the key civilian functionary with broad responsibility for logistics and other services.) Fontanieu was advised on 1 September to expect forty-five battalions of about 30,000 foot soldiers plus sixty-four squadrons of cavalry comprising another 8,000 men. They would use four major routes: the Little Saint Bernard Pass into the Aosta Valley; the Mont Cénis and Mont Genèvre passes into Susa; the Argientière Pass into the Stura Valley; along the Riviera coast, then north over the Tende Pass into the Piedmont.[2]

The French forces were in motion in France before the actual declaration of war but moved into the Piedmont at approximately the same time as the northern army launched its 13 October attack on Kehl. In mid-October the appearance of messages indicating serious problems in troop movement showed that the entry into Italy had begun in earnest.[3] The chief problem seems to have been an effort to put too many men on the trails over the passes at one time. The marshal general of lodging, the marquis de Pezé, effectively the chief of staff of the army, found the daily movements too long as well. The minister of war told him in explanation that General Maillebois, temporarily commanding in Italy, thought that bodies of troops of less than corps strength should not appear in neighboring states and that they had therefore put eight battalions in movement at one time. But the minister wrote to Maillebois the same day indicating his concern, pointing out that there were too many men on the narrow paths. The king did not mean to go so far in keeping troops at corps strength, said the minister—an admission that the original directive had come from Versailles. A few days later, measures were taken in Grenoble to improve the passage of later columns of troops.[4]

Obviously the French had got off to a bad start. But it had been many years since a field army had passed the frontiers of France. Perhaps, also, the minister's effort to explain the situation to de Pezé reflected the fact that the latter corresponded directly with Cardinal Fleury, Chauvelin, and the king.

On 29 October the first column arrived in Turin and the next day a plan for the campaign was worked out by the French staff in the presence of Charles Emmanuel, king of Sardinia. The principal object of the war was asserted to be the conquest of the

Milanese. For this the mastery of the Po was declared essential. Specifically, the following movements were to take place.

Two corps would unite at Vigevano on 30 October, cross the Ticino the next day, and invest Pavia. To the south a force would move from Alessandria and invest Tortone to secure the course of the Po as far as the mouth of the Ticino, and to protect the line of communications with Genoa, whence the supplies not available in Italy would come. A bridge would be built over the Ticino on the twenty-ninth. After investing Pavia the rest of the army would march on Milan and attack its fortified citadel, the chateau. A bridge over the Po would be built at Piacenza. The armies would then cross the Adda and blockade Pizzighetone. Possession of this last fortress would enable the allies to block some of the entries from the Tirol in the north and open the Po Valley as far as the Mincio, where stood the fortified city of Mantua, key defense point of the Austrians in Italy.[5]

Even before Marshal Villars could arrive, while d'Asfeld was temporarily in command, the difficulties with the king of Sardinia began. D'Asfeld wrote to the minister of war that he would be glad to see Villars arrive; Villars would agree, he was sure, that they must besiege Pizzighetone before Milan. But Charles Emmanuel wished to move on Milan immediately, maintaining that the emperor had only 18,000 men, mostly on garrison duty, and did not dare to mount an offensive without reinforcements. It will be seen later that his estimate of enemy troop strength was correct. Nevertheless he agreed to wait for Villars and submit to his decision.[6]

D'Asfeld was also at odds with his own colleagues, generals Coigny and Broglie, who questioned his authority over them.[7] Differences among commanders, often amounting to quarrels, have appeared in all military forces. But it is probable that the eighteenth-century armies in western Europe had more than their share, since most officers then were not true professionals in the modern sense. Especially among the higher ranks they were nobles first and placed pride above obedience, valor above knowledge, and, as a great many surviving messages indicate, refused to submit to command channels in communications.

But things were not all bad for the French. The Austrians were in haste to pull back from their forward bases. There was consternation in Milan, and the emperor's forces were in the process of abandoning all the forward fortresses except Novara, Tortone, Pizzighetone, and the chateau of Milan.[8]

As the French army moved forward at the end of October they were informed that the Austrians had withdrawn from Pavia, leaving thirty cannon behind. So precipitant was the Austrian departure that the guns were left in working order.[9] A few hours later Pavia was occupied and a deputation of citizens hastened to the king of Sardinia to present him with the keys to the city. A surprised Europe saw the emperor's rule collapse in Lombardy.

Meanwhile, Villars was making his way slowly through France toward Italy. He knew this would be his last command, and he savored the honors that were given him. As a soldier serving three queens he received for his hat the cockade of Queen Marie before leaving Versailles; the cockade of the queen of Spain awaited him in Lyons; and the third was placed on his hat after he received it from the hand of the queen of Sardinia when he arrived in Turin. Here it was that he is supposed to have made his memorable response to the queen's question, How old was he?—"Madame, dans deux mois j'aurai MILAN!"

The campaign was under way when Villars arrived in Turin on 7 November and duly announced his arrival by a message to the king of France.[10] We may suspect that Villars was treated with some flattery, for he soon wrote back to the minister of war that he was very happy with the king of Sardinia and his ministers. He would have occasion later to change his views. But the army was on the move by 10 November, about half of it committed to the siege of Pizzighetone under Maillebois, and the other half to an attack on Milan under Coigny. At least initial agreement was achieved with the king of Sardinia.[11]

Villars actually joined the army on 11 November before Pizzighetone. The Austrians had been pulling their troops back to Milan and to Pizzighetone, and in the latter area they had delayed an allied approach by flooding the local terrain with the waters of the Oglio River. Still, it was possible to begin the siege, and Villars must have been happy on the date of his arrival to report back to Versailles, "We opened the trenches this evening." But already he was less sanguine about dealing with the Piedmontese and foresaw difficulties in concerting their projects.[12] Strangely, in the matter of the siege of Pizzighetone an argument developed among the allied military leaders in which Villars was supported by King Charles Emmanuel. Marshal Bernard Rhebinder, a Swede of long military experience then in Piedmontese service, advised only a blockade of Pizzighetone so they might push on with the bulk of the forces to threaten or cut the lines of communication between the Austrian forces in Italy and the passes over the Alps. Although Villars's earlier statements had seemed to favor such a strategy, at this time he demanded a siege, and a heated exchange took place between the two marshals with the result that Rhebinder was removed. Villars explained his change of opinion, not very convincingly, in a letter to his king. The principal reason, he asserted, was the approach of the Spanish army putting forces on his right.[13] Actually, the "approaching" Spanish forces were by no means near at hand.

The question of whether or not there should be a siege of Pizzighetone also pricked the interest of Cardinal Fleury. As a rule the hand of the cardinal is seldom seen in the military dispatches, at least directly. Messages come from the minister of war, the king, even from Chauvelin, but there are few from the cardinal in the military files. Yet occasionally the light pressure of the cardinal's will is felt in military matters and his presence is made known. One of his informants, the marshal general in charge of lodging, the marquis de Pezé, received this letter from him dated 30 October while the question of the siege was under debate.[14]

I read your letter of the twenty-third to the king, who was moved by the pleasure he would have when he knows his forces are in the city of Milan. This does not prevent an appreciation of your reasons to favor Pizzighetone. Marshal Villars, who should have arrived in Lyons yesterday, will presumably join the army before the taking of Pavia, and he will decide. I confess that winter quarters on the far side of the Adda would seem to me quite desirable for the army. Reflect on this and try to put some proposals about it before the Sardinian ministers. Report to me what you think can be done.

The siege of Pizzighetone was to be comparable to the one at Kehl. The town was a small fortified area with about 4,000 people beside a citadel on the left bank of the Adda River, about fifteen kilometers above its confluence with the Po. On the right bank opposite was a fortified suburb called Gera which was connected to the town by a bridge. Like most of the other Austrian strong points it was in poor repair. Field Marshal Lieutenant Count Livingstein, the commander, wrote to Eugene on 5 November, shortly before the beginning of the siege. "In all my life I have never seen a fortress on which His Imperial Majesty had spent so many millions so miserably arranged and so badly supplied." At that time he had a total of 3,696 men (quite insufficient for a place of this size), some forty-five pieces of artillery of various sizes, and three mortars.

As Livingstein later informed the Court War Council, the suburb of Gera was all-important for the defense of Pizzighetone and, once it was taken, the fall of the main fortress would soon follow. But he was determined to make a strong defense despite his eighty-some years. He was said to have answered a summons to surrender from the king of Sardinia with the pointed response that he knew how to keep his sworn oath better than the king, and that threats for an old man who did not have very long to live were not enough to sway him. In harmony with the ideas of his time, he did not say that he would fight to the last man, but rather that he would not surrender without a brave defense.[15]

The allies arrived in force on 16 November. While they awaited the arrival of their artillery by boats on the Po, they put 10,000 workers to digging canals and breaching the dams that gave Gera its water defense. They were in some haste to complete this before rains might make the work impossible. By the twentieth, the attackers were digging the second parallel before the fort. The

artillery arrived and by the twenty-second the firing on both Pizzighetone and Gera was causing substantial damage. On the night
of the twenty-third an attack by grenadiers and workers drove the
defenders from that forward line of defense known as the covered way. Villars, now more confident of the softness of the
enemy defenses, put eleven battalions on the left bank on the
twenty-fifth and opened trenches around Pizzighetone proper.
By 28 November the artillery fire of the allies was much heavier
and the connection between Gera and the main citadel was en-
dangered. Livingstein sent a messenger proposing the surrender
of Gera. The allies refused, but made the counteroffer of allowing him eight days to surrender Pizzighetone, during which period his garrison would be permitted to withdraw. If he refused,
his garrison would become prisoners of war when the citadel was
taken. Livingstein asked permission to send a messenger to Mantua to obtain agreement for his surrender and this was granted.
But in Mantua the commander, Prince Friedrich von Württemberg, proposed that the date for yielding the fortress be set at 16
or 18 December. This proposal was, of course, an attempt to win
time for the repair of fortifications then under way in Mantua.
The allies refused this, and Württemberg ordered Livingstein to
continue his resistance. The resistance could not continue long,
however, and the old commander finally yielded after he had
been granted a delay until 9 December. It was his contention that
the fortress could hold out no more than four or five days if the
attack recommenced and that his delay had won eight days for
the Austrians, in addition to the garrison which, according to the
terms of the agreement, was allowed to march to Mantua and
would supplement the garrison there. So on 9 December Livingstein and his troops marched out, flags flying, drums beating,
arms on the shoulder, with twenty-four cartridges per soldier and
the right to take the most direct route to Mantua. Villars had already reported the terms of the surrender to his king, with stipulations accorded and stipulations denied neatly set off in parallel
columns, a document most carefully drawn up at the termination
of sieges.[16]

The chateau in Milan still held out, but its surrender was only

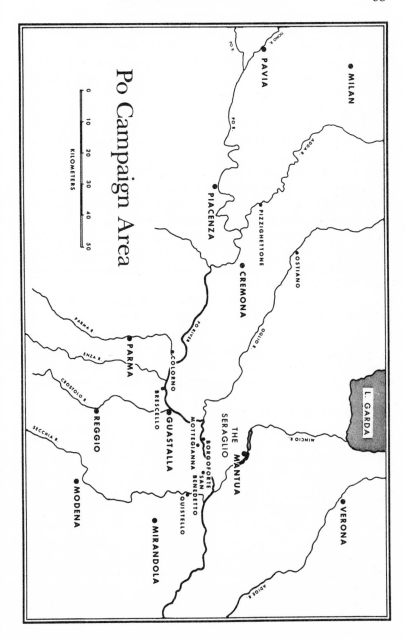

Po Campaign Area

a matter of time. Villars wrote to the king on 4 December: "My first two objectives in arriving in Italy were never to see your army exposed to any sort of peril and to assure the king of Sardinia, according to your orders, the conquest of the Milanese as soon as possible. I arrived on 11 November and on 2 December the two objectives were achieved." [17]

Villars now had some time to give to his ally, the Spanish. The expected appearance of the Spanish forces in northern Italy greatly excited the suspicions of Charles Emmanuel. The arrival of the duke of Liria as a Spanish liaison officer at French headquarters and the passing of communications between Villars and the overall Spanish commander, the marquis de Montemar, caused the Sardinian ministers to state that they had no need of a Spanish ally, and the king of Sardinia demanded the departure of Liria. But Villars seems to have mollified the king after some explanations and regained his confidence, if not always his cooperation.

The initial communication from Montemar came from the Spanish-held state of Parma on 19 November:

I wrote Your Excellency from Barcelona, and I attach herewith a copy, since I am uncertain whether the duke of Liria has arrived at your headquarters. I thought it my duty to inform you of my arrival in Parma where I await your orders with impatience.

I expect that we will soon have the troops from Spain in Livorno and Spezia; they consist of twenty-one battalions of 700 men each and ten squadrons of cavalry or dragoons of more than 120 men each. The rest of the cavalry will come by way of France, embarking at Antibes; eight or nine battalions of those troops in the state of Florence are to join the army which will be composed of thirty battalions and 5,000 horse, with a corps of fifty to sixty engineers, a similar number of artillery officers, fifty siege guns and thirty-four field pieces with all that is needed for an important siege, and twenty general officers.

I have just sent the order for nine battalions at Florence to advance to this side of the mountains; the other troops which will arrive in two convoys from Barcelona and Alicante will follow the same route.

I pray Your Excellency to inform me without delay what this army is to do, whether alone or with the army which you command, and to clarify for me also the other points which I gave to the duke of Liria to put to you.[18]

The note has the ring of a faithful ally to be. But Montemar would prove to be even more difficult for Villars than Charles Emmanuel. Villars soon received word from the French resident at the court of the Infant in Parma, the marquis de Bissy, that Montemar was taking a very sticky attitude and had presented him with a number of reasons why he could not come to a conference with Villars or the king of Sardinia.[19]

As Montemar indicated in his communication, he had under his command both the newly arriving troops from Spain and the Spanish forces in Tuscany already present under a previous agreement with the emperor. He would have roughly 26,000 troops to contribute to the attack on the imperial forces. While the French were before Pizzighetone, that part of the Spanish forces ordered north was moving up the coast from Tuscany taking forts evacuated hastily by imperial troops during the last days of November. At Aulla, near Spezia, the Spanish forces faced a determined Colonel Nothelfer and a small detachment that refused to yield. It was late December when the attackers went through the formalities of digging the trenches and mounting cannon, after which the garrison surrendered and the 140 defenders were made prisoners.[20]

Despite Montemar's earlier insistence on his independence, he did in fact cross the mountains for a conference with Villars at Sabbionetta on the Po on 11 December. This meeting was to fix the responsibility of the Spanish to operate on the lower Po, below the confluence of the Oglio, and to occupy the fortresses of Guastalla, Brescello, and Mirandola with ten battalions. Basically it was a strategy to assure that northern Italy was firmly won before the Spanish should undertake a projected attack on Naples and Sicily. Villars wrote to Louis XV on 12 December and outlined the results of the conference. He had explained the importance of securing the Po to its mouth and argued that it would not be difficult with Spanish assistance, particularly since the Po was very broad below the Oglio. Did Montemar agree to this? Villars thought he did. "He [Montemar] understood well that one could not carry out an attack on Capua and the kingdom of Naples since our first objective must be to close off Italy."[21]

The French strategy was quite logical. The duchy of Parma lay on the right bank of the Po and would be open to an Austrian attack unless the lower Po were secured. Since Parma was ruled by the Spanish Infant, Don Carlos, it was assumed that Montemar was vitally concerned for the security of this prince and the territory of his state. It soon became clear, however, that Montemar did not intend his forces to be used to help the French campaign at all if he thought the campaign did not directly assist his own. More likely he felt that the defensive measures the French asked him to contribute were those which the French could and would undertake whether or not he assisted them. Letters from Villars to Montemar reflect the old marshal's fear that Spain did not understand how vulnerable the lower Po would be if the emperor decided to reinforce his army. The imperial forces could cross the Alps quickly, warned Villars, and we could have 80,000 men upon us. But if the Po could be held, he reasoned, the imperials could be prevented from penetrating deeply into Italy, and the allies would have the grain of the Ferrara area instead of the enemy. Villars had also heard that his old foe (and personal friend) Prince Eugene was coming to take the command in Italy. It was a false report, as it turned out, but it must have increased Villars's concern. Villars also begged Montemar to write to him in French, which Montemar understood better than Villars understood Spanish, but there is no evidence that Montemar even granted him this concession.[22] The Spanish answer to Villars's plea for cooperation was an agonizing delay until the nervous marshal decided to move on and occupy Guastalla with his own forces. Not until 15 January 1734 did a force of 7,000 under the duke of Liria appear and occupy Brescello and Mirandola in the name of the king of Spain.[23]

At the same time Villars's relations with King Charles Emmanuel were deteriorating rapidly. Both the subsistence furnished the French troops and arguments over strategy poisoned the situation. General Vaulgrenant wrote to Chauvelin, sending him a memoir on the poor state of both men and horses as they entered the month of December. The Piedmontese, he said, maintained that the treaty did not permit winter quarters or contributions in the Milanese. The message has a desperate tone. There was not a moment to lose, he stated; the army was threatened with a complete wasting away ("un dépérissement, presque total").[24]

Presumably the crisis was overcome. Versailles did not seem to have been particularly worried, nor did the minister of war or foreign affairs appear to back up his subordinates in this, or in other instances, with great energy. On 28 December, Danger-villiers told the intendant not to press the matter with the Sardinians in spite of the possibility that the Sardinian intendant was pocketing part of the money paid for troop subsistence.[25] Coalition warfare is not easy.

Villars was reminded of his subordinate position in the greater plan of things when Charles Emmanuel on 11 December made a ceremonial entry into the city of Milan. A deputation from Milan had already presented itself at the allied camp and asked for the king's protection. An ancient custom authorized Milan to surrender when an enemy army crossed the Ticino on the west or the Adda on the east, and on the night of 3–4 December, French and Sardinian troops entered the city. The Austrian forces retired to the chateau and elected to withstand a siege.[26] According to a French report, the king of Sardinia was received with a ceremony comparable to that given the kings of Spain and emperors of Austria. Fontanieu's wry comment at the time was that the entry of the king did not rouse great joy in the people, who would choose to be ruled by Spain, France, the emperor, the devil, or the king of Sardinia—in that order.[27] A hundred years later, the king's descendant, borne on waves of Italian nationalism, would receive a more enthusiastic welcome on entering Milan.

Charles Emmanuel now had most of what he wanted and he wished above all to hold on to it. He set about, to the extent that he was able, to direct the strategy to that end. Poor Villars felt the effect soon when he was forced to wait an hour for the king in an antechamber and finally left. By 23 December he showed a deep anxiety as he recounted to Louis his difficulty in securing any cooperation from the king of Sardinia. "As for me, Sire, when I think of the army of the emperor arriving in the Tirol, I realize that the king of Sardinia could cause the loss of our own army and consequently put your kingdom in peril."[28]

But the war had to go on, and another opening of trenches was announced for the siege of the chateau of Milan. About half of the French army was in the Milan area but the siege would be a polite and relatively restrained undertaking.[29] It was arranged with the commandant in the chateau that the French would not attack from the city side, and he in turn would not fire from that side. On 20 December a great ball was held with Villars dancing a minuet at the opening. The orchestra was to begin the music when the first cannon was fired at the chateau. The officers could go from a tour in the trenches to the opera or balls during the thirteen days the chateau held out. But it was an active siege in which the imperial commander, Field Marshal Hannibal Marchese Visconti, gallantly defended his position until, as the French dug their parallels and mounted their batteries, he was faced with a hundred cannon and had only five of his own still in action to reply. With the opening of a practicable breach Visconti held his council of war, beat the chamade, and raised the white flag. His capitulation permitted him to withdraw with full honors to Mantua with six cannon, two mortars, and six covered wagons. Departing with 1,389 men, he lost 475 to desertion before arriving in Mantua with fewer than 900 men.[30]

The end of 1733 thus found the French militarily successful. In less than three months the Austrians had been pressed back into the area around the fortress of Mantua. But the Austrians would not be content to let the matter rest.

On the day the white flag was raised over the chateau of Milan, 29 December 1733, the emperor and his advisors sat in a long Privy Council meeting in Vienna. They had been taken by surprise by the defection of the king of Sardinia and his alliance with the French and simply did not have enough troops available to defend Lombardy. The dependence on a friendly or neutral Sardinia was so complete that not only was there no planning for early hostilities in Italy but there had been troop reductions, as previously mentioned, and grain was still being delivered from

Lombardy to the armies of the king of Sardinia while the latter was urgently preparing for war. Although Prince Eugene used the establishment figure of 21,000 imperial troops in Lombardy in one of his presentations for the emperor, the detailed reports of units, taking into account sickness and desertions, yielded only 13,340 effectives in northern Italy.[31]

The overall commander in northern Italy was the governor of Milan, Field Marshal Count Wirich Daun, one of the older and more experienced generals of the empire. Daun initially desired to hold the forward strong points, notably Pavia and Novara, and force the enemy to dislodge the forces there by the usual cumbersome and lengthy siege methods. His second-in-command, and general in command of troops, Prince Friedrich von Württemberg, a much younger man, wished to withdraw the forward garrisons to the base at Mantua as a final redoubt and keep a cavalry force in the forward area for observation, ready to fall back as need be or meet the enemy in open field. So the Austrian defense of Italy began with a disagreement between the two top commanders in the area.[32]

By the end of October Daun was forced to act along the lines argued by Württemberg and had ordered the evacuation of Pavia. One by one the strong points fell or were given up by their inadequate garrisons, in most cases with the agreement that they be permitted to fall back on Mantua rather than be taken prisoners of war. Daun must have felt uneasy about the rapid collapse of his positions, for in late October he left for Vienna— apparently of his own volition—to justify himself. He presented his case to the emperor in a letter that was passed on to Prince Eugene for advice on the matter.[33] Daun would not return to his command.

Prince Eugene, ailing though he was, came to life during these initial months of the war and began the mobilization of the imperial armies and the resources to supply them. The emperor's handwritten note at the end of Eugene's 25 October briefing was couched in confidential and affectionate terms.[34] On 14 November Eugene in a note to Marshal Bevern stated that already seventeen battalions were in movement toward the Tirol. By the end of the month he informed a garrison commander in Italy that a new overall commander in Italy had been chosen.[35] On 4 December he briefed the emperor on the situation, showing impatience with the three reluctant imperial princes, especially the elector of Bavaria, and stated that the army of the new commander in Italy, Field Marshal Mercy, should be fifty battalions and ten or twelve regiments of horse, plus two hussar regiments. Eugene also wished that his forces could fall upon the French along the Moselle Valley or from Luxembourg, but this could not be done without a "Reichskrieg"—that is, a war voted by the Diet in Regensburg, and with the approval of the sea powers, England and Holland. Eugene saw it all in the darkest terms: "For I see it all too well that this is the crisis for the house of Habsburg, upon which its future fortune or misfortune depends."[36] Perhaps Eugene exaggerated somewhat. The house of Habsburg would survive this war and the accompanying defeat with less strain than succeeding struggles. Cardinal Fleury was not an antagonist who sought the death or even the severe laming of his opponent.

Although the great concern of Eugene and the War Council in October was the protection of the areas north of the Alps— hence the hasty movement of the Pilsen corps to the West—the emphasis had changed by December. This change was due to the fact that the French on the Rhine were going into winter quarters after the taking of Kehl, and doubtless the rapid loss of the Italian strong points must also have invited reconsideration of the Italian strategy. The Privy Council meeting of 29 December 1733 with both the emperor and Prince Eugene in attendance, took up as their first point on the agenda the north-south military situation. Bartenstein's "Protocoll" of the sense of the meeting, prepared for the emperor on the following day, reads as follows: "There should be consideration of the unavoidable necessity for the most rapid creation of two armies, one in Italy and the other in the Empire. And since in the first area the danger is greater than in the second, and because delay there would entail broad and damaging consequences—indeed if the enemy is allowed still more time the evil may become irreparable—so first of all everything possible must be done to bring about early operations by the army under the command of Field Marshal Mercy."

The disadvantage of the Italy-first defense, as discussed in the protocol, was that the campaign in the Empire would have to be delayed. The French were already insinuating that the army of Marshal Bevern was only a token ("Schein") to induce the German states to commit themselves by a declaration of war in the imperial Diet, after which declaration, according to the French, they would find they had little protection given them by the emperor. Efforts must be made to convince the German states, went on the Bartenstein protocol, that neutrality with the French would enable the enemy to penetrate the inner lands of the empire.[37]

The beginning of 1734 saw a stream of messages going out from the Court War Council and from Eugene personally in a great effort to set the lumbering machine of the Austrian empire in motion and produce a field army for northern Italy. The intentions of the French in Italy were probably quite clear to the Austrians. In any case the Austrian embassy in Paris had reported the French strategy to be that of marching with the bulk of their army across northern Italy to the defiles of the Trentino, obliging the Republic of Venice to declare itself, occupying the city of Verona, and thus preventing imperial troops from entering Italy. It was the Villars strategy. Moreover, said the Austrian dispatch from Paris, the French were prepared to send 20,000 additional troops to Italy.[38]

With the capitulation of Milan at the end of 1733 the French were apparently free to move on against the last imperial strong point in Italy—Mantua. But the king of Sardinia from this point on would act as a brake on French movements. He saw the war as a struggle to maintain the possession of Lombardy and thought that any move east or south might imperil his position. The French saw security in a larger sense as requiring the defeat of the Austrian forces in Italy and, if possible, the blocking of Austrian reinforcements. It is very likely that Villars could have taken Mantua had he pushed on. Pajol points out that the marshes around the fortress were dry; there were few defenders, and these demoralized. In his opinion the French should not have permitted the garrisons of the several surrendered strong points to join the Mantua garrison, and the French should have acted to prevent the Venetians from letting more Austrian troops pass down the valleys of their republic to the Po Valley, since the principal entry led through Venetian territory.[39]

Before the arrival of Austrian reinforcements, Villars continued to have trouble with his Spanish ally. The problem arose with the intention of Montemar to withdraw his army from northern Italy—it had hardly arrived!—for an attack on Austrian territory in Naples. While this intention had been no secret to the French, the timing was important. Villars wrote to his king on 8 January 1734, noting that Montemar had agreed in writing to put himself under his orders but had not reported to him in thirty-four days what his intentions were. There were reports that the Spanish army was preparing to leave for Naples, said Villars. A few days later he wrote to the king of Spain, asking him to replace those troops which were being sent to Naples.[40]

On 18 January Villars learned from Bissy at Parma that Montemar had refused to reveal whether or not he was leaving for Naples. Villars then wrote a strong letter to Montemar reminding the Spanish general that he, Villars, was supposed to be commanding, and reminding him as well that the campaign of 1706 was lost to the Austrians under Eugene because of poor generalship involving the loss of Milan, Naples, and Sicily within three months.[41]

Villars then traveled to Parma and visited the Infant, Don Carlos, the son of Elisabeth Farnese, queen of Spain. He reported that the Infant showed "amiability, prudence, and timidity, especially for the orders of the queen his mother." Montemar's orders, according to the Infant, instructed him to march on Naples and to take the Infant with him.[42] Villars wrote to Montemar, noting his conversation with the Infant, and stating that he had advised the Infant to tell Montemar to go ahead. (Could Villars have done otherwise?) But Villars did ask who would cover Parma and Piacenza and mentioned the reports that the road from Trent over the Alps was covered with imperial troops. But it was no use. Montemar had avoided Villars by absenting himself from Parma. Apparently the Infant intended to be absent too but was detained by a mild illness.[43]

In February Villars had more bad news. Not only did Montemar intend to leave Parma but he intended to withdraw his troops from the garrisons of Revere and Mirandola. It was now the turn of the ministry to mollify the old marshal before he went too far in his protestations. A letter from the king to Villars noted that of course the decision of the Spanish "est tout à fait un contretemps" but that he must avoid a quarrel and not bring it out in public.[44] The ministry was making good use of young King Louis to deal with the angry and frustrated old marshal.

On 25 February, after the departure of the Spanish forces, Villars wrote his strongest protest to Montemar, asking him whether the withdrawal of the Spanish troops from the Po without advising his allies was not enough, if publicized, to suggest that Spain was reconciled with the emperor. But he had also received another letter from the king, who reminded him that the Spanish had not concealed their plans for Naples. What was new, said the king, was the way they had abandoned their forts on the Po. "I am sending a message to Madrid on their conduct and to ask strongly that the troops now being embarked in Spain be sent to the Parma area."[45]

But for a time the Spaniards disappeared from the war theater in the Po Valley. The old marshal must turn to other frustrations. He sought to push on across the Oglio to the east but his generals checked him with an appeal for troop rest and, since the area had been struck by a heavy and unexpected snow, he agreed. He was now resigned to wait until March for a move toward the Mincio and Mantua. In the meantime the Austrian strong point of Tortone had surrendered in early February. The last fort west of Mantua had now fallen. Villars knew what should be done. "We should put ourselves between the garrison in Mantua and those who will come from Germany."[46] But he must wait.

Villars also wished to place some of his forces on the right bank of the Po to compensate for the loss of the Spanish forces, and he sought to build a bridge. In this project he hoped to have the support of the king of Sardinia. But by 26 February we find that his intendant was complaining that the king was not doing his part and that in order to get started he had sent General Broglie and 10,000 men to begin the work on the bridge.[47] Finally, however, Villars did succeed in placing a corps on the right bank under General Coigny.

While Villars struggled with his allies, the new commander of the imperial forces in northern Italy was moving his reinforcing troops over the Alps. Field Marshal Count Claudius Florimund Mercy had served his emperor for fifty-two years in peace and war. In addition to having a history of extraordinary personal gallantry in combat, he had been a successful administrator in the Banat. But at this time he was sixty-eight years old, blind in one eye and short-sighted in the other, suffering from gout (and probably from his many wounds), and unequal to the task of commanding a field army. But he was not to be denied his last command and set off via Innsbruck, where he held talks on supplies, across the Brenner Pass into Italy. Arriving at Rovereto on 5 February, he met his predecessor traveling north from Mantua and was informed of the military situation. On 13 February he moved on toward Mantua with some of the reinforcing columns. They moved through Venetian territory in the Verona area. The Venetians, in order to give the French less grounds for complaint, had already asked the Austrians not to use their neutral territory for troop movements. But it was too difficult to reach Mantua by any other route, and Prince Eugene ordered the use of the road through Verona stressing order and discipline among the troops.[48]

Villars was forced to watch the buildup of the imperial forces. On 27 February he wrote that Mercy could make himself master of the Po with the 20,000 men in Mantua plus the 12,000 newly arrived reinforcements. For the next several weeks he would worry about the enemy crossing the Po and turning the exposed flank where the Spanish had departed, and about how to secure better cooperation from the Sardinians in placing a major part of his forces on the right bank of the Po. A gentle warning against dividing his forces came from Versailles in a letter from the king, who supposed that Villars would hold his army together and not try to cover the Parmesan although he might occupy the posts the Spanish had evacuated.[49] It was one thing to put garrisons in fortresses in an area from which they might have to be withdrawn, but quite another to split a field army and place a part of it several days' march away with a river between. Dangervilliers, writing a few days later, seemed to suggest that Villars not extend his lines further. "We think you will have to assemble your forces to dispute the terrain." He went on, saying that the enemy would not fail to bring the war into Modena and, if possible, Parma. He also explained to Villars that the king of Sardinia might resist moving out of the Milanese for fear of a new German corps coming over the mountains and putting itself along Lake Garda in the land that had been taken for him. And with regard to the Spanish, the minister added that, although they had gone, the alliance was in a common cause.[50]

It was well that Villars had been given permission to occupy the strong points on the right bank because he had already done so. Broglie had been given the task of replacing the Spanish garrisons and had occupied Guastalla, Revere, and Mirandola to secure crossings over the Secchia and the Parmeggiana rivers in case a retreat should become necessary.[51] On 14 March a letter from the king applauded the move, saying that Villars had profited by the negligence of the imperial forces who could have stopped the move. Probably in response to this approval Villars in late March placed five more battalions on the right bank.[52] By March the king and court at Versailles were probably aware that the old marshal's health was giving way. During the month the king wrote him three letters, gently reproving him in one for writing to the king of Spain and generally showing him more than usual consideration. On 26 March Villars wrote to the king that he was badly "enrhumé" and coughing, that he must use opium to ward off fatigue and for travel. He begged the king to let him return; he was not fit for defensive war, he said. The ministry finally seemed to understand that Villars needed more backing from the French court, and he was informed that the cardinal had written to the king of Sardinia requesting better support for the French forces.[53]

The result of all this lack of agreement was that the French and Sardinian forces did not take the opportunity to strike at the imperials during those weeks in early spring when the latter were building up, and they would now have to await an imperial initiative. By April the imperial army was formed in sufficient strength and could select its area of operations. "The fear of a crossing of the Po by the imperials is so widespread in the States of Parma that the furniture had been removed from the palace at Colorno, which the advance party selected as our headquarters." So wrote Villars to the king on 8 April, going on to say that he had reassured the Infant and Parma and then must reassure himself regarding the defense of the Oglio on the left bank where, once again, he was unable to persuade the king of Sardinia to move his forces forward. Charles Emmanuel's position was that the line along the Oglio was too long and he therefore would bring his forces only up to the Adda.[54]

By 19 April Villars's complaints have a shrill tone. From Colorno he writes: "I am extremely sorry to be obliged to explain to Your Majesty the dangerous and forced position of your army." He explained that the dispositions of the allied forces did not deter the enemy, whose strength he then estimated at 55,000, but rather encouraged him to attack. The fault was, of course, that he had no support from the Piedmontese forces. "If the enemy army has a general with any sense at its head it will march promptly against the Oglio."[55] The king of Sardinia did in fact bring his forces up to the Oglio before the end of April, but the attack was not to come in this area.

The French and Piedmontese might have been less anxious, although not justifiably so, had they known that the new Austrian commander had completely lost his sight in what may have been an epileptic attack. Eugene wrote Mercy on 20 March that he, Eugene, would not come to Italy but would command the army on the Rhine. After urging Mercy to a speedy recovery, Eugene asked whether in his opinion they should operate on only one side of the Po, or on both, and whether they should send a force to counter the Spanish attack on Naples.[56] Shortly after, Eugene was in contact with Mercy's second-in-command, Prince Ludwig von Württemberg, to say that he was in agreement that no help should be sent to Naples and that they must act with force in the north to cross the Po or the Adda. In any case, "you must leave no more time to the enemies to reconnoiter and fortify further, but act with the utmost vigor, and in such a way that the army, or at least the greater part of it, will be assembled."[57]

But by 14 April little has happened and Eugene is impatient. He wrote to Mercy: "I hope to learn from Your Excellency what form the operations are really taking, since the season is well advanced and it would be an undeniable shame to remain inactive with such a fine and strong army when one has superiority over the enemy. The enemy is deployed over a vast terrain along the Oglio and the Po and so separated that indeed a part of his forces can easily be cut off from the others."[58]

This was enough. On 2 May at dawn the imperials began crossing the Po above San Benedetto in boats. Coigny and his eight battalions were camped across from the mouth of the Mincio and had become used to the lack of activity. Possibly they enjoyed it—on both sides.[59] Now, however, they found the imperials moving in behind them. They retired rapidly upstream toward Guastalla. The imperials now threatened the state and city of Parma. Villars wrote to Louis: "The king of Sardinia has twice ruined the project which might have caused that part of the emperor's army which is in Mantua to perish by cutting it off from all help from Germany." And he added, somewhat plaintively: "I think that I have a great deal to complain about in my zeal for Your Majesty's service and that which concerns my reputation."[60]

The imperials expected a response from Villars by some sort of attack on the left bank of the Po toward Mantua, as they watched the French on the right bank retreating—hastily and in disorder. Villars did in fact throw a column across the Oglio on 4 May, driving the imperials from Borgoforte. But the French thrust soon lost momentum and, when countered by a brigade of imperials, quickly returned across the river. Although a rumor swept the Austrian forces that the entire French army was assembled to cross the Oglio, it was soon discovered to be false. It was a critical period. Not until 9 May did Fontanieu state that, for the first time since the retreat began, their positions were stable, with Coigny placing his left on the Po and his right toward the city of Parma.[61]

In retrospect it seems rather obvious that Villars's dispositions had become vulnerable to attack. Prince Eugene saw it and suggested the weakness to his commander on 14 April. Even a trusted distant correspondent of Eugene was aware of it. The marquis de Prié, in Baden, wrote to Eugene that he had heard from Lombardy that Villars was over the Po with a large force and the rest of his army was in the Cremonese with its lines on the Adda. It is possible that these two corps could be attacked while unable to assist one another, thought de Prié. He must have had rapid intelligence from Italy, for on 5 May he wrote again to Eugene stating that what he had described as possible seemed to have occurred.[62]

Was Villars really able to command in these last days? He must have been nearly broken by the constant debate. Claude Sturgill, writing of him in the War of the Spanish Succession, found him a commander who took hostages from the civil population, fired into cities, and used wounded as cover. Villars was also the only general of Louis XIV strong enough to disobey his master on occasion.[63] But this was now an older Villars.

The king of Sardinia threatened him with that article of the treaty which provided for a council of war to settle a diversity of opinion. "I have never held councils of war," wrote Villars, "and my health is too changed to permit such a burden." On 26 May, with the front stabilized, he was permitted to leave at last and made his way to Turin. He would get no further. He wrote again from Turin to the court: "It is possible that they may say I am feigning illness, the more so because I have taken care to conceal the change in my health." However, added Villars, the cardinal would get the report of the physicians.[64] On 17 June 1734, in Turin, he died.

There was always something of the boastful player about him, and not infrequently something of the unwitting comic. He was unquestionably vainglorious and sought honors unashamedly, making himself a splendid target for sneering courtiers. When not in the field he was truly a courtier himself. He was derided, privately of course, as virtually illiterate and, in fact, his personal signature of several heavy strokes suggests a man unused to written language. But in an age when valor among officers was taken for granted and was sometimes the only qualification an officer had to recommend him, Villars had more than his share.

With Villars's passing, the war in Italy would take on a new color. The armies are in motion and both the French and Austrian courts would ask for more definite results. The old military leaders were leaving the theater. Daun, Livingstein, Visconti, and Villars were gone. Mercy would soon be gone. The war as a minuet, as a dance of forces from one fortified place to another, was over and the armies would clash in earnest, if not intentionally.

✠

CHAPTER SEVEN

# The Siege of Danzig

The war in Italy and in the Rhineland was led by elderly generals who proceeded about their business much as they had done in the battles that had made them famous twenty or thirty years before. It was unlikely that any striking tactical or strategic surprises would occur. Above the aging military commanders on the French side was the even more venerable and cautious figure of Cardinal Fleury, playing his diplomatic cards with great finesse; while above the Austrian commanders was the frustrated emperor, calling for assistance to German princes who did not wish to hear. The overeager, but eventually dampened, actions of the subordinate French commanders, Maurice de Saxe and the marquis de Belle Isle, would be the only notable contrasts.

In what might be called, from a military point of view, the Danzig sideshow, there were, however, actions and personalities that contrasted sharply with the character of the main theaters of the war. In Italy and the Rhineland it was the same generals taking the same fortresses again that they had taken years before, but no prior stage play had been written for the Danzig affair. It took place in a newly emerging subsystem of military and diplomatic power, one which had a few years before experienced the Great Northern War in which Charles XII of Sweden and Peter the Great of Russia were pitted against one another. British sea power and growing Prussian military strength were the other elements in the balance of this area, which was on the fringes of both Austrian and French influence.

During the early months of 1733—long before Stanislas Leszczynski took refuge in Danzig in October—the French ambassador to Denmark at Copenhagen watched the growing crisis that followed the death of Augustus II at Warsaw. He was Louis Robert de Bréhan, Count Plélo, born in 1699 a member of the old Breton nobility. His military career had ended with his falling into debt and the necessary sale of his commission. He would have returned to provincial life had not his brother-in-law, Count Maurepas, then minister of the navy, arranged for his appointment in 1728 as ambassador to Denmark.[1] Plélo had some claim to literary background and was a member of a small circle that included well-known French literary figures, but had apparently some misgivings regarding his preparation for a diplomatic career. He accepted the appointment, however, and en route to Denmark in 1729 was sufficiently humble to write to his minister, Chauvelin: "Guide my steps in a career in which I have as yet only my goodwill to conduct me, and in which I feel that I still lack greatly in perception."[2]

Plélo would show considerably more confidence in his own abilities in months to come. Already, in September 1729, we may deduce from a letter he wrote to Maurepas, that he was reproached for his eagerness. Another letter to Maurepas shows his increasing desire to propose a more active strategy in the North when he asks why it must be the English and the Dutch that are the "maritime powers." Why can't France send a squadron under a brilliant commander like Duguay-Trouin?[3] It was a question he would ask again, but one for which he would never receive a satisfactory answer.

Still, it was not thought likely that the eventual resolution of the Polish question would involve him. His instructions on assuming his post were principally concerned with the complicated Schleswig-Holstein question and ignored Poland. When Augustus II died on 1 February 1733, Plélo was resigned to playing a bystander's part. In February he wrote to his ambassador colleague in Warsaw, the marquis de Monti, whom he had known personally in the army. There is nothing exciting here, he said, but the death of the king of Poland had opened a "grande scène" for Monti. He hoped that Monti's role would be brilliant and fortunate. His own role, he observed, would be that of trying to secure the neutrality of the Danes as France began to assume an aggressive stance toward the emperor. "One cannot imagine that the interests of Denmark require that she follow the will of the court of Vienna. . . . We want to be assured of Danish neutrality in this affair."[4] This was an example of Plélo's guidance from Versailles.

During the next several months Plélo strove to secure the desired neutrality. But the Danes had a defensive alliance with the emperor and would not be strictly bound. They told him they would remain neutral unless France attacked the emperor in Germany. With regard to Stanislas, they had no objection to him and would not try to prevent him from passing through the Sund, the narrow waters between Denmark and Sweden. But the minister made it clear to Plélo that the king of Denmark, in case of some action by Russia or Austria, would not "go beyond the attitudes which we should like to observe" ("traverser les ressentiments que nous en voudrions marquer.") It was vague and careful language befitting a small country, but Plélo became so impatient with these statements that he burst out: "The Danish ministry is one of weakness, bad faith, lack of resolution, and inconstancy, which does not permit us to count on it from one moment to the next. . . . On the other hand, the imperials and the Russians spare neither the promises, threats, money, nor lies to seduce it, and the terrain is well prepared."[5]

But the Danes could go only so far to oblige France and probably assumed that France had already determined to attack the emperor. In the meantime the Danes observed the apparent preparations to bring Stanislas to Poland via the Danish Sund and the city of Danzig. Plélo was very busy. The king of France had written him another reminder that they needed reassurances before French ships could be sent into Danish waters.[6]

By 13 July, Plélo had better news. In a carefully worded document the Danes not only gave approval for the passage of French ships but welcomed them in Danish ports. The document observed that the king of Denmark was sure that "the intentions of His Christian Majesty, in sending this squadron to the Baltic, is not to disturb or give offense, much less attack any of the powers which are allied to him." [7]

Plélo may have thought that his strong pretensions regarding French sea power had been effective. He had reported to the king of France in June that "this talk of a squadron and of vessels ready to appear from one moment to the next, repeated by me to satiety, made an impression on these people here." [8] Or was the youthful ambassador overestimating the effect of his statements and the Danish respect for French sea power? At any rate no squadron arrived during July or August, and the Danes turned their attention to the question of their alliance with the emperor under the 1731 Treaty of Copenhagen. Plélo found that the imperial ministers had asked the Danish minister in Vienna to have the troops of the king of Denmark ready to march. When Plélo pressed the Danish foreign minister as to what Denmark would do if things came to the "dernières extremités" he was told that if the Russians should enter their troops into Poland, France would have a right to declare war on them. But the Danish minister thought only the Swedes would support the French, and knowing the Swedish constitution he very much doubted if they would take action, and even if action were taken it would probably be against Livonia or some other former Swedish province lost to the Russians. [9] Just don't attack the emperor unless he attacks you, said the Danish government to Plélo; otherwise the Danish king is forced to fulfil the terms of his alliance with the emperor. In spite of the fact that both Sweden and Denmark were guarantors of the liberties of Poland, this was all the comfort Plélo could get from the Danish court.

Early in September Plélo was delighted to learn that a French naval squadron was actually on the way. Twelve vessels had departed for the Baltic. It was the squadron that presumably was bringing Stanislas to Danzig. We are not seeking a quarrel with the Russians, said the French ministry, but we will tolerate no "mauvaises manœuvres." The ambassador rushed to the Danes with his news, incidentally finding that they had already heard it from other sources. "I can't tell you how great an effect the projected arrival of a squadron has produced in this area already. . . . Danish Minister Plessen spoke to me in laudatory terms about the firmness which seems to mark our actions. We must follow through to the end." [10]

The squadron arrived at Elsinore on 15 September with three vessels missing and proceeded to Copenhagen. The news of the election of Stanislas in Warsaw arrived at almost the same time, and the deception regarding the travel route of Stanislas was ended. Plélo's messages showed an increased fervor and the word "zèle" enters his correspondence. In his enthusiasm he remarks in one dispatch to his minister: "Vous connaissez le cœur francais, tant ce qu'il a de zèle, et s'il m'est premis d'employer ce terme, de tendresse pour son prince." Already the ministry at Versailles must have had some misgivings about the enthusiasm of their representative in Copenhagen, for a 26 September message from Versailles counseled moderation. But Plélo was playing the "French presence" for all it was worth. He asked that the king of Denmark receive the officers of the squadron, and he announced in court the election of Stanislas. The Danish king's response to the announcement must have been a short comedy scene with the king responding in a very low voice. The ministers from Saxony and Russia pressed as close as they dared to hear the king's answer but, as Plélo admitted afterwards, he could not understand the answer either. [11]

At first it appeared that the French squadron would return immediately to France. Plélo seemed ready to agree, probably after talking to the commander, the chevalier de La Luzerne, and discovering how precisely the latter's instructions from the Ministry of the Navy were stated. As a matter of fact, Plélo was even willing to instruct his ministry in naval strategy, as he noted in a message that there were three reasons for the arrival of the squadron, first to cover the movements of the king of Poland, second, to show the northern powers that they may be visited by water, as friends or enemies, and, third, to salute the Russians as friend or foe ("de gré ou de force"). The season was too far along to go into the Baltic, he agreed, and nothing could be gained thereby. But this was before the rumors of a retreat of Stanislas to Danzig began to arrive. On 8 October, under pressure of this new information, Plélo wrote to his minister that, although he understood that the squadron must not be risked in the Baltic on the basis of a rumor, he proposed that two frigates be sent to reconnoiter Danzig. The next day he wrote to Monti explaining that the squadron would have to return because of the strict orders it carried but that he wished one or two frigates could be sent to Danzig.[12]

In the next few days Plélo seems to have let his zeal carry him on. Unable to make La Luzerne detach two frigates for Danzig, he had himself carried out to the squadron in a small boat just before the sailing and stressed to La Luzerne that something might happen to the king of Poland for which La Luzerne might be blamed later. The commander could not be moved. Plélo demanded a council of war and following this was able to hold three frigates. He explained it all to his minister, hoping this action would be approved. He must have realized quickly his impropriety, for in a message to the king he asked for pardon and admitted that he yielded to his own zeal.[13]

He had indeed overstepped his authority. A message from Versailles told him that he had only compromised the position of Stanislas in Poland by holding the frigates. The rumor alone had produced a bad effect, said the minister, giving the impression that the king of Poland expected these ships in order to escape, and it would have been even worse if they had arrived at Danzig. Whether Plélo accepted this reasoning or not, he duly informed Monti that the three frigates were sent back to France on 21 October.[14]

Both the Russians and the English were watching the French squadron. Lord Forbes had hardly arrived in Saint Petersburg to upgrade the English mission to an embassy when Count Osterman informed him in July that a French squadron was to pass the Danish Sund—and what would the English do? Forbes answered that he thought the French vessels were too small in number to be a problem and the season was already late for any operations in the Baltic. Osterman hoped that the English would send a squadron. Forbes was happy to be told later from London that he had given the right answer and that operations at this season would be indeed precarious. A few weeks later Forbes was informed that the returning French squadron had been sighted off Dover.[15]

Plélo had lost a battle but believed that there was something he could do. The king of Denmark had told him that Denmark must help the emperor with whom he had an alliance. France had now attacked the emperor, and the king of Denmark must keep his word. Plélo's suggestion to his government to counter the sending of a Danish military contingent to the emperor was to offer the Danes subsidies to delay, or better still, hire the soldiers for France. Ten or twelve thousand troops going into Poland would be useful, thought Plélo; most of the Danish ministry was imperial at heart, and only money could balance it. Paying the Danes would be expensive, he admitted, but it would mean fifteen to twenty thousand troops and ten to twelve war vessels, and there is the possible opposition of these people to the passage of French ships into the Baltic. "I only await orders," he concluded.[16]

Actually, he sought to do a great deal more. A few days later, on 10 November, he forwarded a memoir outlining a plan which was, to say the least, bold in scope. His project had several parts, but the object was to stop the Russians. First, the Turks should attack the Russians. Plélo admitted that he did not know how to bring this about. Second, a squadron should be ready to sail about the end of April with fifteen or sixteen vessels of the line, ready for a five-month campaign and with six or seven thousand men, including cavalry. The Swedes would be subsidized to have pilots ready to aid the French ships and to strike in Finland. The French fleet would go straight into Livonia and Courland which, according to Plélo, had poor defenses. French troops would land and pillage the country while ships would bombard Riga and Revel. The desolation of these lands should make the Russians in Poland return home. This must be done, emphasized Plélo, or Denmark will go along with the Russian view and the Swedes will be prevented from acting for us.[17]

Did Chauvelin and his staff pass this memoir about from one man to another and shake their heads? It would be interesting to know what they said, and what the cardinal said after reading it. The message of 3 December to Plélo was presumably an answer and it noted dryly that an expedition to the Baltic such as that projected in the memoir could not be undertaken without great difficulty and expense. The original draft text said baldly that it would not be sent because the English would put a fleet to sea, but this statement was lined out and a longer explanation was given. The notion of interference by the English remained in the text, however. The ministry also commented on Plélo's suggestion that the Danes be bought off from their aid to the emperor by noting that France was not accustomed to paying people for not working against her but for working actively in her favor.[18]

In the meantime, after the reproach from Chauvelin, Plélo was also trying to explain his holding the three frigates. In a letter to his brother-in-law Maurepas and to Abbé Alary he showed his bitterness at the reproach he had received. He sent letters from Monti and from the Swedish ambassador in Stockholm to support his claim that it was not a "zèle inconsideré," which made him desire to hold the squadron. "The risk to the vessels was uncertain; the danger to the king of Poland was actual. . . . My zeal is great, I admit, but it is not blind."[19]

Chauvelin was obviously ready to drop the frigate matter. "We credit your motives and good intentions. Do not worry about this. It is a closed matter." Chauvelin went on to note that the king of Denmark, in spite of his protestations, was the first to declare for the emperor and to find the Polish affair a "cas de son alliance." Because the attitude of the Swedes may depend on the way the Danes are handled, France will consent to a six-month payment of subsidies. He then added, in an apparent attempt to encourage subtlety in his impetuous ambassador, the king of Denmark may not respond either to the approach of the king of Poland or to that of the elector of Saxony. "You do not need to ask for a direct answer."[20]

As to the attitude of the Swedes, whom Plélo seemed to believe eager to reassert themselves in the Baltic, the French ambassador in Stockholm was of another opinion. If the Swedes are to be moved by glory it will take a long time to persuade them, noted the ambassador. He pointed out several cases of Swedish circumspection and added that the Swedes wished that any sales of munitions for Stanislas in Poland be only through the account of a private merchant.[21]

Plélo may seem immature and reckless in his actions, but in

other ways he was aware of traditional limitations that have worn much thinner in the twentieth century. At the end of 1733 he was approached by one Treschler, a Danish officer of Saxon birth, with a plot to assassinate the elector of Saxony. Plélo immediately turned the officer over to the Danish government, a move later approved by Chauvelin.[22]

Stanislas was received with enthusiasm in Danzig in October 1733 and seems to have felt confident in his position there. In a letter to his daughter on 3 October, the day after his arrival, he mentioned that the Russians would soon have the Turks and Swedes to be concerned about ("sur le bras") and that France would keep the emperor occupied. He was thoroughly satisfied with the marquis de Monti and expected to have a tranquil reign.[23]

Stanislas was accompanied to Danzig by several politically important figures. These included the primate, Theodore Potocky; Stanislas Poniatowski, who had given up his own candidature; and five Czartoryski princes. His own intimate staff was a more interesting group. First there was Tercier, the secretary of Monti's embassy. He was later to direct the secret correspondence of Louis XV and the duke of Broglie. Pierre Joseph de la Pimpie, chevalier de Solignac, became a secretary of Stanislas and stayed with him, later guiding his literary pretensions. Stanislas Zaluski was a chancellor of the Polish crown and bishop of Plock. After Danzig fell, he was kept in office and became an intimate counsellor to Augustus III. Finally, Joseph Zaluski, who was sent to the Holy See by Stanislas after the fall of Danzig, later came back to Poland and played an important role there. These, all men of letters, were the intimate staff.[24]

Many weeks were to pass before the Russian army arrived in the Danzig area. During this period the French publicly made great protestations of support for Stanislas while privately they showed little resolution. Boyé, in his masterful work on Leszczynski, lays it all at the door of the cardinal. "He was, we will see only too clearly, the sworn enemy of the father and the daughter." There were splendid exchanges of compliments between them, says Boyé, but Stanislas was always the dupe.[25] If Stanislas was an enemy in the cardinal's eyes—and Boyé may have exaggerated this—he would not find any favor with the cold Chauvelin either. In a letter of 8 November Chauvelin advised him to assemble troops.[26] This was hardly the kind of assistance the besieged king was expecting. In December and January as the winter set in, his letters to Marie showed him far less serene about the future. No help came in this season, of course, but neither did the Russians. But a definite promise of help came in a 15 December message sent by Louis XV to the Danzig Magistraat.[27]

Very dear and good friends,

We see with pleasure, from your letter of the 18th of last month, and from the accounts of our ambassador the marquis de Monti, all the indications of fidelity and zeal which you have shown toward the king of Poland. The threats made by his enemies and ours have not been able to diminish the sentiments which will transport your glory to succeeding centuries and which make you so dear in our eyes.

Several powers already show an interest in your preservation, but none will be able to extend this as far as we desire to do, since we regard your interests as our own, and we intend to neglect nothing which our strength and goodwill can encompass.

In the light of the decisions that were taken in the next few months this effusive and categorical statement should have troubled someone's memory at Versailles. Nor would it be the last such statement. It was quite enough to convince the burghers of Danzig, and in a 3 February sitting the city agreed to keep their royal guest. It was after this that they assembled a garrison of about 6,000 men. In addition there was a "garde bourgeoise" and some volunteers. About 5,000 troops were allocated to the outer forts. The Swedish Colonel Stackelberg, with the title of adjutant general of the king of Poland, was put in charge of the fort at the mouth of the Vistula below Danzig, the Weichselmünde fort.[28]

Lacy, commanding the Russian forces, had difficulty in assembling a sufficient force for the attack on Danzig. According to the British resident in Saint Petersburg, who was kept well informed by the Russians, Lacy had stayed at Thorn to provide his troops with boots. The troops were worn out with long and painful marches and the need to repair bridges, which were everywhere destroyed. Lacy announced that he intended to start for Danzig on 31 January 1734 with 24,000 troops, descending on both sides of the Vistula.[29] Manstein, in his memoirs, asserts that the besieged in this case outnumbered the besiegers three to one and should have used their superior numbers to fall upon the dispersed Russians as soon as they arrived.[30]

Whatever his numbers, Lacy and his force arrived in Danzig territory in early February and approached the city. On 20 February, Monti wrote to Plélo, "A party of Muscovites appeared at the first defense line. We beat a general alarm and everyone took to arms."[31] Lacy demanded the delivery of Stanislas. When this was refused, he set to work cutting off the water supply of the city while waiting for his superior, Marshal Muennich, who arrived on 10 March. Muennich wrote to the Magistraat giving them twenty-four hours to recognize Augustus III as king and on the same date made an attack on a redoubt called the Hagelsburg. Here 800 Poles and Danzigers repulsed the attack with severe losses for the Russians. But the Russians gradually seized the outer defense points, with the exception of the Weichselmünde, and cut off the city from all land access.[32]

An important element in the siege was the attitude of the king of Prussia, since the Russians could bring in heavy artillery only by crossing Prussian territory. In spite of the protests of the French, permission was granted, and the larger guns came by sea through Pillau into the inner bay known as Frisches Haff and from there to the Danzig area.[33] When told of this, the British resident in Saint Petersburg wrote to London: "Count Muennich's military eloquence has prevailed on the king of Prussia to let the cannon pass."[34] On 30 April a heavy bombardment began to fall on the city.

What were the Poles doing elsewhere? Was there any organized effort to aid the king so enthusiastically acclaimed a few months before? Messages tell of skirmishes throughout the country, but the organized forces were few and unreliable. The largest force appears to have been that of Joseph Potocky, palatin of Kiev and a brother of the primate, who had forces in the Cracow area. These were of little help in the siege of Danzig and apparently held to the Cracow area in order to have an avenue of retreat into Turkish territory if needed. Boyé mentions that a force of 10,000 under Tarlo advanced toward Kalics in February, but after an encounter with the Saxons near Warta, fell back in disorder.[35] Manstein tells of a battle between Lacy's forces and an estimated 10,000 Poles, who were dispersed on 17 April in what was the only serious effort of the Poles to relieve Danzig. The British resident in Saint Petersburg was not far wrong when he reported that the only Polish troops were 8,000 rabble in the Danzig area. Woodward in Warsaw heard that the castellan of Czersk lost nearly 600 men in a clash with the Russians six miles from Danzig.[36]

How could so large and populous a nation become helpless before so small a force of invaders? André Corvisier analyzes it as a failure to place its military nobility at the service of the state. Precisely the opposite phenomenon was occurring in the neighboring state of Prussia, where the nobility was militarized and incorporated into the army. Poland was at the other extreme, the military institutions of the monarchy having declined to the point that the royal army comprised only a few companies and fortresses. The nobility in Poland, to use Corvisier's expression, escaped "domestication."[37]

Actually there may have been a moment when Danzig itself could have broken the siege. An attack in early May by Muennich on the Hagelsburg cost the Russians several thousand casualties compared to insignificant losses for the Danzigers. Had a sortie been attempted at this time, the siege might have ended. The slow but steady movement of the Russian forces and their acceptance of casualties gave the impression of an inexorable force, but the messages of the British in Saint Petersburg reveal that the Russian court felt considerable apprehension for possible French and Swedish actions. Biron was uneasy, reported Forbes, and must steady the tsarina. There was talk of having to raise the siege for some reason and "drawing the stake out of the play." On 15 May, when doubtless the Russian losses around Danzig were known in Saint Petersburg, Forbes reported that Biron and Osterman were ready to quit Danzig if the Saxons did not do more.[38]

But the French were probably unaware of any lack of resolution on the part of the Russians. This left the possible lifting of the siege up to the cardinal at Versailles. At some time in late February or early March, Danzig received another reassurance from France. A letter signed by Louis on 18 February said: "You may rest assured that we will neglect nothing to sustain against all foreign efforts your just and proper sentiments, and to protect you against threats which may be made."[39] Matters were becoming desperate in Danzig and words were not enough. Was this letter intended to keep up the spirit and resistance of the city until that promised help arrived? We might expect rather serious preparations.

The decision of the French government as to what was an appropriate force to send to the Baltic did not begin to take concrete form until early April 1734. It was to be a modest force, even by the standards of that day. Plélo had recommended in March that a French army strike through to Saxony and, as we shall see, Belle Isle and others must have been encouraging such a plan. But the orders from Versailles were to assemble and embark a force of 650 men from each of three regiments—less than 2,000 men in all. A communication from the port of Calais acknowledged a 4 April order from the ministry to embark the men of the Périgord and Blaisois regiments.[40] Those of the La Marche regiment would follow a little later. A steady exchange of communications continued between Segent, the *commissaire* for the expedition to Danzig, on the one hand, and the ministry of the navy on the other. The *commissaire*, in charge of administration and supply, filled the role of intendant at lower levels of command.[41] The reports of the commander-designate of the expedition, one Brigadier La Motte de la Peyrouse, also began to appear in the files.

La Motte was sixty-six years old and an experienced officer. His actions and reports suggest a stiff and cautious man. A biographer asserts that he was known to Dangervilliers, who wanted to employ him.[42] Another source insists that Cardinal Fleury offered the post to several colonels who refused unless granted certain "gratifications." La Motte left this up to the cardinal and was accepted.[43] La Motte may have needed employment. The rank of brigadier had been devised for competent lieutenant colonels who were unable to purchase a regiment and become colonels. The brigade, enabling a brigadier to command, existed only during hostilities. By this route a man could become a general without ever being a colonel.[44]

La Motte and Segent, on the two warships added to the expedition, were delayed by contrary winds and did not arrive in Copenhagen until early in May 1734. Four French troop transports arrived there on 23 April, however, bearing the men of the Blaisois and Périgord regiments. Plélo was shocked at their lack of provisions, both food and powder, and set about making local purchases. Moreover, his reaction reflected disbelief that the expedition could be so small and poorly equipped, and his messages warned that the measures undertaken were inadequate. He apparently chose to believe that the ships arriving at Copenhagen were only an advance guard and so informed Monti and the French ambassador in Sweden. In his message of 24 April he stated that officers of the expedition who came ashore told him they were followed by 20,000 men. Is it possible that he believed this? Probably not. In the same message he lectured the ministry, saying that with twenty-four or twenty-five war vessels and 12,000 to 15,000 men "we will be on top of our affairs in three months and the North will tremble for a long time. What glory for France, Monseigneur, if this can be done. But also what shame if our people, too weak to save Danzig, arrive only to share in its fall." He understood the risks, added Plélo, but the present circumstances required taking chances. "There are those occasions when one must win or die" ("vaincre ou mourir").[45]

On 1 May, still awaiting the two warships bearing La Motte and Segent and the remainder of the troops of the first two regiments, Plélo became more desperate in his appeals. He warned that they must send more than twenty vessels and more than 15,000 men. Three or four battalions may encourage the Danzigers and cause them to defend themselves, but it cannot prevent their defeat. The honor of the king and of the nation are at stake, he told the ministry.[46]

La Motte and Segent arrived at Copenhagen on 4 May. The commander immediately wrote in his own hand to the ministry, giving due credit to the efforts of the ambassador in equipping his troops. He expected to leave the next day for Danzig. One may wonder whether La Motte had serious misgivings about the expedition he was leading into the far reaches of Europe. Acknowledging that he might find obstacles at Danzig, he added that they would surmount them with "the help of the Lord and the will of our troops." It then occurred to him to insert the phrase "and our precautions" after the word "Lord."[47]

On 8 May the six vessels left Copenhagen for Danzig. The fort at the mouth of the Vistula with its Swedish colonel was no longer in direct communication with the city, but there were agreed signals regarding the arrival of help and for sorties of the garrison. Here on an island in the river, under the guns of the fort, the little force was landed on 11 May. They did not remain long. La Motte found that he could not reach Danzig because of Russian entrenchments which had been thrown up between the fort and the city. He also found the supplies in the fort disappointing and held a council of war, following which, on the fifteenth, they reembarked the troops and returned to Copenhagen.[48]

La Motte probably could not anticipate the reaction of Plélo when the expedition reappeared at Copenhagen. He had taken action, like any conscientious commander, for the security of the forces under his command and doubtless felt that he knew the difference between prudence and showing faint heart before the enemy. Plélo had been busying himself with further provisions for the expedition. He reported the arrival of three additional vessels bearing the troops of the La Marche regiment and he offered his advice on the tactics to be employed at Danzig. He was obviously stunned to find on 20 May that the expedition had returned to Copenhagen. He went on board the warship *Achille* where he wrote a report to the king stating that the expedition had made no effort to reach Danzig, that a panic of terror had seized the soldiers, then the officers, and even the commanders. They could not speak without trembling, he wrote, and La

Motte he found was a man "shocked, befuddled and absolutely incapable of any vigorous decision ("etonné, battant la campagne, et absolument incapable d'aucune résolution vigoreuse"). Only the naval officers were worthy of their king. "I saw only one thing to do, Sire, to put myself at the head of your troops and to attack the enemy. . . . We left, then, Sire, with the five vessels of war, four transports, several landing corvettes, and the three regiments." On the same day he wrote to Chauvelin: "I don't know yet whether we will succeed but the shame, the infamy of what happened can only be effaced by complete victory or by all of our blood. . . . Whatever happens the king will see that I am worthy to serve him."[49]

Perhaps La Motte was made to feel that he had not shown sufficient vigor and did not resist the demand to return to Danzig and the virtual taking over of his command. Not all the officers had been in favor of the return to Copenhagen. Baraillh, the naval commander, was critical and wrote to Maurepas on 20 June that he thought they had been too fearful in their reaction.[50]

It seems doubtful that Plélo took over the command as completely as his message suggests, but at any rate the expedition returned to the mouth of the Vistula and disembarked on the same island as before. They were now, in effect, obeying the orders of Plélo and Monti, although the messages of Segent and La Motte suggest that the decision to return was taken as soon as they encountered the third battalion that was to join them, and La Motte later describes Plélo's role at this time simply by saying that "Count Plélo wished absolutely to come with us." On 25 May, from the island in the river, La Motte wrote that he was awaiting orders from Monti, from whom he had received a letter. Had he received this at the time of the first landing, he added, he might not have made the decision which he did and which "gave rise to the suspicions which have since appeared."[51]

The order from Monti to attack the Russian defenses soon came. They were to attack at nine o'clock on the morning of the twenty-seventh, at which time a sortie from the city would be made.[52] The greater part of the three battalions, with an overall strength of probably 1,200 to 1,500 men marched on the Russian lines. They found themselves in trouble. La Motte reported it as follows:

We were first obliged to cross an area with water up to our waists. We didn't expect this since we had been assured there was nothing as deep as the ankles. This caused many powder cases and arms to be wetted. After this we entered a wood where after a thousand paces we came to the fortifications of the enemy before which there was a great defense of felled trees. Our grenadiers threw themselves on this with all the valor possible but most of the officers of these two units had already been killed or wounded by the heavy fire of the enemy, and being unable to extend to the right or left because of the narrow way in the woods, almost all of the first troops perished there. Two redoubts, which we had not been able to see, and which struck us from left and right with cannon fire, broke the column, which was not in complete formation.

The soldiers, astonished to find such an obstacle in a place where they expected to surprise the enemy, were obliged to fall back as they saw the large body of infantry troops which came to reinforce the area. This caused me to pull back to the protection of the fort, and by a misfortune for which I will never be able to console myself, M. de Plélo, who wished to follow me in spite of my wishes and the efforts I made to prevent this, was killed here.[53]

Segent duly reported the loss of 7 officers and 90 soldiers killed, and 24 officers and 112 soldiers wounded. La Motte commented further on the engagement, saying: "I foresaw this catastrophe, which was against all the rules of war which my experience taught me . . . but the ardor of Count Plélo and the orders of the marquis de Monti prevailed."[54] A letter sent by the chevalier de La Luzerne, commander of the men of the Périgord regiment, to his brother a few days after the engagement probably gives us a clearer picture. According to him, both Plélo and Monti, in spite of the genuine obstacles which were pointed out to them, insisted on an attack on the enemy in his entrenchments in an attempt to force through to the city.

We executed their orders on the twenty-seventh of this month and we had our nose bloodied. The regiment, and that of La Marche and Blaisois, have lost more than 130 men and all of our grenadiers, a number of officers killed, a great number wounded, of which I am one by a ball which cut a vein from the temple to the ear. I have been bled twice but hope there will be no further consequences. I forgot to tell you that M. de Plélo, who wished to come with us, has remained here.

What throws me into despair, my dear brother, is that we are here with people more dangerous for us than for our enemies, and that they would sacrifice us all without being able to execute our commission, that of rescuing the father-in-law of our king. We are about to die of hunger, abandoned by everyone, and worse than ever before.[55]

From this time on there is little spirit in the expedition and, except for a sortie from the city on 1 June, which did not change the situation, no further actions. La Motte and his men, like the besieged in Danzig, await rescue from some quarter. Plélo and Monti have played their cards and lost. The reckless flash of feudal chivalry has given way and the ways of eighteenth-century military custom have reasserted themselves. Plélo, who was willing to sacrifice his life and the lives of men under him but would not plot to assassinate the head of an enemy state, was dead. It is very possible that he was killed by his own men. The account of the battle indicates that the French retreated before they had actually reached the enemy entrenchments, certainly before they had attacked them in hand-to-hand fighting. Yet Plélo's body bore bayonet wounds when it was returned by the Russians.[56]

But success had been closer than would appear from the forlorn attack of Plélo and La Motte. As we have seen, the Russians were threatening as late as 15 May to abandon the siege if the Saxons did not assist them. The Saxons arrived—eight battalions and twenty-two squadrons—on 25 May, two days before the engagement. The Russians also decided to commit their fleet at precisely the right moment, and it arrived on the scene before Danzig at a time when the luckless French expedition was hoping and expecting a French relief squadron to appear.[57]

The expected French relief squadron was a casualty of Cardinal Fleury's determination to keep the war within bounds—bounds which he had chosen. A decision to prepare a squadron of ten warships at Brest had been made and Duguay-Trouin was given the command. Duguay set about his work with great energy but partly because of a breakdown in his health and partly because of the irresolution of the French government no squadron ever sailed. It became a phantom squadron, awaited by the desperate Monti, La Motte, and, until his death, Plélo. Monti sent a letter via Copenhagen to Duguay. Plélo's successor in Copenhagen, Malbran la Noue, by this time aware that the fleet would never sail, simply held the letter. La Motte seems to have believed that help was coming after the unsuccessful attack. He reported: "While awaiting the arrival of M. Duguay-Trouin I have withdrawn the troops into the camp on the island." On 1, 3, and 11 June he continued to mention in communications that he awaited Duguay-Trouin. His situation was desperate but he did not dramatize it. "I am very impatient to see M. Duguay-Trouin arrive."[58]

What had happened to the will of the French? The answer is clearly a fear of involvement with the English. Chauvelin wrote on 29 May to the already dead Plélo, praising the measures he had taken but noting the uneasiness of the English and the need to show them that France was acting in moderation. On 14 June the ministry wrote that the Council of State had decided that with the uncertainty regarding the English they could not send more than five vessels, which it was hoped would raise the siege with the two battalions on board.[59] A more quietly dramatic revelation of the attitude at Versailles comes from the interlineations on Segent's report of 28 May which acted as a cover letter for his report of casualties. The notes written between the lines and in the margin may have been those of Dangervilliers and quite possibly were made during the council meeting noted above. We find the following: "We must disabuse ourselves of M. Duguay-Trouin since the English might follow him into the Baltic and he would not be sure of returning."[60]

So no help came to the little camp of soldiers at the mouth of the Vistula. The five transports with two additional battalions failed to arrive before the French expedition capitulated. In any event there was no intention to send them past Copenhagen unless an escort of vessels of war was at hand.[61] Baraillh waited with his five transports at Copenhagen in case he was needed to reembark the expedition. He awaited Duguay-Trouin, according to Malbran, but instead was sent orders from Maurepas on

11 July to return to France. The expedition had surrendered and he was not needed.[62]

Monti had not been ready to give up after the failure of the 27 May attack and continued to communicate with La Motte and plan attacks. La Motte's reply to this call for further action was that he was waiting for Duguay-Trouin and that they had little bread left. Monti agreed to try to send provisions. The attack had failed because La Motte had attacked in the wrong place, said Monti, but "ce qui est fait, est fait." In a postscript to his message of 18 June he added that if La Motte would try another attack, he would send an officer who knew the country.[63]

But it was too late for another attack. They were under attack themselves on their exposed island. The Russian fleet had unloaded cannon and ammunition and begun a bombardment of the Weichselmünde fort while pushing their works closer. On 18 June the French officers held a council of war in which each stated his opinion. Most were ready to send an envoy to Marshal Muennich to ask for terms. Conveniently, the next day Muennich sent a demand for surrender to La Motte. But while this capitulation began to take form La Motte was embarrassed to receive a letter from the king of Poland, countersigned by Monti, the burden of which was that La Motte should not surrender if the king did not. It was a last effort to prolong the siege, but it had no effect. La Motte's response, signed also by his officers, was that they found it impossible to execute the orders.[64] A representation of the expedition was sent to Muennich with full powers to negotiate and by 23 June a document showing the requests of the French and the answers by the Russians in parallel columns had been drawn up. The next day Marshal Muennich, the duke of Saxony, and Admiral Gordon, commander of the Russian fleet, came to the French camp. On the twenty-sixth the French went on board the Russian ships.[65]

The French surrender was with all the honors of war. The principal condition of the Russians was that the Russian ship *Mittau* and its crew, taken earlier by the French in the Baltic, be returned. Although it was agreed by the Russians that the French would be returned to Copenhagen, they were taken to the Russian naval base at Cronstadt until the French returned the *Mittau*.

It was only after great hardships, including a shipwreck for some, that the survivors and La Motte reached France in the spring of 1735. Boencourt estimated that only about 200 of each regiment returned of the 650-man regiments sent out. La Motte was promoted to marshal de camp and made governor of the citadel of Valenciennes. Certain "gratifications" in small sums of money were given to the officers.[66] We find nothing to indicate that Louis XV ever concerned himself with the memory of the man who so zealously, if imprudently, sought to save his king's honor, Count Plélo.

After the surrender of the French expedition the city did not long survive. As early as April there was evidence that the leaders of the city were seeking an "honorable capitulation." According to an unsigned document in the Austrian files, dated 15 April in Berlin, the city of Danzig had approached the king of Prussia in terms "forts lamentables" asking his assistance. They sought in exchange for submission to Augustus III a general amnesty, the retention of their old privileges, no garrison and definitely not a Russian one, permission for Stanislas and his adherents to leave under Prussian escort, and withdrawal of the Russian army from the city and its territory.[67]

Prince Eugene was shortly thereafter in possession of this approach to the king of Prussia through Seckendorff in Berlin. He gave his opinion to the emperor that to restore the peace of the North nothing would be better ("nichts Gewünschteres zu sein") than to get Stanislas out of Poland and let him withdraw to France. Eugene, who at that moment had just arrived in the Rhine area to take command of the forces there, may have felt that his master would be unable to dismiss Stanislas so easily, and he added that of course there might be circumstances of which he was unaware and the emperor might be better able to decide.[68]

By May the British were looking ahead and suggesting clemency for Danzig, a port of considerable importance in the Baltic trade. Forbes pointed out to the Russians that such clemency would reflect honor on the tsarina and would, in view of the trade between Danzig and British ports, be viewed favorably by the king of England.[69]

The city capitulated on 30 June 1734. Muennich received letters in the most humble terms from the important Polish leaders in Danzig, accepting Augustus III as king. Monti became Muennich's prisoner, delivered up by the burghers of Danzig according to one report, but Stanislas was not to be found, and the leading Poles disclaimed knowledge of his escape.[70]

Stanislas had left the city secretly with a Swedish associate, General Steinflicht, and one other person. Although they became separated, Stanislas was able to cross into Prussian territory and was recognized in the town of Marienwerder on 4 July. He had asked the king of Prussia for protection, and the king was sufficiently annoyed by the elector of Saxony to refuse to take any action against the refugee king. As a matter of fact he permitted Stanislas to set himself up in the old castle of the Teutonic grand masters in Königsberg where the supporters of the exiled king began to gather round him.[71]

Monti and the primate were less fortunate. Monti was considered by the Russians to have lost his diplomatic immunity by his actions at Danzig. It must have been disagreeable for the French to ask the British to intercede for them to recover their soldiers and their ambassador, for the British had quietly but firmly opposed them in every court in Europe, but they did so, and asked the help of the Dutch as well. The Russians were willing to release the French troops when they received their frigate from the French, but Monti, they said, was not accredited to the Russian court and had violated international law by bearing arms and acting as a French general, which could be proved by intercepted messages.[72] The British and Dutch intercessions were met with a declaration detailing the violations committed by Monti and stating that he deserved to be treated as an enemy of the empress of Russia.[73] Monti remained a prisoner at Thorn for eighteen months and died shortly after his release and return to France.

The primate remained in prison for a year. He wrote personally to the tsarina without result. The pope pleaded his cause with the emperor who interceded with the tsarina to secure his release.[74]

Stanislas remained at Königsberg as a government in exile.

After some fleeting success in starting a new uprising under Adam Tarlo, and a further effort of Steinflicht to organize a mass levy in Podlesia, his efforts ceased. He would be forced to remain in Königsberg while the negotiations involving him took place without his concurrence.[75]

The city of Danzig was saddled with a great debt by the terms of the agreement of capitulation, and its representatives were still pleading with the Russian court through the British for an abatement of the sum when the war ended in 1735.

Poland now recedes from view. The attention of the great powers and their diplomatic and military efforts move back toward the West. The spotlight on the side stage has been extinguished. And it is easy to agree with Boyé when he says that Fleury and Chauvelin had a great deal to answer for in what he calls the false treaty of Danzig.[76]

✠

CHAPTER EIGHT

# The War in the Rhineland in 1734

Military activity north of the Alps in 1734, apart from the matter of Danzig and a few small encounters, would be restricted to three French initiatives: a siege of Trarbach on the Moselle River, an attack on the Ettlingen Lines near present-day Karlsruhe, and a siege of the great Rhine fortress of Philippsburg. It was a fairly modest effort considering the strong French forces available, but the efforts of eager subordinate commanders to extend the conflict would be set against the strong will of the senior commander, Marshal Berwick, and that of the old cardinal at Versailles.

During the winter months of 1734 military operations in Italy had slowed and in Germany they had virtually ceased. The weather permitted limited operations in Italy during the winter months but in the Rhine Valley the armies, like a modern circus, went into winter quarters until the roads became passable in the spring and grass for the horses began to grow. Military posts in the Rhineland reported and evaluated the strengths of enemy forces and any other intelligence they could secure, particularly any construction of defenses that might change the military balance. Since France was the aggressor, the problem for the French was to decide how and when they wished to engage the imperial forces when weather permitted a resumption of operations. The emperor's problem was a defensive one—how to secure the contingents of troops from the German princes and provincial assemblies in accordance with the declaration of war which would be made by the imperial Diet at Regensburg, and how to build up the imperial army to meet an attack. It was hoped that he would also receive help from his allies, England, Holland, and Russia.

According to an official French version of the 1734 campaign published later in that year, the French government initially wished to undertake no projects on the Rhine and intended to remain on the defensive, drawing only upon French resources for the supply of the army. But a later decision was made to engage in some operations before the emperor could assemble his army, since it was not believed that he could field a significant force before June. The town and fortified chateau at Trarbach had been used for sorties against the French in a previous war, and Belle Isle proposed a siege of both Trarbach and the city of Luxembourg. The latter objective was not approved but a siege of Trarbach appears to have had conditional approval early in the year. In view of the requirement for early action, colonels were ordered to their regiments by 1 April and generals by 15 April.[1]

Two memoirs in the French military archives probably represent the attitude of the ministry of war in the spring of 1734. Both are dated 8 April and, although they differ somewhat in proposed operations, the basic concepts are the same and French operations in 1734 were in general responsive to them.[2]

Both documents stress that the principal effort must be made in Italy. One memoir notes that the object of the war is to injure the emperor and reduce his power. "Success in Italy is enough." There are no conquests to be made in Germany, the text continues, and the war on the Rhine is only a strong diversion of which the success is of only secondary importance. It is necessary to cross the Rhine and open the eyes of the German princes so that they will bring pressure upon the emperor. The other memoir takes a similar point of view, adding that enterprise in Germany will stir jealousy in England and fear in Holland. The principal difference between the two memoirs is that one seems to fear an imperial riposte on the lower Rhine and proposes that Coblenz be taken to check the movements of the Danes, Hanoverians, and Hessians, while the other sees this area as too far north to consider. This less aggressive memoir finds disadvantages in almost any French move that can be made. Philippsburg can be attacked only in September, it believes, because high water floods the area earlier in the summer. The Ettlingen Lines close the roads to those who cross at Kehl or Fort Louis. To cross below at Philippsburg one must have Mannheim and the Elector Palatine there does not appear ready to receive us. Breisach and Freiburg lead nowhere. Luxembourg is part of the Lowlands, and the king of France has accepted the neutrality of this area. In the Moselle Valley there is only the chateau at Trarbach which "belongs to the elector of Trier who has not definitely declared himself yet." Some hand, possibly that of Dangervilliers, changed the language in the quoted passage to "belongs to the Empire," which probably reflected that the memoir was being overtaken by events, since General Belle Isle and his forces entered the city of Trier on 8 April, the date of the memoir.

The recapitulation at the end of the memoir makes the following points as recommendations: 1) have 40,000 men in Alsace by 20 April ready to cross the Rhine at Mannheim or above; 2) leave 10,000 men to occupy Speyer and mask the move towards Philippsburg; 3) use the magazines at Landau for the troops, then those of the Elector Palatine; 4) put 10,000 men in the area of Luxembourg to contain the imperial garrison and support an action at Trarbach; 5) the 16,000 men that were destined for Flanders can replace those at Luxembourg when the attack is made on Trarbach; 6) see Philippsburg always as the end of the campaign.

Thus the only feasible initiatives foreseen were attacks on Trarbach and Philippsburg. In short, the French, although the aggressors, contemplated only the taking of a fort on the Moselle and another on the Rhine. And the last point above put a definite period to the military campaign.

As the French planned the timing of their 1734 campaign, they had two main factors to consider. The first was that the emperor and Prince Eugene were using all their considerable influence to get the military contingents from the German princes in motion to join the imperial army. Until these various contributions arrived, the imperial army would be extremely weak. It was an excellent time for a French attack. On the other hand, spring campaigns were limited by the grass available for the horses, and the supply was not usually adequate until late May. As the memoir noted: "This is the most important restraint of all." Some compromise between the two factors was needed.

In view of the need for early operations Berwick was back in Alsace at the end of March, and messages signed Berwick began to emanate from Strasbourg. The intelligence he received led him to believe that the enemy was assembling forces behind the Ettlingen Lines, and that the fortresses of Breisach, Freiberg, and Philippsburg were lightly garrisoned. In messages to his subordinate in the Moselle Valley preparing to attack Trarbach, he called attention to this assembly of imperial troops. Berwick was also informed that imperial couriers had been sent to hasten the arrival of the Hessian and Hanoverian forces, and from the French ambassador in Berlin came the news that the Prussian regiments promised to the emperor had been withdrawn from Prussia and Pomerania and had arrived in Berlin in preparation for a move toward the Rhine.[3] The French were pressed by these reports to move as soon as they could.

The remains of the fortified chateau of Trarbach still cling to the steep hill above the town of Trarbach and its sister town, Trarben. The lovely Moselle winds through the valley in deep curves. Where the high steep banks did not face the sunless North, they were covered with vineyards, then as now. With both Coblenz at the mouth of the Moselle and the fortified city of Luxembourg to the southeast in imperial hands, the chateau at Trarbach represented the controlling center of a corridor which led directly, if somewhat tortuously, into France. The Moselle frontier was a sensitive one for France. Belle Isle's elaborate defense plan for this sector, as shown in Chapter 5, was too ambitious to be put into action. But throughout the war French commanders would worry about keeping the imperial forces directly before them in the Rhine Valley and fear an attack around their northern flank through the Moselle and Meuse valleys. Luxembourg is closer to Paris than Strasbourg is.

A French military memoir dated 12 April 1734 discusses the problem of the Moselle, stating that this was the most threatened frontier. The solution recommended was to put enough troops in the triangle formed by the Moselle and the Rhine to eat up the subsistence there. This would keep the enemy on the other side of the Rhine until the grass was growing, according to the memoir. The general would spare the country as much as possible, but it was indispensable to take the hay and grain. Straw and wood was needed for the soldiers. "We need a great deal of wood for cooking bread and may have to go as far as to demolish houses to get it. And we need cows to infinity."[4]

Belle Isle assembled his army—probably approaching 20,000 men—on the plain above Sierck on 7 April and moved into Trier, which was unfortified and whose gates were thrown open by the citizens. The elector of Trier had only a few troops and these were in Trarbach and Coblenz. Belle Isle sent his brother, the chevalier de Belle Isle, ahead from Trier to take the walled city of Trarbach. This was accomplished with little resistance on 15 April. But the chateau, to which the military forces in the town withdrew, had bombproof underground defenses. Although it had no forward works about it, its crenelated walls allowed the garrison to put up fire without exposing themselves.[5]

After Belle Isle had moved into the territory of the elector of Trier he was given permission to besiege the chateau at Trarbach, but the final decision was left up to him and on 15 April Berwick asked him if he had definitely decided to go ahead with the siege. There was always the chance that some of the units of Hessians, Prussians, or Danes moving southward toward the imperial army might be diverted towards the Moselle. The duke of Noailles, who commanded the army of observation that moved between the Moselle and Berwick's main force near Speyer, called this to Belle Isle's attention, adding that Berwick had even talked of giving up the idea of a siege at Trarbach and changing the positions of his army. On 20 April Berwick also cautioned Belle Isle, suggesting that he watch a movement of Hessian troops near Schwalbach.[6]

But Belle Isle would get his siege and make the most of it. The messages from Berwick reflect some of the impatience of the old marshal with his bumptious subordinate. Berwick could be sure that his cautious policy was that of the cardinal, but Belle

Isle too had friends at court. Dangervilliers was one who sought Belle Isle's friendship and criticized the marshal's decisions. He assured Belle Isle, in a letter of 6 April, that the imperials could not assemble a large force in early spring. "We will be the masters during April." He then went on to cast doubts on the intentions of Berwick. "If, in spite of all appearances, the marshal should not consider it appropriate to make any significant operation, I confess to you that I should be very sad to see only these movements." The marshal is only using up forage, he observed, and if he is not going to do anything it will ruin the lands of the Elector Palatine with whom we are not angry. But, he added finally, perhaps the marshal has a plan.[7]

Belle Isle must have been amused to receive a letter of this sort, with its confidential tone, from his war minister and another with the same date, but with quite a different tone, from his superior, Marshal Berwick.

I have your letter of the fourth saying that you will not be able to have the regiments leave until after the expedition of the chevalier de Belle Isle. Until I have news of what is happening at Trarbach and what you recognize as possible to do this month I cannot make a decision. But in order not to lose time have the goodness to advance (illegible word) troops over to this side in accordance with the letter which I sent you the day before yesterday. I pray you in the future to follow to the letter what I tell you.[8]

It is strong language from one senior general to another. One is tempted to believe that Belle Isle may have held the two communications before him at arms length, one in each hand, and laughed. Lee Kennett was correct when he observed that Belle Isle "always had difficulty distinguishing the functions of a minister from those of a general," although he was speaking of Belle Isle as war minister a quarter-century later.[9] Dangervilliers also offered advice, telling Belle Isle that the chateau at Trarbach was more difficult to take than it had been in an earlier campaign. It will take from twelve to fifteen days to position the artillery, he noted. They could hold out a month and take you into June. It is not expected that you will be interrupted by the enemy, but it appears that the marshal has other plans and you may have to join him. After Trarbach is taken, concluded the minister, the marshal will be *à son aise* along the Rhine. A few days later he advised Belle Isle that there were troubles at Speyer and the marshal had hanged four soldiers. "Keep your troops in a condition in which you do not have to do the same." Belle Isle could feel himself on fairly firm ground. The minister was corresponding directly with him and with his younger brother, one of his subordinate commanders. And Belle Isle's letters had been read to the king, Dangervilliers told him.[10]

The siege itself could not have been a very difficult one. Some 40 members of the town's garrison were captured. The garrison of the chateau was composed of 600 men furnished by the elector and 100 imperial troops sent in from Luxembourg. During the first few days the French tried a number of methods to force entry but were thrown back and on the 25 April began the standard procedure of opening the first parallel. Other normal procedures were followed. For example, the French agreed not to attack from the town side and the garrison agreed not to fire from that side. By 2 May, after 2,687 shells had fallen in the fort and all but two of its cannon were out of action, the white flag went up. The garrison marched out, drums beating with two cannons and a mortar and were allowed to proceed to Coblenz. There the elector of Trier, in his great Rhine fortress of Ehrenbreitstein, wrote to Prince Eugene of his great satisfaction with the performance of both his own commander and the imperial representative at Trarbach. The imperial officer himself was of a different opinion and so unhappy about the defense undertaken that he would not sign the capitulation. The French report noted a French loss of 200 men to only 10 lost by the enemy and suggested that the unexpectedly early surrender of the fortress at Trarbach might have been related to the fact that the commander was young and newly married.[11]

And Belle Isle made the most of it. Berwick consented—we may assume without enthusiasm—to the return of the chevalier de Belle Isle to Versailles to report personally to the king. Belle Isle also enjoyed a note from Chauvelin, who hoped he would take Coblenz as easily as Trarbach. Dangervilliers threw in his flattery and even the cardinal felt compelled to tell Belle Isle that the king was well satisfied with his conduct and was impressed by the taking of Trarbach and other achievements.[12]

But Berwick now took firm hold as the theater commander, moving his main forces on 1 May. He gave Belle Isle clear orders on 6 May that as soon as he was finished with Trarbach he was to join him on the Rhine. On 11 May he told him to blow up the two forts of Trarbach and Kirn on the Moselle.[13] Belle Isle left Trarbach on 15 May to join Berwick. The final razing of the Moselle forts was accomplished only after several further weeks of discussion.

The position of the elector of Trier must have been a painful one. The colonel commanding the elector's forces at Coblenz wrote to Belle Isle concerning the officer and men who were taken prisoner in the town of Trarbach. He called attention to the fact that there had been no declaration of war on either the French side or that of the elector. Since the soldiers were simply for the protection of the town and not for hostilities, could they not be released? If not, would he discuss ransom terms? The French answer from Belle Isle was that the elector's vote in the imperial diet at Regensburg had been against France and the men would be considered prisoners of war. Still, this was not total war. Although the plundering of the population in the area was undoubtedly severe and workers were forced into the digging and construction required by a siege, there were at least some promises of restitution. Belle Isle told the elector that he regretted taking the forage but that it was unavoidable and he would give a receipt as in France.[14]

The elector of Trier was not alone in his discomfort. The Austrian files contain the apologetic letters of smaller German sovereigns who found that as close neighbors of France they could not be supporters of their emperor. One letter to Prince Eugene in 1734 poses the dilemma:

This will inform you of the things which I cannot report to you [officially] so that you will not think ill of us. As you know, the emperor wrote to our prince to send a contingent of troops. His Majesty believed that he should respond and on the nineteenth of last month he did, asking him to accept money rather than a contingent because we have no troops. We have had no response from the emperor.

If we should try to put troops on foot they would melt like snow in the sun. We would never get any from the king of Prussia or the electors of Cologne or the Palatinate.

To avoid the ruin of the country we have done as the other princes of the empire bordering France in trying to arrange with France a treaty of contribution.[15]

An imperial rescript of 8 June 1734 would recognize the problem and allow princes who were prevented by enemy action or other causes from sending a contingent to pay in money.[16] Thus the unfortunate princes must count themselves lucky to pay their "contributions" to the French and to the emperor simultaneously.

The fall of Trarbach and the absorption of Belle Isle's separate command into Berwick's army would end the attempt of the subordinate to take a large share of the action, but he was already marked as "un homme d'une ambition démesuré." In a personal letter the aging and renowned military theorist, the chevalier de Folard, congratulated Belle Isle on his siege of Trarbach and noted that although the French had by this time crossed the Rhine he did not think they would take proper advantage of it. What should be done, said Folard, was to "detach a corps of 20,000 men, commanded by yourself, and have it march straight into Saxony. Nothing easier. And it would greatly disturb the Muscovites and the duke of Saxony."[17] Rumors of such a possible move must have been current, for Prince Eugene's representative in Baden wrote that the French were spreading rumors of a corps of 30,000 men under Belle Isle attacking through Hesse into Saxony. Eugene, picking up the story from this source or some other, passed it on to the emperor. As Eugene saw it there could be an army of 25,000 under Belle Isle passing through Hesse into Saxony while Berwick placed his army between the Main and the Neckar to engage Eugene.[18]

Belle Isle would push the cardinal into such a project in a fu-

ture war, but at the moment he must be content with the siege of
Trarbach—a classic siege if a small one.

Berwick kept his own counsel on what he intended to do. His
subordinate, the duke de Noailles, when ordered to move toward the Rhine with the army that had been supporting Belle
Isle, told the latter that the marshal kept the plan secret but that
he could not be prevented from guessing. He hoped it would be
something "grand et décisif." A few days later Noailles found
himself across the Rhine with the advance guard, moving on the
Ettlingen Lines, while Berwick wrote to Versailles: "I began today to cross the Rhine." [19]

Berwick's plan was to cross the Rhine with two armies, one
above and one below the fortress of Philippsburg, and descend
upon that strong point from two directions. The actual numbers
of men involved in these operations is impossible to determine
with great accuracy, since the actual strength of units varied
greatly and even the numbers of units reported in different periods is difficult to interpret. In general the French forces were
building toward the 100,000 mark for Berwick's entire command. At the beginning of May about 20,000 were still in the
Moselle Valley under Belle Isle. French order of battle reports
during the last of April show more than 100 battalions and 150
squadrons of horse in Berwick's army, including those on the
Moselle. On 24 April there were 38 battalions at Speyer with 14
coming from Homburg and 24 more expected, making a total of
76 battalions available for the Rhine crossings. With the attached
cavalry squadrons Berwick probably had up to 80,000 men for
the crossings—which was the estimate made by Eugene. [20]

One army at Speyer was placed under d'Asfeld, who had recently arrived from Italy, and the other under Berwick himself
began crossing the Rhine at Kehl and over a new bridge at Fort
Louis. This latter body was the army that would confront the
Ettlingen Lines.

The Ettlingen Lines figured strongly in the French communications, and in the months preceding the campaign French
intelligence gleaned all the information about the lines they
could obtain. Basically, the lines were a linear fortification that

stretched from a point on the Rhine River in or near what is to-day the city of Karlsruhe in an irregular series of obstacles across the lowlands bordering the river and into the hills. They were in existence during the War of the Spanish Succession and had been broken by Villars in 1707.[21] Since then, and particularly during the winter of 1734, efforts were made to reconstruct and improve the lines. In the flat country they were strengthened by trenches, blockhouses, and even by an area which was to be inundated in case of attack. In the hills there were trenches—still to be seen today—and felled trees. In its greatest concept it was to be a long diagonal from the Philippsburg area, through Karlsruhe, to terminate in the hills near the town of Spessart. Actually, although there were posts along the Rhine above Philippsburg, the serious effort to create a line of obstacles which could be defended was limited to the fourteen kilometers from Daxlanden near the Rhine, across the lowlands south of Ettlingen, and up into the hills. Already in January 1734 the French noted the improvements which had been made and a message from General de Quandt to Marshal Du Bourg estimated that the lines would embarrass the beginning of a campaign and that the end of the line in the hills probably could not be turned. Five thousand men, peasants and soldiers, were working on the line, he had reported. The imperials had indeed been busy. General Freiherr von Schmettau had worked from 26 December 1733 to March 1734 to put the lines into a defensive condition.[22]

By 26 April Eugene had arrived in Heilbronn, some fifty kilometers east of the army headquarters at Waghäusel. He had come by way of Nuremberg to avoid, as much as possible, the Bavarian lands. He wrote to the emperor that he did not yet have information on enemy movements and had not yet had the opportunity of talking to the commanders, Bevern and Württemberg. His chief concern, he emphasized, was to get the promised reinforcements from the empire—the auxiliary, circle, and Reich troops, the arrival of which he hoped to hasten by letters directly to the several courts involved and by the efforts of Seckendorff and Küfstein. The offer of the king of Prussia to send more than his promised contingent of 10,000 men, which was mentioned as early as July 1733, had been renewed and forwarded to him by Seckendorff.

According to the latter the king of Prussia suggested sending his entire army—which the ambassador thought meant an additional thirty battalions and eighty squadrons above the 10,000— into the Moselle Valley, and he asked Eugene whether the offer should be accepted. Eugene's reaction, in his letter to the emperor, was that the promised 10,000 must be started on their way first; this should not in any way be delayed by the possibility of sending a larger force. Moreover, although it would be a fine thing to have the king of Prussia produce such a diversion against the French, it was unlikely that he would allow his entire army to move so far while there was still animosity between him and the elector of Saxony and while he had difficulties with the Russians over the movement of artillery.[23]

The next day Eugene arrived at the camp at Waghäusel, near Philippsburg, to take command of the army. He found the imperial troops stretched over a line from the Black Forest to Coblenz. Of a strength of sixty-nine battalions, forty-one grenadier companies, and sixty-nine squadrons of horse, he had only thirteen battalions, eight grenadier companies, and forty-four squadrons in the camp as a field army to meet the French attack. After he had examined the situation he wrote: "In spite of all these effective troops available, they were beyond my reach by their deployment, and I had to make do with the 15,000 men at hand."[24] He awaited the reluctant sending of princely contingents, some of which would never come at all if their princes felt themselves threatened and elected to hold their forces at home. Some even asked for troops from Eugene, who countered with the argument that there would then be "the danger that an invading enemy would cut off one part of the forces from another and consequently one corps after another would be lost."[25]

After Eugene learned on 1 May that the French had crossed the Rhine he received several contradictory reports which caused him to delay his decision for action. But in the night of 3 May he had positive information that a strong French force was approaching the Ettlingen Lines from the south and ordered troops into the lines. However, on the morning of the fourth he made a personal inspection of the lines and found them untenable. The troops then in the lines were ordered out and a general retreat began.[26]

Not an impressive reaction on the Austrian side. But when this conflict is seen from the French side it represents a daring attack upon a formidable defense line commanded by the most feared general in Europe. It was precisely at this moment, when it was recognized that the physical powers as well as the influence of the great Eugene were slipping away from him, that a young and energetic leader entered the scene opposite him as an enemy subordinate commander. This was the opportunity for Maurice de Saxe, the illegitimate son of Augustus II of Saxony and later one of France's greatest generals, to win the recognition that he had been so avidly seeking. Maurice, then a colonel, was the eager subordinate of Noailles in the force that approached the Ettlingen Lines. At some point in the day of 4 May Maurice and Eugene must have been quite near one another. The events of the day were reported to the ministry by Noailles on 8 May in a fifteen-page message, and were dramatized in the journal of Noailles's command for the days 1–5 May.[27]

*2 May.* We crossed the Rhine and camped at Iphintzaim [Iffezheim]. M. le Duc de Noailles and M. le Comte de Saxe were detached with two regiments of dragoons, the Hussars, 400 gardes du corps, and 14 companies of grenadiers. . . .

*3 May.* The army marched in 3 columns to a place near the Lines of Oethlingen. The duc de Noailles had left Rastatt at dawn to reconnoiter the lines. Count Saxe advanced with the Hussars and a detachment of dragoons through the woods which cover the lines up to within musket range. Several cannon shots were fired at him and the Hussars carried away 1,200 sheep which were at the edge of the enemy entrenchments. At three in the afternoon the duc de Noailles marched toward the mountains and stopped at the foot of them. Count Saxe used the little daylight left to find a passage in the mountains and a terrain suitable for assembling troops. With four Hussars and twelve dragoons he penetrated up to the top of the mountains by a trail where one could pass only in single file, and there he found a space large enough for the troops. . . . The troops climbed up in single file at dawn on the fourth by this path. It took them an hour to climb up and two hours to assemble . . . after which they began to march toward the line in good order. . . . Count de Saxe placed himself before the grenadiers sword in hand and cried, "Battalions, March." What a proud moment! . . . Firing was heavy and stubborn on both sides. Finally the weight of valor and numbers carried and the enemy was obliged to retire in confusion. . . . The enemy who feared, with reason, that the French would arrive on the plain by the gorge of Ettlingen . . . abandoned all their works and retired to the trenches with the rest of their army. Prince Eugene himself was in the lines.

5 *May*. Marshal Berwick entered the lines with the cavalry and took up his headquarters. . . . If Count de Saxe had not carried the lines we would have been obliged to have recourse to delaying expedients, perhaps to that of retiring some leagues because the troops of Prince Eugene were arriving very rapidly.[28]

It is not too much to say that this exploit made the career of Maurice de Saxe. On 19 May, Dangervilliers sent him a letter of commendation, noting that his performance in the attack on the lines had been called to the attention of the king. On 22 May a short note from Cardinal Fleury to Maurice acknowledged his attack on the lines.[29] Like Belle Isle, Maurice was wild for advancement.

Farther downstream the army of d'Asfeld had crossed the Rhine near Mannheim. The count of Bavaria, who was a part of it, was surprised that there was no real resistance, but he hesitated to criticize the great Eugene. He learned on the sixth of the success of Maurice, which he noted in his diary without comment.[30] We may wonder how these two generals in the French army regarded one another. Maurice was the natural son of the late elector of Saxony and Bavaria was the natural son of the elector of Bavaria. While their half-brothers were reigning German princes, both these men would serve France as soldiers.

Eugene was well aware of Berwick's strategy. He retreated with his outnumbered forces north to Bruchsal and then eastward to Heilbronn where he wrote that his enemy on the right bank of the Rhine now numbered over 100,000 strong in two armies and intended to catch him between them. He had pulled back to Heilbronn, he explained, where there were adequate supplies and awaited reinforcements.[31]

Eugene had explained it to his emperor in a message of 5 May, noting that he had only 20,000 troops at hand and was facing, as he thought, an enemy with three or four times as many. He was uncertain and "in such uncertainty we remained the whole of the day before yesterday until during the night, about one o'clock, further news came that the enemy was only a half-hour from our lines and his troops had been issued powder for an attack on the following morning." Eugene was drawing troops to himself rapidly, he related, to protect his crossing over the Neckar and prevent "what would be the worst of all, to be cut off from the still awaited troops." He assured his master that he had not lost spirit: "The greater the danger the greater attention I can give to it." [32]

The emperor responded on 14 May assuring Eugene of his trust and support and of his understanding of the need to concentrate his forces to avoid being cut off. "My confidence in you is complete, and in this matter I do not expect you to ask my prior approval." [33]

Eugene was reaching in all directions for the needed troops. Even the commander at Philippsburg received an abrupt and unmistakable order. "Mein Herr Feldmarschall-Lieutenant, as soon as you receive this and without the slightest delay send 800 men from the imperial battalions so that they arrive here today." [34]

The French were in an extraordinary position to shatter the emperor's only field army while it was still nearly helpless. It must have been difficult for many to understand why this opportunity was not taken. The Count of Bavaria could not see why a better attack was not made after breaking the Ettlingen Lines. The enemy could reassemble, he pointed out. Had the French proceeded to the Neckar, to deprive the enemy of subsistence, they could have returned to besiege Philippsburg when there was no more to be had. But d'Asfeld would not move although he admitted to his minister that the decision not to attack Eugene was not well taken by the younger people in his command. [35]

There is no doubt that Eugene's situation was critical, very likely more critical than his messages showed, although these revealed strong concern. In one message of 20 May he asked the emperor not to take things too much to heart, for God had spared his house often in the past and would do so again. Hardly a reassuring report from a commander. In another letter of the same date he was franker:

> I confess that in spite of all the dispositions taken to cope with an attack on the rear guard, I really don't know how matters would have turned out if the enemy had done what he could have and should have done. Nor do I understand why he has remained twelve days inactive, undertaking nothing of importance, while he exacts contributions. He has given me time to refresh my tired men and horses, send heavy supplies forward, and draw troops to myself so that in a few days I will have about 30,000 effectives available.[36]

Did Berwick hold his hand because of the great renown of Prince Eugene? He wrote to Belle Isle on 9 May that he had been assured that Prince Eugene had retired to Heilbronn but that he wished to know positively. A few days later he wrote that he was sure. Does this betray more than the usual concern of a commander for the security of his forces? The Austrians may choose to lay great stress on the fear of Eugene, but Berwick's actions, after all, are in keeping with the plans made months before.[37]

Berwick was still in favor of a siege of Philippsburg and sent his opinion to the minister and to the king. It would be a long affair, he said, requiring both armies under his command, one for the siege and one for observation. The king must decide. Noailles too was in favor of a siege for the reason that the troops were inexperienced in conditions of actual warfare. After an interruption of twenty years the troops needed to become accustomed again to gunfire, said the general. On 11 May the minister answered that the king believed the siege of Philippsburg was the most important but suggested that sieges of Mainz and Coblenz be considered as well.[38]

The Ettlingen Lines were broken, the emperor's army scrambling in retreat, the legend of Eugene fading rapidly. The French might have destroyed the imperial army, cowed the German princes, and pushed into the Habsburg hereditary lands, even towards Vienna. But instead the victorious French army would move a few miles north along the Rhine and begin the massive diggings for the siege of Philippsburg.

Perhaps the French had forgotten how long and difficult a siege might be. Kehl and Trarbach had been short actions with few casualties and fitted in nicely with an army of cautious commanders and inexperienced troops. Philippsburg would remind them that a siege of a key fortress defended by a determined leader could be painfully expensive in human and material resources.

Philippsburg today is a town on the flatlands of the Rhine Valley halfway between Mannheim and Karlsruhe. The Rhine has been canalized so that the river no longer passes the town, and there are today no visible remains of fortifications. But in the eighteenth century Philippsburg with its great bastions facing north on a bend in the river, surrounded by woods and swamps, was one of the key defense points of the Empire. The site of a Roman castellum in the third century, it was besieged by the Swedes in the Thirty Years' War and by Marshal Turenne in 1644, and in 1688 Vauban directed a thirty-two-day siege there against imperial forces. Since the summer of 1733, when the probability of hostilities with France became clear, work had been under way to put the defenses in better condition. Although Seckendorff was the titular governor of Philippsburg and would normally have been expected to take over the defense, he could not be spared from his post as ambassador in Berlin. General Freiherr von Wuttgenau was appointed commander in the fall of 1733 and set about his task with great energy. He dug out trenches that had filled with earth and rebuilt ramparts and he restored the Rheinschanze, a detached fortification on the left bank of the river connected with the main works by a suspension bridge. When Prince Eugene arrived in late April 1734 and inspected Philippsburg he reported that Wuttgenau had done such a splendid job in so short a time that the enemy would not find it easy to challenge the fortress. Wrote Eugene to the emperor: "[It was] difficult to comprehend how this work, which assures us a Rhine crossing, was carried out

with Berwick's camp only an hour away, when it could easily
have been obstructed by only a few thousand men."[39] This may
have been more of a criticism of Berwick than a commendation
for Wuttgenau, but the fortress was in relatively good condition.
Moreover, it was commanded by a competent and determined
man with a garrison of 4,000 men.

Prince Eugene very properly regarded the French decision
to besiege Philippsburg as unexpected luck which would give
him time to strengthen his army with more incoming troops.[40]

The French began the siege on 26 May with work on the "cir-
cumvallation" line around the fortress and a boat bridge across
the river below the site. On the same day 150 cargo boats came
down from Strasbourg with the siege artillery, consisting of 162
bronze cannon, 196 iron cannon, and 123 mortars. Then came
the diverting of the normal water supply of the garrison. After
this the first serious effort was directed against the Rheinschanze
as the most vulnerable point.[41]

Berwick put the greater part of his cavalry on the left bank
and divided his infantry into an observation army that remained
outside the fortifications and trenches, and a siege army that
manned the trenches and batteries. It was an army of over
100,000 men in all. But it was difficult for the French to believe
that Eugene was not preparing some kind of attack or diversion.
Noailles mentioned this to Dangervilliers on 8 June, suggesting
that Eugene might cross the Rhine toward Luxembourg to draw
off a large part of the French forces. But in Versailles there was
now less caution and a desire for some achievement. Dangervilliers wrote to Berwick that to counter what had occurred in
Italy—by which he meant the crossing of the Po by the Austrian
forces in early May and the subsequent retreat of French forces
in a near rout—it was "bien nécessaire" that some good news
come from his area. Eugene was under the same pressure and
wrote to the emperor that a "fortunate major engagement"
either in Germany or Italy was needed to give things, which
looked so evil on all sides, a better appearance. Until this happens we can expect only disadvantageous and "disreputable"
peace proposals from France and her allies, added Eugene.[42]
But Eugene did not make the diversionary effort expected. Did

he believe that Philippsburg was truly important? After all, he had not thought the Ettlingen Lines worth defending. Yes, he did, as the following message shows. "The evil consequences which the loss of Philippsburg will entail I understand all too well. It will make the Schwäbisch and Fränkisch circles unsuitable for operations. Wherever one turns he will have to leave an army corps to observe the garrison of Philippsburg, and he will have to leave even greater numbers because we can then not depend upon Mannheim. After Philippsburg much will be lost and the enemy will be able from Philippsburg to operate against this army in any direction, if not this year, then in some future year, before we can assemble."[43]

By 3 June, Wuttgenau was forced to give up the Rhein-schanze. He quietly withdrew the 400 men across the river during the night. It was also on 3 June that the French began the first parallel against the fortress itself. But progress was slow with the French effort, which was directed mainly against the detached hornwork and crownwork. Berwick hoped that this might be the means of reaching the covered way, a significant step in reducing a fortress.[44]

Detailed reports fill the files, using the siege terms that are now quaint or completely unfamiliar. But the intensive detail, the naming of units and commanders in their positions in the siege operations, and the careful descriptions of the small conflicts that took place from time to time—all these are convincing witness that the siege was a formalized and highly skilled operation. The count of Bavaria's diary exemplifies the patient attention to siege detail as he notes the precise names of men and units and their locations in the trenches. If the meeting of mailed knights represented the warfare of the feudal period, and the dogfight of fighter pilots typified an aspect of twentieth-century warfare, the language, expertise, and daring of the siege expressed the spirit of eighteenth-century warfare even more typically than the marching of close-packed columns of men.

In a siege the high-ranking officer might have cleaner work than the soldier who dug and fought in the trenches but, if he inspected his troops, he was exposed to fire nearly as often since there were no true rear areas. On such an inspection, on 12 June

1734, Marshal Berwick was killed by a cannonball. Christopher Duffy suggests that as the besiegers approach a fortress the batteries of the parallels behind could not lend close support without an appreciable risk of removing the heads of their own men —and this probably explains how the marshal was killed at Philippsburg.[45] There is a story that in Turin the dying Villars was informed of the death of Berwick and responded: "That man was always lucky." Soon only Eugene would be left of the famous names of the War of the Spanish Succession.

Prince Eugene's army was increasing. The contingent of 6,000 from Hanover arrived in the early days of June along with the 10,000-man Prussian force. The commander of the Danish troops sent assurances that he was coming in two columns to Frankfurt as rapidly as he could.[46] By the first week in July, Noailles noted that the imperial army was as large as the French and the cavalry more numerous.[47]

The reason Eugene did not make a serious diversionary effort as his strength increased and Philippsburg began to falter was, if we can believe his communications, partly the doubtful quality of his troops. It may have been this same lack of troop quality that caused the French to hesitate to exploit their victory over the Ettlingen Lines.

Atrocities are a reflection of the quality of the troops. Since the crossing of the Rhine by the French forces in May, reports of atrocities were sprinkled through the communications. Those committed by the Prussian contingent when it passed through the Würzburg area were so outrageous that, even at a time when Germany was threatened by a foreign invader, there was concern that a people's insurrection might occur against the "Hilfstruppen" of the emperor's German allies. Eugene complained without notable success to the king of Prussia. Eugene also had complained of the atrocities of the French and in a letter to one of his commanders on 15 May spoke of the unbelievable excesses and cruelties of the enemy troops. Reports on atrocities had reached the French court as well, and a 15 May letter from the king to Berwick asked for more rigorous measures to stop depredations.[48]

These atrocities were, of course, incidents that went far beyond the excesses often attending the levying of contributions, the foraging, and the forced labor in the siege operations. For example, the authorities in Durlach complained to Eugene of marauders who had plundered all the villages between the Alb River and the Saal Creek (roughly the area of operations of both armies in May) on 8 May and committed unbelievable excesses. On 15 May a letter from Ignaz Koch, the privy councillor and secretary to Eugene, to Count Küfstein probably describes the incidents which Eugene refers to as unbelievable. "The sacred Host thrown on the ground . . . children of four and five years slashed in the face and, most horrible, women nailed to a cross with both hands and in such a cruel condition raped to death." [49] These have the ring of atrocities from the Thirty Years' War and may or may not have had some religious overtones.

There is also a recurrent tone of complaint about discipline from commanders in both armies and some tendency for each to believe that discipline is better in the opposing forces. The years of peace, we are assured, are at least partly to blame. Eugene admits frankly to the emperor, "I understand completely how your troops used to be and how they are now." He goes on to explain that many general officers had not served in a campaign or had served only as junior officers and that many had forgotten a great deal. And the circle troops were mostly made up of newly raised companies. All this imposed a caution on his decisions, added Eugene. [50]

It is not difficult to understand how atrocities will follow rapidly upon relaxed discipline, given the source of the troops. The eighteenth-century army was composed of men largely from three sources: first, foreign troops who might be labeled mercenaries or soldiers of fortune; secondly, men recruited, often by force or fraud, in goodly proportion from the criminal or "sturdy beggar" elements of society; and thirdly, militia elements that were, usually temporarily and often illegally, hustled into the regular army to meet a critical need instead of defending their home areas from invasion. Some such militia units were serving with the French forces. There was no regular conscription to disrupt the productive manpower of these societies, which were still basically agrarian at this time. The army, at least below the officer ranks, was a slice of the bottom of society. The high rate of desertions suggests a high percentage of men who were either forced unwillingly into service or were thoroughly disenchanted by the experience. The separation of the common soldier from his officer (and a great many officers were needed to check desertions) was probably never as great as during this period. He had no spiritual link with his commander as he may have had during the religious wars, nor did he have a reason to feel any national sentiment during a dynastic war in an army where his superiors were from an international nobility and he himself may have served more than one sovereign. His chances for advancement into the officer corps were probably as low as they had ever been. Vagts points out that the monopolization of officer posts by the nobility in this century had almost put the noble back in the position he enjoyed in the Middle Ages.[51]

This gives us a large organization of men—although by no means as large as modern armies—whose spokesmen for us today are only the officer/noble class, since this class alone possessed enough education to write. We seek in vain for diaries of private soldiers or noncommissioned officers in the War of the Polish Succession.[52] It was all the more likely, in an organization so clearly separated along class lines, for the directing elements to have no feeling of empathy for their troops and to undertake without hesitation the most severe measures when they believed them necessary. For example, Wuttgenau was so enraged at the performance of one body of 112 men defending a part of Philippsburg that he wanted every twentieth man condemned to be shot, later altering this to have them run the gauntlet six times.[53]

The lack of response of the soldier class, except by desertion or mutiny, probably allowed the noble class to, as Friedrich Heer put it, play out the war-leadership ritual for the baroque period of European society. "It is of the essence of archaic, courtly, knightly, personal-subjective societies that play, feasting, celebration, war, cultus and art all hang together. . . . Prince Eugen and his opponents in the European theatre of war were still 'playing out'—with great intelligence—the war-leadership ritual."[54]

In a great siege, such as that of Philippsburg, we see the game element in full play in a monstrous theater on the Rhine where the players, largely out of view of their own civilian leadership, carried out their assigned roles on a stage all their own.

In late June, Charles VI still hoped for a victory of some kind: "A fortunate masterstroke either in the empire or in Italy is the last human means to rescue me, my house, and all of Europe from the domination of the house of Bourbon."[55]

But the siege went on with only small actions. An attempt was made by the Austrians to burn the French boat bridge by floating fireboats against it from upstream, but the scheme was poorly carried out, only one of the boats reaching the bridge, and was unsuccessful. French artillery fire increased steadily in effectiveness. The Rheinschanze, across the river, was now the location of a French battery.

As the French efforts against the hornwork and the crownwork intensified, Eugene moved his army, now much greater and representing the contingents of more than a hundred princes and assemblies, into Bruchsal, about fifteen kilometers from the French lines around Philippsburg. On 30 June he gave the march order to move closer on the following day. It was in great detail and began as follows: "Tomorrow, God willing, the army shall break camp at Bruchsal in six columns and march in the following order." The French watched Eugene's army march toward their lines. General de Brou wrote from Philippsburg that Eugene appeared ready to attack. On 2 July d'Asfeld reported the movement drawing closer to his lines and listed the measures he was taking. Another message of the French staff reported Eugene's army at Wiesenthal within sight of the French lines.[56] The great drama was ready for a fitting climax with a clash of the armies of the major commanders before probably the greatest fortress in Europe. But Eugene did not attack. By 3 July the French understood that he did not intend to attack.[57] The great moment passed.

The French then continued their attacks on the hornwork and by the fifteenth they were successful. There were 360 men inside, reported d'Asfeld. They made no resistance; all had been killed or drowned except for 110, now taken prisoner. So after seven weeks the two most important forward defense works had been taken. There remained the inner bastions of the fortress itself. And the Rhine, which had been rising since the first of the month, swollen by heavy rains, was now falling.[58]

Wuttgenau knew it was the end. On the seventeenth he sent an officer to d'Asfeld with a letter for Prince Eugene giving the conditions in the surrounded fortress. D'Asfeld refused to forward the letter and Wuttgenau held a council of war with his officers. A second effort was made to arrange a suspension of hostilities and siege operations, but d'Asfeld insisted that there could be no capitulation at all if a day's delay ensued. After another council of war the surrender conditions were drafted. They were completed at three in the morning of the eighteenth and sent to d'Asfeld, who in turn sent his capitulation draft to Wuttgenau and proposed a meeting for the nineteenth. Wuttgenau might have held out for one or two more days, but the garrison would then have been lost.

Under the terms of the surrender, the garrison was allowed to march out with honors of war, taking six cannon and twenty rounds of shot for each man, and was permitted to retreat to Mainz. As a special mark of recognition for the brave defense, d'Asfeld gave Wuttgenau the finest cannon in the fort, a culverin cast in 1521. The garrison left on 21 July. Casualties had totaled 1,017 men. The rest, 3,526 strong, reached Mainz on 27 July. French casualties were considerably more. The Austrian staff study estimated them at 10,000. The count of Bavaria detailed them carefully, including 32 officers killed and 211 sick and wounded, 1,130 soldiers killed or died of sickness, 4,655 sick or wounded, and 2,734 deserters.[59]

Eugene and his army were literally within sight of the fortress when it capitulated. Since d'Asfeld refused to let any communications pass between Eugene and Wuttgenau until the garrison had withdrawn, Eugene had been reduced to an ignored spectator during the last days of the siege. What must have made it doubly painful for the greatest military leader in Austrian history was that since earlier in the month of July the king and crown prince of Prussia, with a number of other Prussian princes, had been his guests at the camp at Wiesenthal. He had hoped to use this personal encounter to draw both father and son away from their French sympathies and figuratively back into the emperor's camp. He seemed to have struck some sympathetic chords with the king but thought that with the crown prince the French poison had taken deep root. The crown prince, however, who was destined to become Frederick the Great, would cherish this early meeting of several weeks with the old leader as a valuable master-student relationship that would serve him well in the future.[60]

With the fall of Philippsburg the great scene for this theater of war had now been played out, and the actors would show caution and fatigue for the rest of the campaign season. Eugene must, of course, explain his actions, or rather lack of them, to his emperor.

He had weighed all the means of relieving the fort and reconnoitered in person, wrote Eugene. A great part of the army was composed of inexperienced troops and this was one of the principal circumstances that restrained him from a general engagement. This solution, if it failed, would not only lose the army, but under the circumstances, make it impossible to bring another army together, and the enemy would have four or five months to exercise his strength where he chose. Moreover, a misfortune to the army on the Rhine, with Bavaria and other princes ready to join the French, would require a complete withdrawal from Lombardy and the emperor would have to accept blindly the demands of the enemy. He concluded: "So long as the army holds together, it protects the hereditary lands, holds Bavaria in check, opposes further progress of the enemy's campaign, allows us to undertake some measures according to circumstances—all these considerations weighed so strongly with me that for Your Majesty's service it was better to see Philippsburg lost, however difficult for me, than to risk the army in a dangerous attack and see it lost as well."[61]

It is hard to fault this reasoning. But in his early days Eugene had fought and won campaigns in which he was seriously at a disadvantage. Many hoped in vain that he could achieve another such stroke at this time. It was not to be.

But Eugene was not idle. On 23 July he already had in hand a requested estimate by Quartermaster General von Schmettau examining French intentions in the post-Philippsburg period. Schmettau thought that the French had the choice of attacking

Breisach in the south or Mainz in the north. But since the Philippsburg garrison had been allowed to proceed to Mainz, and since Eugene had control of the Neckar bridges, he tended to rule out Mainz as a French objective. It was more likely that Breisach would be attacked, he thought, since its fall would release a considerable number of French troops committed to strong points throughout Alsace. He recommended substantial strengthening of the garrison. Eugene agreed with him and ordered the commander at Freiburg to send reinforcements to Breisach.[62]

It was a logical but incorrect conclusion. After the capitulation, d'Asfeld promptly moved his army back across the Rhine and forwarded to the minister his own estimate of enemy capabilities which suggested that he intended for the French forces to play a passive role. Eugene had three alternatives, thought d'Asfeld: 1) he may descend the Rhine to Mainz. I will position myself so that I am not committed to action; 2) he may remain opposite me to prevent my crossing the Rhine; 3) he may ascend the Rhine to consume the forage and cover Württemberg. D'Asfeld thought that Eugene would choose to stay along the Rhine to observe him and to prevent a crossing at Philippsburg or Fort Louis.[63]

But others were distressed by this lack of enterprise. Noailles, now also a field marshal, although he had earlier shown himself cautious now felt that the move of d'Asfeld back to the left bank would be interpreted as timidity.[64] Although Dangervilliers's communications initially seemed to indicate that defensive measures were uppermost in his mind, a change in attitude came from Versailles by 11 August, and d'Asfeld was virtually ordered either to move on Mainz and accept combat there or to cross the Rhine and march on Heidelberg and Heilbronn. The memoir of early 1734, which saw Philippsburg as the end of the campaign, seems to have been forgotten in the enthusiasm of a victorious siege. This must have shaken the aging d'Asfeld (he was now the senior marshal in the French army and would retire after this campaign), for he had written to the minister that it was time to think about winter quarters.[65]

Nevertheless, d'Asfeld did not move against Mainz. Actually the campaign was sputtering to an end on both sides. Sickness and desertions plagued them. The only action of the fall months would be a brief occupation of Worms by imperial troops during the last days of October. In October both d'Asfeld and Eugene left their armies. Noailles, after a trip of inspection, also took the road home where he found himself named commander in Italy for the coming spring campaign. The armies on the Rhine, French and imperial, were now in winter quarters.

✠

CHAPTER NINE

# Military Climax and Denouement

The War of the Polish Succession reached a climax of ferocity in Italy in mid-1734 and then dwindled away in all theaters, both north and south of the Alps, until an armistice was signed in late 1735. Perhaps the most intriguing question is how the restraints which had so formalized the war up to mid-1734 could have failed and allowed two pitched battles to occur which were of doubtful value to either side.

When Marshal Villars left his command in May, the acceleration in activity had already begun with the crossing of the Po by the Austrian army. The emperor could be resigned, if fearful, over his reversals on the Rhine, since he was losing no territory, but it was otherwise in the Po Valley where he had been forced out of some of the richest land in Europe. The ten-week buildup of imperial forces in the Mantua area and the appointment of an aggressive new commander brought about the first notable riposte to French progress when Mercy crossed the Po in early May and drove back the ill-positioned French columns on the right bank toward the city of Parma.

This Austrian initiative was checked in a few days by the French, and there followed a period of caution by the commanders on both sides during which their superiors in Vienna and Versailles became more and more impatient. The French commanders found that their Spanish and Sardinian allies were of little value to them. The former had disappeared into the southern part of Italy when the Spanish army marched away to take

Naples and Sicily, and the latter, King Charles Emmanuel and his Piedmontese army, played an active role in deflecting any aggressive French strategy. With the taking of the Milanese and the Cremonese this sovereign had gained as much from the war as he could reasonably expect and saw every further French initiative as leading to a possible defeat which could lose at a stroke the lands he had occupied. It was a fairly obvious geographic problem. If the allied French and Sardinian army were committed in any serious degree on the right (or south) bank of the Po, then the Austrians, by a sudden shift in direction, might launch an attack along the left bank into the Cremonese. It would be a revolving-door action in which the push on the right side would bring about a corresponding and opposite push on the left. Apparently Charles Emmanuel was governed by this strategic *fixe* and he frustrated as far as possible every French move to engage the Austrians on the right bank.

Now that the Austrian crossing of the Po had been a success, both Eugene and the emperor expected further movement. But the Austrian command situation was unstable. Since March, Field Marshal Mercy had had recurrent attacks which left him blind and speechless. In May he was struck down again and retired to Abano, where there were thermal baths. General Prince Ludwig von Württemberg took over, but Mercy was not definitively relieved of his command. Eugene, then in the Rhineland with his army, wrote to Württemberg expressing the hope that energetic measures would be taken before the enemy had time to strengthen himself.[1]

Eugene maintained a certain influence over the events in Italy although he admitted on several occasions in messages that he was not always sufficiently well informed to make judgments. Indeed at this time he must have been almost entirely preoccupied with the unhappy state of affairs in his own command area. But we find that there was a direct traffic between him and the commander in Italy throughout 1734 and 1735. Eugene remained, of course, even while in the field, the chairman of the Court War Council.

The emperor too was writing to his commander in Italy, doubtless guided more and more by Bartenstein. He had pressed

Mercy to seek a decisive victory. If some decisive action is not accomplished soon, pointed out the emperor, the English will not only fail to carry out their commitments but will soon bring out highly disadvantageous peace proposals. "And if the sea powers turn to this idea it will not be an easy matter to bring them away from it. Later progress will not alleviate the evil as much as some early encouragement for their depressed spirits. Some early good news from Lombardy would yield a basis for hope that England, and then in consequence the States General, would enter the stalemate."[2]

At the time this message was written, the emperor probably had the news of the loss of the Ettlingen Lines and the withdrawal of Eugene's army from the Rhine, with all the discouraging effect this would have upon the German states friendly to him and the encouragement of those opposed to him, such as Bavaria. But that was not all. The emperor was then losing his two kingdoms in the south, Naples and Sicily. In March 1734 Eugene mentioned the possibility of sending reinforcements to Naples from northern Italy but realized that it meant giving up the additional strength needed to operate on the right bank of the Po. By April he noted in a letter to Württemberg that it was better to act with all the force possible in northern Italy.[3] Of course the commanders in southern Italy had appealed urgently for reinforcements, but they could not agree on the use of the limited forces they already had at their disposal, a disagreement reminiscent of the difference between their counterparts in northern Italy when the French-Piedmontese invasion was imminent in 1733. Field Marshal Prince Caraffa wished to assemble the imperial forces and meet the Spanish army arriving from the north. General Count Traun desired to hold the strong points with garrisons and wait for the relief he was sure would be sent. It was Traun's strategy that won out and the Spanish, with a land army and a fleet operating unopposed offshore, were able to defeat the emperor's forces piecemeal.[4] It took time to capture the various fortresses but there was little doubt of the outcome.

Naples itself, lightly defended, hastened to send the keys to the city to the approaching Don Carlos. It was news worth a special messenger to the queen of Spain, and by 27 April the count of Val Hermoso had arrived in Madrid from Naples with the information that the Neapolitan parliament had taken the oath of allegiance to Don Carlos. It had, according to the Gaceta de Madrid, "given expression to the love, loyalty, and devotion they felt for his Royal Highness."[5]

Montemar and his forces continued their cleanup operations. Near Gaeta he defeated an imperial corps of 7,000 and left a force to lay siege to Gaeta itself. Here again is an example of the formalities of siege warfare. In July the duke of Liria demanded the surrender of Gaeta from its imperial commander, Count Tattenbach. The latter, in the presence of several of his officers, responded: "It is not yet time, since no batteries have been formed and no cannon are in place which would be a cause for surrender. The general must be patient for a while."[6] The attitude of Tattenbach was correct. The relief would never come and he would surrender as soon as he could—barring the loss of his honor.

With the pressure of these events weighing on the emperor and transmitted to Mercy and Württemberg, it was difficult for them to remain on the defensive. After considering the danger of exposing his communications by a move on the right bank, and weighing the possible advantages of an attack up the left bank against the strongest part of the allied forces, Württemberg on 17 May began to move forward on the right bank southwest from San Benedetto, with forty-four battalions of infantry. By 26 May his army, without fighting any engagements beyond reconnaissance clashes, had crossed the Enza River at Sorbolo and was only a few miles from the city of Parma with its right wing on the Po. Mercy, from his spa, continued to meddle in the strategy and wanted an attack across the Po against the allied flank or rear along the Oglio. Finally the emperor ordered him to cease his direction of the army until he recovered. Württemberg was to command until the new commander-designate, Count Königsegg, arrived. But Königsegg was not in the best of health either. Although a competent and experienced soldier who had the confidence of Eugene, he was over sixty years old and was unable to take over his command for many weeks because of a severe attack of gout. In spite of the emperor's order the unhappy shifting of command back and forth from Mercy to Württemberg would continue.[7]

On the French side the minister of war was by no means happy about the French retreat by Coigny, and his messages to that new commander would have a much sharper tone than he was accustomed to use with such senior commanders as Berwick and Villars. On 1 June he observed to Coigny that they had at the same time lost the subsistence in the Modenese and "a part of our reputation." "And why is it," he asked, "that after the enemy has been across the Po over a month we have forgotten to supply this location [Parma] and to put in order the limited fortifications it has? This is incomprehensible. You know the king told you to oppose the taking of Parma if you were free to act." It is rather strong language for a minister to use with a major commander but Coigny was not, like Villars, a marshal of France who had carried his baton for Louis XIV. In another letter of the same date to General Broglie there is further criticism. The army is in a poor position, he emphasized; although we have a superior force we are reduced to letting the enemy do as he pleases.[8]

The fears of the king of Sardinia were probably responsible for the inactivity that provoked this wrist-slapping from Versailles, but at last on 2 June Coigny was able to report that he had convinced the king to cross the Po with his whole army. The buildup of the Austrians before the city of Parma had become serious, and if the city were to be saved, something must be done. Coigny was afraid that the city, under a Spanish commander, would surrender without a stand. He had a letter from Montemar to the commander in Parma permitting the latter to yield the city when he saw cannon, and to yield the citadel when the first breach was made. Princess Dorothy did not want to leave and did not want to expose the inhabitants to pillage.[9]

On 3 June Coigny crossed the Po with his forces augmented by those of the king of Sardinia. They were quickly in substantial conflict with the Austrians near Colorno on the fourth. The next day Coigny was able to give details of the battle and state that he judged the enemy wanted to retreat. His plan was to follow the enemy and force him across the Enza and the Crostollo. Two days later, however, he had to report that the enemy had not retreated back across the Enza, nor could he get the king of Sardinia to aid in an attack. At about this time he must have received the letter from the king of France dated 5 June. It reminded him that there was an agreement with Spain to protect Parma and Piacenza and expressed the king's pain that territory had been lost and that the enemy was still in the Parmesan. "I want you to move on the enemy and to attack him when you are able to do so with the superiority you should have from the number of troops which have been given to you."[10]

Again strong language to a commander who has just taken charge. Is this the old cardinal speaking in the name of the young king? It seems a little too forthright. There are occasions when the fine hand of the cardinal seems to recede and the policies are expounded in more direct terms. Dangervilliers sent a dispatch of his own to Coigny on the same day, noting that he was aware of the message from the king. Very likely he wrote it. Dangervilliers obviously felt that the headquarters spirit in Italy needed reviving. When we have an "unfavorable success," said the minister, it doesn't mean that all is lost. Here we think it is possible to regain all that has been lost and that we can oblige the enemy to reenter the Seraglio and be sufficiently weakened to remain there for the rest of the year.[11] The Seraglio is the low plain between the Po and the city of Mantua.

But the enemy retreat that Coigny had expected after the battles at Colorno had not occurred. The king of Sardinia took the position that he had crossed the Po to prevent a siege of Parma, but he did not want to risk a major engagement by an attack.[12] So the June days continued to pass without serious action on either side.

The powers at Versailles had begun at last to understand that Coigny was doing all he could and they turned their attention to the king of Sardinia. Coigny was sent a sealed letter for the king. It will conform to your thinking, he was told. Other correspondence showed that Versailles was placing pressure on Charles Emmanuel, but there was no evidence that it was effective. On 18 June, Coigny admitted that he had proposed three possible courses of action to the king to no avail. On 25 June, Coigny was instructed to examine, with Broglie, other possible measures to push the enemy back and, if the king remained negative, to send a special courier with details.[13] As it turned out the movements of the Austrians would dictate the decisions of the allied commanders, and Coigny found it unnecessary to carry out these instructions. Happily for the French, when the moment of decision arrived on 28 June, the king of Sardinia had gone back temporarily to Turin because of a serious illness of his queen.

Looking back then, we have a mounting pressure from Versailles for roughly six weeks, and a similar pressure building up on the Austrian side. Both courts pressed their commanders for action. The Austrian army in the Parmesan was weaker than the allied army opposing it, mainly because it had peeled off many troops to man the various strong points as it moved forward. But by 25 June Württemberg was resigned to making an attack. His moves up to this time had been to avoid, if at all possible, a general engagement. As he began his forward movements, Mercy appeared unexpectedly, having had a restoration of sight, and immediately ordered Württemberg to march at night and attack the enemy at dawn on the twenty-sixth. Württemberg was able to parry this order with a need for reconnaissance, which showed that a move around Parma on the north was not practical but that a march around the south was possible. The imperial army then crossed the Parma River just south of the city and camped southwest of it on the night of the twenty-eighth. The French, uncertain of both the movements and the objectives of the imperial army, held a midnight war council after which it was decided to attack. The French and Piedmontese forces began before daylight on the twenty-ninth to move south along the Parma River toward the city. By six in the morning the advance guard was across the Parma-Piacenza road and reconnaissance parties sought to discern the movements of the imperial army which they now knew was south of them and already west of the Parma River.[14]

On this same morning Mercy, ignoring the counsel of his generals, made his own dispositions of the troops for an advance to the north toward the allied army. "Ich will selbsten den Feind à la tête meiner armée recognosciren; je vois clair et je ferai les choses à ma mode," cried Mercy. By eleven o'clock the imperial advance guard came up against enemy positions. Württemberg believed—correctly, it turned out—that this was the main defense line of the allies. Mercy thought it a small corps and ordered him to attack. Württemberg delayed, waiting for more units to come forward to join him. Finally, impatient with the delay, Mercy ordered the advance elements to attack, leading them himself, and ordered Württemberg to support him. Shortly after, Mercy came under heavy fire and fell dead from his horse. But now the battle, so long avoided, was joined. Mercy is supposed to have said: "Il faut diner à Parme ou souper en Paradis!"

Both sides now drew units forward and a full-scale engagement followed, including four separate attacks by the imperial forces, until evening brought a lessening of firing. By nine o'clock it was over; both armies held their place and began to count the heavy losses. There had been virtually no terrain gained or lost, although the imperials had for a time threatened to break the allied center. According to Austrian sources, the imperials, after a council of war, fell back the next day to their camp of the twenty-eighth; there was not enough ammunition to continue the attack. According to Pajol, Coigny and Broglie likewise held a war council and decided to retreat the next morning, meanwhile fearing a night attack by the imperials, and with Coigny even sending a message to his king that the battle was lost. It was only after reconnaissance and deserter reports that Coigny realized that the imperials were badly damaged and were retreating back across the Parma River.[15]

After Coigny realized the imperials were withdrawing he estimated enemy losses from eight to ten thousand. They were not as high as that, but were finally given as 6,237 men and 800 horses, more than one-fifth of the army. The French losses alone, not counting the Piedmontese, were in round figures 4,000 men—1,245 killed and 2,757 wounded.[16]

The military high point of the war was reached in this battle. Another serious clash was to occur some weeks later but would only confirm the results of the Battle of Parma. If we review the messages and movements leading up to the battle we note a striking lack of eagerness among the commanders on both sides to bring their armies to a head-on decisive encounter. But there were impatient orders from the French court in the name of the king, and there were equally impatient directions from the emperor and Prince Eugene. The king of Sardinia on the French side and Prince Ludwig von Württemberg on the imperial side represented the moderating forces that were finally overcome—the king, by being absent from headquarters at the decisive moment and Württemberg by the wild passion of his commander.[17]

Now the French moved forward in pursuit. "The enemy has marched day and night since the battle, and I have followed them for two days. When they crossed the Crostollo at Reggio I held up here," wrote Coigny from Guastalla. It was to be a short delay while he awaited supplies, but apparently the momentum was lost, for eight days later, on 13 July, he reported that he was unable to cross the Secchia for lack of bread. The French built ovens for their bread, and Coigny probably meant that he was as far ahead of them as he could advance.[18] For a time the king of Sardinia was not the obstacle; he had returned to the army on 30 June following the battle, and approved the pursuit of the Austrians on the right bank.[19]

On the Austrian side, Field Marshal Königsegg, appointed in April, finally arrived on 11 July to take command. Because of the losses at Parma and the hardships of the retreat he found that his army, apart from the necessary garrisons, numbered only about 20,000 foot soldiers and 8,000 riders. He set up his camp near the mouth of the Secchia with boat bridges over the Po and maintained a strong reconnaissance on the right bank of the Secchia.

The French forced the surrender of the city of Modena from the Duke of Modena, a prince who had made the mistake of relying on the Austrians for protection. This left the fortress of Mirandola still in Austrian hands, and the objections of the king of Sardinia to further action reappeared. He refused to agree to a crossing of the Secchia and a siege of Mirandola. The French were again frustrated. Dangervilliers informed Coigny that Louis XV had written the king of Sardinia of the shame he felt in not besieging Mirandola. "You should act on your side with all the force possible to convince the king of Sardinia." But the king was a stubborn man, and his possession of a considerable part of the needed artillery forced the French to submit. Even a personal letter from Cardinal Fleury was not enough to move him.[20]

It was fortunate for Königsegg that the French were for the moment unable to act. His strength continued to drop. Sickness and desertions increased, and his numbers probably did not exceed 17,000 infantry during the month of August. On 4 August he wrote to Eugene: "My principal need is money," he said, while not neglecting to explain his other needs. He placed his camp at the mouth of the Secchia in order to defend Mantua and to use the Po and the Mincio for grain supplies coming by sea and by the Adige River.[21] The Austrian army's money needs had become so severe that he reported his officers and men in the infantry eating together in their misery, while the cavalry was reduced to plundering and stealing in order to eat.[22] Apparently his strong reports to Vienna brought some aid, since by 20 August he wrote again to Eugene that a considerable sum of money had arrived, and if it continued to be sent, they could survive. As a matter of fact, as money and reinforcements began to arrive, Königsegg began to think of some kind of attack on the enemy positions. He had noted that the actions of the forces opposite him were such that they obviously did not believe him capable of any initiative. The French had moved the greater part of their cavalry away for better foraging and their lines along the Secchia had great intervals between the battalions. "I have already made several reconnaissances and will again reconnoiter the area and the banks of the river to see if it is possible to attack. If the thing is feasible I will make a dawn attack."[23]

The desire to attack lay not simply with Königsegg. The pressure for a victory continued from Eugene and the emperor. Eugene wrote on 27 August: "To press the enemy can only have a good effect. In the relationship in which we now find ourselves, it is always a great advantage to show the enemy by a sure and decisive attitude that we do not fear him."[24]

But Königsegg did not attack immediately. The French tightened up their defenses again by bringing the cavalry back, increasing patrols, and keeping their men under arms at night. Königsegg wondered if this was prudence or if from the reports of spies (of which they have plenty, he adds) they had some pre-sentiment of attack. But the French will relax their precautions, he reported. As of 10 September Königsegg seemed discouraged, complaining of the heat and new money shortages. The men "are so weak from sickness and so crushed by the heat, which is worse than ever, that both officers and men, if they are not actually sick are hardly able to drag themselves about."[25] Perhaps this message was intended for interception, for Königs-egg must have been actively preparing for a major attack at that time.

In the meantime the French continued to argue with the king of Sardinia. They had given up the idea of advancing fur-ther by early September. A memoir was sent to Charles Em-manuel outlining a plan to hold the Secchia for the winter with thirty-seven battalions and forty-two squadrons. The king was asked to supply a part in proportion to the strength of his forces. But the answer came back that the king did not want any of his forces on the right bank of the Po and would consent to all of the troops guarding the Secchia being French.[26]

The ministry at Versailles accepted abandonment of a cross-ing of the Secchia and of a siege of Mirandola with reluctance. If we cannot advance, suggested the minister, we should at least make some diversion in the Seraglio.[27]

Königsegg was right in expecting the French to relax some of their precautions, and despite his own weakness, on 15 Septem-ber at dawn he launched a strong cavalry attack across the Sec-chia. It was a complete surprise. Marshal Broglie, in a house that was overrun by the enemy, was forced to flee before he had time to dress, but managed to save himself. The image of a high-ranking officer running for his life in his nightshirt is one that delights all ranks, and the phrase "il s'est sauvé en chemise" is repeated in the reports with relish, even by Coigny. The French reeled back toward Guastalla where their carefully defended bridges across the Po awaited them, and drew up their army un-der the guns of the fortress of Guastalla.

Königsegg during the day dashed off a message to his em-peror from Quistello where he had set up headquarters. "Since I have with God's help succeeded in attacking the enemy army and in driving it back from the Secchia with the loss of their camp and much baggage, I send Your Highness the adjutant chevalier St. Pierre who has been constantly with me and with whose service I am very well pleased, to report to you orally until I can prepare a thorough written report for Your Highness." [28]

Coigny reported it all sadly on the 17th: "It is with sadness, Monsieur, that I have the honor to tell you that the enemy has put me to the necessity of abandoning the Secchia. You know the reasons which a month ago forced me to send away my cavalry for lack of subsistence. On the morning of the fifteenth the imperials surprised the house of M. the Marshal de Broglie by a column of grenadiers who had crossed the river by fording and he saved himself only *en chemise*, unable to be aided in time by the Brigade Dauphiné which camped nearby. By means of the column of grenadiers the enemy put a corps of eight to ten thousand horse across in the interval between the Dauphiné and Picardy brigades." [29]

After noting that the fort of Quistello was abandoned in orderly fashion except for fifty Piedmontese who were "forgotten," Coigny stated that they had lost only about 400 men killed or wounded and believed that the imperials had lost a like number. Further on in his message he remarked that he had also forgotten to mention two Piedmontese battalions which were unaccounted for and were discovered later to have been captured. Finally, Coigny reported that he proposed to the king of Sardinia an immediate counterattack, which the king had countered with a request for a council of war. At the end of the message Coigny wrote in his own hand that the king believed it would be useless to attack since the principal object was to protect the Parmesan and the Cremonese.

So there was no counterattack and the Austrians sought to press the attack further. Early on 19 September they attacked the French lines, before the fortress of Guastalla and a bloody battle similar to that at Parma lasted all through the day until five o'clock, when the imperials gave way and began a retreat. By the end of the day Coigny knew that the field of battle was his and he committed several units in pursuit. The losses in this battle, he thought, might be equal to those at Parma. [30]

The Battle of Guastalla was the second and last general engagement of the war and the most devastating in human losses. For a time the French at Versailles seemed to relish their victory and Dangervilliers reacted with "grande joie" to the news of the battle and congratulated both Coigny and Broglie. But a few days later second thoughts must have overtaken this spirit and a more severe judgment came from Versailles. On 20 October, Dangervilliers complained to Broglie that, "our victories produce nothing but honor. . . . I wish with all my heart there had been no Battle of Guastalla, and everyone would be better off."[31]

Pajol observes that the minister was right; after two expensive victories the French were in the same positions as at the beginning of the campaign.[32] Perhaps, but this may have been the definitive lesson that both sides needed to move into the period of negotiation, as indeed they did, although without immediate results.

The losses were greater than at Parma. The French reported 1,403 killed and 3,445 wounded, or a total of almost 5,000 casualties. In addition, 1,300 men were taken prisoner. The Austrian losses were given by the French as 4,400 killed and 4,600 wounded, or a total of 9,000 casualties, including the second-in-command, Prince Ludwig von Württemberg, and five other generals.[33]

Although Coigny speaks of the flight of the Austrian army and of his pursuit, this pursuit was evidently a very limited and cautious one. Königsegg, ten days after the battle, wrote that he remained at Mottegiana on the right bank of the Po until 25 September, while the enemy held their positions at Guastalla. He was obliged then to recross the Po to Borgoforte because of lack of forage in an area where armies had been devouring it all summer long. The enemy did not interfere with his movement, he noted, and two days later they also recrossed the Po by their bridges at Guastalla.[34]

The correspondence for the weeks following the Battle of Guastalla reveals that both commanders were extremely unhappy. Königsegg had time to realize that a great victory had been denied him by the failure of his army to pursue strongly the first surprise success over the French on the fifteenth. The French camp had been overrun and a great quantity of booty taken. According to Arneth, the imperial army, instead of breaking up the surprised French forces, itself broke up in search for booty, giving the French time to throw in some Piedmontese to stiffen the positions and enable them to make a stand at Guastalla. In a confidential letter to Eugene, Königsegg does not explain it explicitly as a breakdown of discipline in a search for loot, but notes that he left out of his official report some essential circumstances, because first reports are too widely read. He had been obliged to retreat because his forces, infantry and cavalry, had not done their duty: "I am sure you will agree that after surprising the enemy and completely routing him, taking 4,000 prisoners without losing a hundred men, that I would not stop in mid-road. Who would believe that an army with such an advantage would lose its courage before an enemy beaten and fleeing?"[35]

Königsegg, with his army in the Seraglio, now pleaded for money and reinforcements. He hoped that Eugene, now back in Vienna, would intercede for him and explain the failure at Guastalla.[36]

Coigny was also unhappy as the summer period of field operations drew to a close. A force under Maillebois of eight battalions and cavalry was sent against the last position of the Austrians on the right bank of the Po—the fortress of Mirandola—and was driven away by a relieving force of Austrians. Coigny abandoned an attempt on Borgoforte and by November had to draw his army back up the Po and take positions on the Adda. The enemy was gaining reinforcements, there was no support from the king of Sardinia, and subsistence and forage were growing short. Worn down by the struggle with the king of Sardinia, Coigny left the army in Italy to direct operations in Germany in the coming year.

The end of 1734 and the beginning of 1735 brought about the first strategic review on the part of Austria, the combatant suffering the most serious losses at the present and facing the most serious and ominous portents for the future. The first clashes of 1733 were only the announcement of the struggle. But in 1734 the battles in Italy and the sieges and clashes on the

Rhine, and all that had been lost in these conflicts, must now be assessed. The traditional winter quarters period granted both sides a respite, and the military commanders could return to their capitals. Prince Eugene, back in Vienna since 10 October, saw the need for a decision in a rapidly worsening situation.

The longer we delay, the more our situation will worsen, and it will become at last completely insoluble. Our funds are insufficient by far to face up to such powerful resources. In spite of the personal goodwill of the king of England, there is little hope for help from the sea powers, for England insists that she can do nothing for us without the support of Holland, and the latter will take no part in the war. In the German empire those who incline toward neutrality between the emperor and France grow day by day. The Saxon court does nothing, either for itself or for the emperor. The king of Prussia will live only a short time. The electors of Cologne and Bavaria are strengthening their troops through very substantial recruiting. Their subsidy agreement with France is concluded, six months of it paid, and Bavaria begins to set aside any limitation and to take measures which only too easily could bring us into open conflict during the winter. In Turkey only the grand vizier is with us against war; all the others have been won over by the French ambassador and Bonneval.

Internally, went on Eugene, you know the difficulty, not to say the impossibility

of raising such monstrous sums as are needed to carry on the war. On the other hand, under such circumstances, a peace can only be disadvantageous. For those enemy powers arrayed against us, who see the emperor abandoned by his allies and brought to a point where he may be attacked simultaneously by Turkey and Bavaria, these powers will certainly not give up their conquests but will perhaps put before us still more oppressive demands.[37]

A similar assessment had come from Königsegg in a handwritten message to the emperor who had forwarded it to Eugene on 25 October. It does not appear that Eugene was aware of it in the message quoted above.

Königsegg presented a grim view of the situation and concluded that the emperor could not continue alone against the three allies—France, Spain, and Sardinia. He pointed out the isolation of Austria amid a circle of worthless allies. It was a picture similar to that drawn by Eugene, although perhaps Königsegg laid more stress on the impossibility of carrying on without adequate funds. While the tedious steps in raising money are repeated again and again, the army is falling to pieces, he said. Officers cannot remain in service when they have not been paid for months; soldiers live from plunder and then desert in numbers. There is no question of military operations. The French will soon take advantage of this, and on the eastern frontier the Turks will soon become active. Königsegg begged his emperor to make a sacrifice, even a substantial one, to save the overall situation.[38]

The emperor in forwarding this estimate to Eugene, asked that it be circulated to the Privy Council. On 6 November the available members—Eugene, Sinzendorff, Starhemberg, and Harrach—met with the emperor. Instead of being persuaded to a decision, the emperor asked for their opinions in writing. Perhaps they knew he would not or could not make a decision during the next few weeks. It is otherwise incredible to find that, faced with a grave crisis, they could not finish the preparations of these estimates until early February 1735, by which time Königsegg had been called from Italy to participate in the discussions. Both Königsegg and Eugene, the two field commanders, presented an even stronger case for peace to the emperor and their civilian counterparts. Eugene's written counsel stressed once again the lack of money and credit, and the plight of the army. For example, there were periods of eight to ten days when no bread was issued to the army in Italy. A peace is necessary to avoid the danger of a complete breakdown, went on Eugene, and the best that could be expected would be 1) to hold the present positions in Italy, 2) to prevent the junctions of French and Bavarian forces, and 3) to defend against a breakthrough of the French to the hereditary lands. Of course it would be well if some strike on a sensitive position ("empfindlichen Streich") could be achieved in some way to show that the emperor could carry on another campaign, but it would mean thousands of lives from the hereditary lands and millions more in debts. "Under such circumstances it is impossible to hope for an advantageous peace. In the situation in which through the improper behavior of his allies Your Majesty finds himself, any peace is better than the present war."[39]

The other members of the council agreed on the need for a peace, although Sinzendorff could not forget that in the War of the Spanish Succession they had driven the French out of Italy after five years of discouraging warfare. He seemed to forget, however, that the English and the English financial support were both behind Austria at that time.

Despite this unanimous judgment and the strong representations of the two field commanders, the emperor saw the situation otherwise. Arneth believes that the judgment of the emperor was affected by the "Spanish party" at the Viennese court. Admittedly they had no official positions but they were close to the emperor in private life. These people enjoyed pensions and certain offices reserved to them in Naples and Sicily which would be irretrievably lost if Don Carlos remained in control of the two southern kingdoms. They pressed the emperor for a last try for military success. The emperor clung to other hopes too: for example, that the brisk French rejection of the English peace proposals would lead to the English fulfillment of treaty commitments with him, that the reports of sickness among the French troops on the Rhine and the reports of misunderstandings between Spain and Sardinia might mean serious weakening of the enemy. Eugene and Königsegg had given their counsel. The emperor made the decision to continue military operations, and both commanders must soon return to their armies to begin another campaign in 1735.[40] As to the possibility of England joining the war we have the highly credible story from the memoirs of Lord Henry about Robert Walpole's statement to the queen: "I told the Queen this morning, Madam, there are fifty thousand men slain this year in Europe and not one Englishman."[41]

Going into winter quarters was the opposite of assembling the army. It was a system of dispersal and, in the case of the two armies facing one another in the Rhine area, one that covered a relatively large area. The imperial forces were in camps from the Black Forest in the south northward as far as Westphalia, mostly on the right bank of the Rhine, except at the fortified city of Mainz which provided their only sure crossing point. The French camps stretched from opposite the Black Forest at Huningue, near Basel, north to Worms and west to Trier. In several major camps they recruited and trained new troops and regenerated the spent health of others. It was also a time for prisoner exchange, and an agreement made on 5 January 1735 was carried out during the weeks following.[42]

Besides the recruiting and training there were fortifications to build or rebuild, and each side sought to determine the intentions of the other from the work done at specific locations. For example, the Field Marshal Duke of Württemberg had seventy portable boats built at Freiburg, which gave credence to a possible imperial attack across the upper Rhine into Alsace.[43] But primarily the imperials were concerned with improving the security of Mainz, and work had been continuing on the fortifications there since the summer of 1734. On 14 January General Count Seckendorff, newly arrived to command until Prince Eugene would return in the spring, visited Mainz to inspect and hasten the work. By the end of January there was a garrison of 7,689 men in Mainz, of which only 5,016 were considered effective.[44]

It is easier today to see that the French overestimated the capabilities of the Austrians to begin a serious campaign and that the imperials similarly overestimated the eagerness of the French to launch a serious strike. There was not very much that the French could do that was truly useful to them. They did not want to enter deeper into the Empire and thus, unless the emperor's army crossed the Rhine, they could not conveniently engage his forces. Mainz was a possible target, although it involved attacking still another imperial elector, and it might also be an expensive siege. Add to this the fact that the French were increasingly conscious that the major benefits of the war appeared to fall to the Spanish and Sardinians.

On the imperial side the campaign of the preceding year had been purely defensive. Now, under the pressure of a declining military situation, we see attempts to find military initiatives to enhance the emperor's bargaining power. Thus, paradoxically, the side losing the war sought to find an area for offensive operations while the winning side became basically defensive.

The events of 1734 had taught the imperials that they must assemble their army earlier in the spring. The fact that the French had let slip away from them the advantage of an early beginning of operations made them likewise consider an even earlier assembly date. Eugene predicted in his *Gutachten*, or assessment, of 6 November a very early French assembly.[45] To the prince whose lands lay between the French armies and Bavaria and who foreseeably had the most to lose from French military operations, the duke of Württemberg, the preparations which he observed indicated an early opening of the campaign by the French. He proposed a partial assembly of the imperial forces by withdrawing them from the extended line of winter quarters into cantonments along the Rhine, Main, and Neckar rivers. The original cantonment project would have put the field marshal duke in direct command of a large part of the army, approximately 40,000 men, in the area from Ettlingen to just south of Heidelberg.[46] This was changed, however, and the battalions were allotted in greater strength to the commands farther north. Eugene remained in Vienna, keeping his finger on the preparations as closely as possible. Twice he warned the duke that his forces should be farther removed from the Rhine in case the French should make a quick strike across the river. "The troops in the cantonments should not be so close to Philippsburg and Fort Louis, but better displaced rearwards, in which position they can be supported by the magazines on the Neckar and nearby area, and will not be exposed to an enemy surprise attack, and Your Lordship will have time, whenever the enemy moves, to assemble where necessary."[47]

Eugene's presence was needed with the forces but he did not arrive in Heilbronn until 13 May. Seckendorff was at sword's point with his superior, the duke of Württemberg. The duke was also unable to control the Danes and Hessians, who ignored his orders when they chose to do so.[48] It was time for Eugene to put his still immense influence to work. Doubtless he understood that all was not well among his commanders, but it was the last of his strength that he was using for a last campaign, and he metered it out carefully. The messages from the emperor to Eugene show that Charles VI too realized this, for at the end of his messages, written in German by his staff or even frequently in his own hand, we find almost invariably a few words in French, couched in friendly and affectionate terms, asking Eugene to conserve his health.

Resuming command once again, Eugene reported back to the emperor on 15 May from Heilbronn and stressed that the French army was already in motion with the main army near Speyer being joined by another corps from Upper Alsace. It was too early to predict their intentions, however.[49] Passing on to the headquarters at Bruchsal he found the duke ill but the army in reasonable shape with an assembled strength of twenty-nine battalions and sixty-nine squadrons. The remainder of the army was stretched in a long, thin line from the Black Forest to Mainz. The enemy army he estimated at 120 battalions and 170 squadrons, not counting some militia in garrisons at strong points.[50] By 24 May Eugene was examining the position of the three electors who were not cooperating with the emperor—Bavaria, Palatinate, and Cologne, the three Wittelsbachs. He still saw no chance that Bavaria would cooperate by sending a contingent of troops; rather the increase in Bavarian militia suggested that the elector might be preparing to come to open hostilities against the imperials in an attack in the Tirol. Eugene was not alone in believing the elector might open hostilities. Marshal Du Bourg, on the other side of the Rhine, forwarded to Versailles an unsigned letter from Munich stating that the elector's movements seemed to indicate that he would take part in the coming campaign. There was also a report that made Du Bourg "die laughing" —the fortifications of Vienna were being repaired![51]

With regard to the Elector Palatine at Mannheim, Eugene agreed that it was probably not feasible to prevent various supplies from passing through Mannheim to the French, but it would not be wise to force the elector completely into the arms of the French. From the elector of Cologne Eugene expected a contingent of troops and heard that a money contribution had been offered in Vienna.[52]

A few days later Eugene noted that the tempo of movement in the French army had increased, but that the reports were so confused that nothing more than marching and countermarching could be established. He stated briefly that while a number of choices were open to Coigny, his own responsibility was not to be led into some untimely movement.[53]

Although on the imperial side there was no thought of making an attack at this time, the French were alarmed from time to time by reports of possible attacks. Dangervilliers told Du Bourg on 5 April to prepare for an attack on Worms, for example. When Coigny arrived in Strasbourg on 21 April (a month earlier than Eugene) he received there a letter from Dangervilliers cautioning him to report the movements of the enemy carefully. "Don't spare the couriers," he was told.[54]

During the month of June, Coigny was in motion concentrating his forces and bridging equipment closer to Mainz. If Eugene moved down the Rhine opposite him, Coigny had sufficient forces upstream to make a crossing at Philippsburg or Kehl. But Eugene did not move from his position near Philippsburg. He reinforced Seckendorff, who held the forces between the Neckar and the Main, and except for a short visit to Heidelberg, held to his camp at Bruchsal.

Coigny was under some pressure to cross the river but he did not do so. Instead he moved up into the Mainz area, placing 50 battalions and 131 squadrons in three camps at Weinholsheim, Stadecken, and Gau-Algesheim, which formed a line across the corner formed by the bend of the Rhine as it approaches Mainz and contains that city.[55] But he did not undertake the siege, nor cross the river.

It is clear in retrospect that Eugene, by his refusal to move up and down the Rhine paralleling the French movements, had used his smaller army to the best advantage and probably averted a potential disaster. The French, with their larger army, would sooner or later have caught him out of position had he sought to react to each of their movements. But he was under considerable pressure to undertake operations, if only to increase Austrian bargaining strength in forthcoming negotiations.[56] "The more critical on all sides matters appear so much more complete is my trust in Your Lordship that you will find the ways and means to undertake an important operation against the enemy." So wrote the emperor to Eugene on 28 May 1735.[57]

The answer came back from Eugene in a wide-ranging discussion that was at times elementary in its approach. "To act offensively means either battles or sieges. The first depends not wholly on my choice, but upon that of the enemy, particularly if his army remains on the other side of the Rhine. For if I cross over and he finds it not to his advantage to engage in battle, nothing is easier for him than to withdraw behind the most impregnable lines at Speyer or pull back between his fortresses."

One is struck by the chessboard or sandtable effect of Eugene's statements and can visualize a man with a pointer over a great relief map of the Rhine valley. To be drawn in too deeply or to have an unfortunate battle could leave his army cut off from its bases or destroyed, went on Eugene, noting as well that the only sound crossing point was at Mainz, and to move northward with the imperial army would leave Swabia open to the French and permit a junction of French and Bavarian forces. With regard to sieges, Eugene found that he had insufficient guns and other equipment to attack Neu Breisach, Landau, Strasbourg, or Philippsburg. If the expected Russian contingent were at hand, he added, a siege might be considered but it would come too late to permit such an undertaking this year.[58]

Was Eugene's strategy that of an old man seeking reasons why he should not act? It is possible that a younger Eugene might have been ready to take chances. But against an adversary with so many advantages, Eugene saw the existence of his army as the last defense of the entire empire, the only barrier to the hereditary Habsburg lands, and the fragile block that prevented a combined French-Bavarian army from cutting off the imperial forces in Italy. So the army of Eugene would remain poised but inactive in stage center of the Rhine theater until the last days of summer.

Could the Russians be the saviors of the emperor? They figure large in the Austrian communications as they approach the imperial forces on the Rhine. The emperor was paying for their coming, of course, and the Russian court had been split over the question of helping him. The elements at court friendly to the emperor finally had their way, and 12,000 men of a first contingent were marched slowly from Poland into Silesia and Bohemia and were to cross the Upper Palatinate of Bavaria.[59] Eugene feared that at this point the elector of Bavaria might use force to oppose their passage, and he advised the emperor to be sure that the proper instructions were given to the Russian commander, who was, incidentally, the Irishman Peter Lacy.[60] Eugene was aware that the elector had once again proposed the marriage of his eight-year old son to the eighteen-year-old Maria Theresa as a means of settling all differences, and he was equally aware that this was unacceptable to the emperor. But an intercepted Bavarian message gave the emperor reason to believe the Bavarians would not attack, and he reassured Eugene.[61]

The Russians arrived on 26 August, the first Russian forces to see western Europe. They had crossed Bavarian territory without incident and were visited by Eugene two days later. In a letter to the imperial ambassador in Saint Petersburg he spoke of their appearance and readiness with enthusiasm.[62]

The increased activity across the river brought Coigny to life and he began to assemble his army. He was now under instructions that permitted him to remain on the left bank of the Rhine, but not to refuse combat.[63] Coigny noted that his infantry was superior to that of the enemy. He had 140 battalions and 179 squadrons, although 28 of the battalions and 30 squadrons were detached farther back in Alsace and on the Moselle and the Meuse. With the Russian supplement Eugene now had 119 battalions and 181 squadrons, giving him a rough equality, or even superiority, along the Rhine proper.[64]

It was Seckendorff rather than Eugene who saw that some initiative must be undertaken before the summer dwindled away. He had proposed in July that, after the arrival of the Russians, a corps of thirty battalions and fifty squadrons should cross the Rhine at Mainz or Coblenz, march on Trier, and occupy it. Then, after wintering in the area, they should strike into France in the spring. He prepared a study of the possibilities, probing the various maneuvers by which a detached corps could be supported by the movements of the main army on the Rhine. This was reviewed at a 19 August meeting of generals which took place at Eugene's headquarters at Bruchsal. Eugene was not ready for a major engagement, but he was willing to approve a limited offensive in the Moselle Valley. He did so and left for Vienna while the operation was under way. This may have been because he thought it was bound to fail. More likely he left for personal reasons; he had only six months to live.[65]

On 20 September the operation began with the crossing of the Rhine in the Mainz area and by 28 September there were forty-one battalions and eighty-five squadrons of imperial forces across the river, reported by Seckendorff as 23,327 infantry and 12,840 cavalry in serviceable condition, rather than simply in assigned strength. There were no Russians included; imperials, North German, and Danish troops made up the totals.[66]

Coigny had had a council of war on 3 September and decided to concentrate in the Speyer area if Eugene united all his army. If Seckendorff moved toward the Moselle with 25,000 or 30,000 men, then Belle Isle would be detached with sufficient forces to meet them at Trier. When the latter alternative occurred, Belle Isle formed a corps and marched west on 1 October, passing Kaiserslautern on 2 October, and arriving with some advance forces in Trier on the fourth. But Belle Isle's forces when fully in place were still considerably smaller than Seckendorff's, which were now in the Moselle Valley where they were augmented by troops from the garrison at Luxembourg.[67] Coigny then brought up further reinforcements and took command himself in Trier. On 20 October the two armies made contact along the Moselle River near the abbey of Clausen, twenty-five kilometers below Trier. Without coming to a decisive battle the French, assessing their position as untenable, retreated to Trier. Seckendorff moved after them, but carefully.[68]

In the midst of these cautious movements the two commanders were overtaken by what both may have expected daily—the suspension of hostilities. The agreement had taken place on 3 October in Vienna, and on 10 October Württemberg, the imperial commander after Eugene's departure, was informed. But it was not until 31 October that Coigny informed the duke that he had been notified of the ratification of the suspension of arms agreement, and it was 4 November before Coigny and Secken-dorff agreed to a suspension of arms with the Moselle River between their forces.[69] The last meeting of forces in the north occurred thus in the corridor into France that concerned Belle Isle at the beginning of the war. It was a corridor that would provide entry for German armies in the future.

It had been a complete campaign year without any engagement large enough to be called a battle. Every move or threatened move had canceled out the moves of the other side even to the end in the Moselle Valley. Many of these moves were foraging expeditions undertaken to sustain one army while simultaneously denying food to the other as, for example, when Coigny carefully consumed the forage in the Mainz area in late spring without attacking the city.[70] Indeed, the matter of foraging was so painful to the small states in the path of the armies that a considerable body of correspondence exists regarding the complaints. Since the sovereigns themselves often signed the complaints, and had considerable justification for doing so, the responses could not be simply ignored. The Elector Palatine, for example, was pillaged by the soldiers of both sides while trying to remain neutral.[71]

The movements of the armies during the campaign were basically cautious ones. Still, a commander could have made an error and found himself abruptly at a serious disadvantage before his opponent. But the actions remained within the expected range of professional military activity, and there was no place for such ingenuities as new weapons, as one example indicates. A French officer and a small detachment were taken prisoner after crossing the Rhine and being cut off from their boats. After Eugene learned that they had in their possession a fire bomb ("ordentliche Brandkugel"), he no longer considered the officer an honorable ("rechtschaffene") man and wrote a letter of complaint to Coigny. A satisfactory reply came back in which Coigny denied that he was aware of or responsible for the fire bomb.[72]

So the war along the Rhine was over and the armies would negotiate directly with one another until the suspension of hostilities acquired a more permanent character and the disbanding of units could begin.

Meanwhile in Italy, after the heavy losses at the Battle of Guastalla in September, neither side wished to force another engagement. The French were in winter quarters from 30 December and many troops were hospitalized. Marshal Broglie, then in command, wrote on 3 January from Cremona: "Since the departure of M. de Coigny I have been working on the lodging of troops in this garrison. There is an infinite number of sick. Many die every day."[73]

The allies held the right bank of the Po, including the Modenese, Guastalla, Parma, and the Tortonese. The imperials held the Oglio from its mouth to Ostiano, as well as Revere and, across the Po, Mirandola.

The French, still behind the Oglio after two campaign seasons, were ready to try another commander. Villars had angered Charles Emmanuel by his character and the indiscipline of his troops.[74] Nor did Coigny and Broglie do very much better. The new commander, Marshal Noailles, had found it intolerable serving under d'Asfeld and had been consoled by the promise of the supreme command north of the Alps for the following year. But he later objected to the task of forcing contributions in the occupied areas and was forced to defend himself against criticism of his operational decisions during the campaign year.[75] Arriving at court in January 1735 he found that he was to command in Italy. It was thought that he could deal better with Charles Emmanuel; and he was a captain general in the Spanish service and outranked Montemar.[76]

Noailles arrived in Turin in March and received flattering treatment. He wrote to the minister on 12 March that he was happy over his reception but noted the great sickness among the infantry. One could not count on more than 250 men in a battalion, he discovered.[77] Not that nothing had been done. Considerable effort had been undertaken to make up the heavy battle losses of the preceding summer: an amnesty for deserters was given in exchange for service in Italy, 7,000 militia were sent there, and officers' commissions were given out on a more liberal basis to men who would bring recruits with them. Some 10,000 men were gained in this manner and the minister asked in March why units were still weak in strength.[78] According to the Noailles memoirs, abuses and corruption were a good part of the answer. For example, losses had been greater than reported, allowing captains to make profits on their companies by keeping them incomplete. A kind of anarchy reigned. Dangervilliers sent a strong letter to Noailles with a royal dispatch authorizing him to use his authority to remedy the situation. By 6 April Noailles was able to tell the minister that he had made some progress. But he was not yet ready for operations and ordered Savines, commanding in the Modenese, to avoid action.[79]

While the marshal was struggling with the condition of his forces, he was also involved in meetings to determine strategy. When he arrived in Italy, Broglie presented him with a plan by which the French and allied forces would attack head-on across the Oglio and force the Austrians back on Mantua. It was a plan to finish the war in one major drive. Noailles, cautious as usual, expressed reservations. In answer to the king of Sardinia, who asked for ideas on a campaign, Noailles prepared a memoir which was more a statement of principles than a military plan. Noailles noted the presence of a difficult terrain with many canals, streams, and closed fields, and put forth the following: 1) The enemy can be reduced more easily by ruse and maneuver than by force. Combat will be unavoidable and it will tend to be lively and frequent. 2) The enemy must be pressed as much as possible to prevent him from concealing his movements, and from finding subsistence. 3) Diversions and feints are to be used. The greater numbers on the allied side permit this. 4) Operate so as to be always ready to assemble. Do not hazard separate detachments in adventures. Be ready to attack when an advantage occurs.[80]

It was hardly a plan for annihilating the enemy army, but a reasonable prescription for military action by a professional officer of the eighteenth century whose objective was to defeat his opponent, not to destroy him.

The king of Sardinia approved the ideas in principle during the last of March, but lack of forage and poor cooperation from the Spanish blocked any immediate operations. The Spanish army had returned to the north and Broglie had already asked Montemar to provide fifteen battalions in the Modenese, which the latter refused to do on the ground that there would be inadequate subsistence before May. Noailles then held conversations with Montemar in April and could do little better. Montemar would hold his forces to the south in the Bologna area and near the Tuscan border for forage and subsistence and would give aid if the imperials attacked. Noailles found that he could not refute the Spanish arguments; the matter of subsistence was critical enough with his own forces.[81]

At last in May the three armies were ready to cooperate, after a fashion. On 12 May the French and Sardinian forces crossed the Po and established a headquarters at Guastalla. Königsegg, strongly entrenched at San Benedetto, had about seventy battalions and ninety squadrons. It was more than the French and Sardinians could field but less than the three allied forces combined. Spanish support came at last, and the combined operations of the allies forced Königsegg to abandon the Po and retreat toward Mantua during June. By the end of the month he had left a garrison in Mantua and moved north into the mountains with the imperial cavalry in the Tirol and the remainder of his army in the Trentino. As Dangervilliers wrote to Noailles, Königsegg had taken the "debris of his army" into the Trentino.[82]

But Noailles would not follow the imperials into the Trentino as Dangervilliers recommended. Nor was he ready for a siege of Mantua as the Spanish urged. The weakness of the imperial army permitted the allies to dispute among themselves. As late as 14 October, Noailles was still trying to mobilize action among his allies and, apparently unaware of the agreement in Vienna, spoke of his preparations for the next year's campaign. Happily another solution came in November when the minister advised him of the suspension of fighting. "I add that it is already in execution on the Rhine and the Moselle and it is time to do the same in Italy."[83]

The hostilities were over—that is, they were suspended by a preliminary agreement. There would be relief for the emperor's forces backed up into the Alps. A period of military negotiations—or rather gentlemanly meetings—would ensue before an armistice could be signed among the field forces. The final step, a peace treaty, was far in the future. It is now time to investigate the diplomatic negotiations that were carried out, partly in the open, partly in great secrecy, during the period of hostilities—negotiations that brought about finally the suspension of hostilities and indicated the main points of the peace agreement.

✠

CHAPTER TEN

# The Negotiations

The ritual of military operations must have seemed an end in itself to many participants in wars of the eighteenth century —certainly to those officers who, like La Motte, were lifelong professionals. They were used to long campaigns; they were not impatient; they felt no particular rancor toward their opponents. Valor they knew well and it was seldom lacking. The lists of high-ranking casualties after the battles is proof enough. But they saw no reason for heroic efforts against impossible odds, such as the attack on Danzig, nor could they see the need for head-on clashes and senseless massacres such as occurred at Parma and Guastalla. These were aberrations not of their choosing. But they must do their duty. The 1735 campaigns, rather than those of 1734, were for them the correct and appropriate use of military forces.

Another ritual paralleled the military operations—the diplomatic negotiations, which were almost always active in some form at some level. A contestant who was not seeking the destruction of his opponent found it reasonable to establish negotiations as soon as some military advantage, or disadvantage, was evident. The negotiations were normally as long and tedious as the sieges and the marching and countermarching of the military operations. While the top figures were the hereditary sovereigns and their high-ranking nobles, a less visible professional group acted in their names. Ignaz Koch and Johann Bartenstein had their opposite numbers on the French side. The participants in the negotiations could be patient and secretive, for they were not subject to a demanding press and volatile public opinion.

In the summer of 1734 Austrian fortunes were very low. Southern Italy was lost; Lombardy was lost. But the Battle of Parma was equally expensive for both sides. So the emperor did not regard his gloomy situation as truly desperate, and he was not ready for major concessions. But Prince Eugene, as noted earlier, saw the fading military situation more clearly, and he was already feeling carefully in several areas through his contacts. He made at least two attempts to reach the British sovereign through particular individuals.

The Hessian general Ernst von Diemar was at that time in England and it was hoped that he could use his good relations with the king of England.[1] Eugene's letters to him are bitter over the refusal of England and Holland to assist the emperor. One must also read into his letters to Diemar a willingness to think in terms of an eventual accommodation. "Abandoned by everyone, the emperor will have to yield in spite of himself. To save his lands he must bring himself to decisions that he would never have considered."[2]

Eugene had another correspondent in whom he seems to have placed some hope, an Englishman continually predicting the early fall of Robert Walpole. This was Henry Davenant, an English diplomat who had gone over to the Austrian service and was at this time in Brussels. Although his letters smack of the sycophant and usually terminate with a whining request for money, Eugene sought to send him to see the king of England in London. The king refused to receive him, however. A second project to have Davenant see the king at Hanover was blocked by the emperor. Davenant continued to predict a change in English policy with a fall of the Whig government and sent Eugene letters from English informants to prove his close contact with affairs in England.[3]

These approaches were ineffectual and were really efforts to bring England into the war, as was the offer made through Count Kinsky to appoint George II the commander of the imperial army on the Rhine.[4] One has the general impression that the

Austrians cannot quite accept the diminished and still diminishing influence of the English king over governmental decisions.

What the English offered was their "good offices." It was the least they could do.

The first firm contact among the great powers which brought about serious peace discussions originated with Horatio Walpole, who had been sent as ambassador to Holland in August 1734. He wrote on 19 August to Gedda, Swedish ambassador in France, stating that he wished jointly with the Dutch government to come to an agreement with Cardinal Fleury and M. Chauvelin. The letter was taken to Cardinal Fleury. Fleury answered on 4 September. He was ready to treat with the same open-hearted manner as when they had worked together in earlier days and would confer with any person at any time, or if desired, he would send a confidential representative. But since France had allies from which it would not be separated, there must be inviolable secrecy in these preliminaries. "We accept without difficulty the mediation and good offices of the maritime powers on the basis of their profession of a complete impartiality." The cardinal pointed out that he had used the term "profession" because he felt it would not be in good faith if he did not retain some doubt or suspicion as to the rightness of the intentions of the maritime powers. The cardinal was not yet ready to outline his specific terms, but he protested that France did not wish to increase her territory by even a "single village" although she had been accused of secret designs to extend her frontiers and destroy the equilibrium of Europe.

The cardinal then added a postscript saying that he preferred to deal directly with Walpole in order to maintain secrecy and not to be involved with the British ministry.[5]

After an intermediate exchange of letters, during which time Walpole informed his king of the negotiations, he replied to Fleury on 2 October that he accepted the proposal of a confidential representative and that he and the pensionary of Holland were ready to confer with such a man. He pointed out that the spring would bring on another military campaign and that they must act quickly to prevent this. The cardinal replied on 7 October, emphasizing again the secrecy of their relation. As to his own representative: "I will think from now until Tuesday to name a reliable man." The cardinal was not yet ready to mention specific matters, but he noted that the three powers involved were the only ones that did not seek additional territory and could thus be impartial. The only interest of the king of France, he insisted, was in the Polish affair.

Walpole advised the cardinal to send his man to a hotel in Delft, informing him in advance the day of his arrival and the name he would use. Walpole would see that matters would be conducted secretly from this point. Fleury would send Jannel, who had been secretary of the Congress of Soissons some years earlier. Again the cardinal stressed secrecy and added that if no accord were reached he would not make use of anything that occurred. "You have the right as of now to deny anything that I might let escape of our negotiations."

Then on 24 October Fleury became more specific. First he wished to assure Walpole in general terms regarding his commitments to his allies. "I can tell you that our treaties have to do with the Two Sicilies in favor of Don Carlos and the Milanese in *statu quo* for the king of Sardinia. There are no other stipulations regarding the other lands of the emperor, not even Mantua." There was no desire on the part of France to aggrandize herself, said Fleury, and only the matter of Poland interests her. France is against the Pragmatic Sanction which it regards as against its interests and a threat to the liberty of Europe.[6]

"I begin with Poland," wrote the cardinal, admitting that there was little hope that Stanislas could be replaced on his throne. But this may depend to what extent England is involved. If your court, he told Walpole, has no commitments, there should be a way to save the honor of France.

With regard to Spain, the cardinal found this a difficult area because of the inflexibility of the emperor on the one hand and of the queen of Spain on the other, over the two kingdoms of Naples and Sicily, the Two Sicilies. One solution might be for the emperor to give his second or younger archduchess in marriage to Don Carlos. The Two Sicilies could be given her as a dowry with reversion to the older sister if the younger had no children. But the emperor probably would not agree, and the queen of Spain would not wish that the Two Sicilies, taken by conquest, be subject to reversion to Austria if Don Carlos had no children. There is also the fact that the other states of Europe might be alarmed by the possibility of all the lands of the emperor in Italy falling under the rule of a Bourbon prince, one who, in addition, could inherit the crown of Spain. The cardinal went still further. He was convinced that it would be better if the emperor had no lands at all in Italy because as long as he kept a foothold he would always be occupied with recovering the territory he had lost. Was this intended as a humorous comment?

Then came one of the smaller points that are always on the edge of discussions over the larger ones. The port of Leghorn should not remain Austrian or Spanish, thought the cardinal; it should be a free port open to all nations and be either a republic or ruled by a weak prince. The English had no trouble agreeing to this.

With regard to the third area of importance—namely, how to satisfy Sardinia—the cardinal admitted that he was leaving out this article for the moment. One does not put all the cards on the table at once in a diplomatic exchange.

Fleury then turned to an accusation that obviously embarrassed him from time to time—that he was working to bring the Turks into hostilities against the emperor. The cardinal was ever aware (and his later correspondence with the emperor made this more obvious) that he was a Christian and a churchman dealing with a Christian opponent. The French embassy in Constantinople did not compromise the emperor, said Fleury; the proposals had been for the Turks to act against the Russians, who were apparently to the cardinal not quite the same kind of Christians. However, complained the cardinal, the emperor did not scruple to use the barbarian Cossacks and Kalmuks to ravage Poland.[7]

Walpole responded a few days before the arrival of Jannel. His first item was to seize upon a remark made by the cardinal that England was augmenting its troops to be able to put some on the continent. Walpole was "astonished" at this accusation and felt it necessary to justify his country's policies in a somewhat injured tone, educating the cardinal regarding their relative military situations. In times of peace, he said, we do not have active troops, *sur pied*. When there are wars in which we have allies, and to which we are not indifferent, we must augment our forces for our own defenses and to be ready to help our allies. These prudent measures, thought Walpole, should not reflect on the rightness of our intentions; France is always prepared to take umbrage against those who make provision for their own security.

It was obvious that both parties were volleying back and forth on minor points, while touching the major ones very cautiously.

Jannel arrived in Holland and the meetings began. They were pleased with his candor and frankness, said Walpole later to the cardinal. Jannel was less happy over the cover story used to explain his presence. He was identified as a Frenchman who had been involved in an unwholesome affair which required him to seek refuge in Holland.[8]

No substantive issues were raised in the first meeting on 5 November. On the sixth Jannel sat down with Walpole and the high pensionary, Slingelandt, and from their silence saw that it was up to him to begin. He opened with a little preliminary fencing, mentioning a claim by the Habsburg court that mediators must propose nothing that had not already been ratified by that court. Walpole and Slingelandt denied the existence of any such agreement. Jannel then touched on the Polish question under three headings: to sustain the honor of the king of France, to assure the security of the state of Poland, and, lastly, to protect the liberty of the Poles.[9]

In the third conference on 7 November they began to touch the more specific issues. Walpole suggested that Stanislas be recognized as king by the emperor, the elector of Saxony, and all the powers. He would then abdicate and call upon his son-in-law to cease his efforts in his behalf. Then Stanislas would be given a pension befitting his dignity. Jannel noted that these external items did not compare with the possession of a great kingdom and that Stanislas had a legitimate title. They were unable to advance on this point and turned to Italy and the overall question of equilibrium. When asked what he claimed for his allies, Jannel answered that for Don Carlos he wanted all that he was in possession of—namely, Naples, Sicily, Parma, and Piacenza, and the eventual possession of Tuscany. The two ministers thought this entirely too much.

On the subject of what was to be given to the king of Sardinia Jannel said that this would be obvious if you gave Parma, Piacenza, and Tuscany to the emperor, meaning, of course, that there would be nothing left for the king of Sardinia but lands in the Milanese. The question was whether the emperor could be satisfied with Parma and Piacenza for the loss of lands in the Milanese. The ministers of the maritime powers felt that the emperor must also be given Tuscany. In addition, they argued that he was so angry at the conduct of the king of Sardinia that it might be difficult to get him to cede any of the Milanese.

When the matter of the Pragmatic Sanction came up it was in connection with Lorraine. Walpole said that England would not consent to have Lorraine under a prince who would become emperor. The Pragmatic Sanction thus could not be accepted purely and simply. Jannel went further, saying that France could accept the Pragmatic Sanction, but only provided that the Lorraine would never be in the family of the emperor. After a meeting on the eighth, Jannel returned to Paris and explained his differences with Walpole to the cardinal.[10]

The principal points had now emerged regarding the claims made for Spain and Sardinia. It would be a question of gradual adjustment to bring the sides together; nothing new would be added. But the satisfaction of Stanislas and the honor of the king of France were not yet brought within range of specific articles.

The cardinal fenced a little more with Walpole in his letter of 22 November in which he indicated that he wished to send Jannel back with new instructions. Fleury protested again the matter of increased armaments on the part of England and Holland, noting that they were also allies of France. He recalled that when England would not give France reassurances when France wished to send a fleet to the Baltic, France did not take the risk of enlarging the war. Finally he responded to a remark by Walpole regarding his age, a remark which presumably questioned the assurances in a treaty with a man who might abruptly depart the scene. Fleury may have been a little nettled by this and protested his good health. "The young, like the old, can never count with certainty on the length of their days, but when God wishes to terminate mine, I shall have the consolation of leaving the king with sentiments of justice, truth, and love of peace, which should be the spirit of the conduct of princes. I must add to this that the keeper of the seals, whom the king has given me as an assistant, thinks as I do and holds the same principles."[11] The old cardinal, at eighty-two, still had eight years to rule as first minister.

At last, on 3 December, Fleury outlined the provisions that might be acceptable in the Polish situation. These form the expedient, said the cardinal, which seemed to him most natural and most reasonable to save the honor of the king and satisfy at the same time the emperor and the tsarina. 1) Stanislas is to be recognized as king of Poland by all the powers after he has been notified of his election; 2) he will then ask his son-in-law to permit him to abdicate; 3) in consequence he will publish universals to assemble a Diet for abdication, which will accept the abdication and will then announce the free and unanimous election of the elector of Saxony; 4) Russian and Saxon troops are to be withdrawn from Poland; 5) the Republic of Poland will send a deputation to Stanislas regretting his abdication; 6) there will be an amnesty for all past actions—notably Danzig will be reestablished with its rights; 7) all the acts of Stanislas will be recognized as legitimate; 8) Stanislas will retain the rank and title of king of Poland and grand duke of Lithuania; 9) troops will be forbidden to enter Poland in a future election; 10) the emperor will send Stanislas a solemn embassy to congratulate him on his sacrifice for the peace of Europe; 11) Stanislas's estates will be given back and he will be given a pension for life by the Republic.[12]

In both substance and theatrics it was enough to keep European courts busy for months. If it seems strained and overwrought, it must be remembered that, although the cardinal was confident of his ability to maintain his relationship with the young king (and intimated this strongly to foreign diplomats), he must nevertheless from time to time satisfy the members of the Council of State.

The cardinal was also forthcoming on the question of Italy. Give the emperor Parma, Piacenza, and Tuscany, and most of the Milanese, he recommended; but, of course, the emperor must take care of the damages to the Duke of Guastalla if Mantua is not returned to him. Finally, the cardinal counseled the maritime powers as to procedure. Nothing should be proposed to the emperor or to Spain as coming from France. That would compromise us, said Fleury. Rather they must form a general plan of peace as coming from the maritime powers.

Thus, two understandings were involved. First a secret one between France and the maritime powers, and second a peace plan ostensibly prepared though the good offices of the maritime powers for submission to all the powers in the conflict. This would be the Plan of Accommodation.[13]

Jannell then went back to Holland with two basic principles in his instructions. There must be no increase directly or indirectly in Austrian territory, and Lorraine must not be in the hands of the emperor or his family. And there was the admonition from the cardinal that yielding to the Pragmatic Sanction must not come lightly but in the sense of a great sacrifice. After all, as he pointed out in a message, a guarantee of the Pragmatic Sanction by the king of France tends to make the empire hereditary. Perhaps in the back of the cardinal's mind was the claim of the elector of Bavaria as a likely candidate for the imperial crown, a claim he would seek to exercise in a few years.

In summary, it may be said at this point that France had placed the pieces of the Italian puzzle on the table. They might be pulled together in any way subject only to the proviso that the emperor must suffer a net loss. Now the cardinal could shift his attention to the terms required to satisfy France rather than those required for his allies.[14]

At the Hague the conference proceeded with firmer positions and a seriousness and urgency evidenced by meetings on 24, 25, 26, and 27 December. On the question of Poland the cardinal's points would have to be scaled down. It was impossible to have Stanislas abdicate before the Polish senate or have a new election. The maritime powers would not go beyond their for-

mer position. On the Italian questions they were closer. Don
Carlos must give up Parma, Piacenza, and Tuscany if he holds
Naples and Sicily, and the emperor must have damages for Tus-
cany during the life of the grand duke.[15]

A package was now taking shape. Actually, the question of
Lorraine was still open, but Walpole assured the cardinal in a letter of 28 December that something would be done for France if
the duke of Lorraine became emperor, but he would not go so
far as Jannel demanded, namely, that the house of Lorraine be
forever excluded.[16]

Walpole now proposed that they proceed to the Plan of Accommodation but it was about this time that the negotiations fal-
tered. The documentation does not indicate precisely what went
wrong, but one thing was clear—the cardinal felt that he had
overcommitted himself and sought to retract some of his positions. The negotiations continued but never recovered from this
setback.

Waldegrave, the British ambassador to France, was brought
into the talks to keep them alive; he had been only partly informed on the details up to this time. He reported a session with
the cardinal on 8 January 1735 and felt that the cardinal was
now sensitive to criticism for being too compliant on matters
touching the king's honor, that is, on the Polish quesiton. However, the cardinal did not insist on Lorraine, said Waldegrave,
only that the duke not be emperor and at the same time hold
Lorraine. The cardinal also told him that the emperor and Spain
were seeking accommodation and that a monk had been sent by
the emperor to Spain in secret. He had died on the way, passing
his secret to another monk, from whom France learned of it.[17]

Fleury had already answered Walpole on 6 January. He admitted they were in agreement on the principal points but wanted the Polish article more precise and wanted the elector of
Saxony proclaimed king a second time. This, of course, would
imply that the original proclamation was invalid. Fleury also
backed away from an agreement on "reciprocal neutrality." This
was a concept to put greater leverage on the belligerent powers
to accept the Plan of Accommodation when it was submitted to
them. Under such an agreement France would become neutral

if her allied belligerent powers rejected the plan, provided that the British, in turn, would remain neutral if the emperor rejected the plan. Then the cardinal added a remark that may have been the key to it all—that he expected to have trouble with the Council of State in a meeting on the ninth.

The conferees at the Hague, including Jannel, were surprised. According to Le Dran, Chauvelin had participated in this reply. Jannel had been given authorization to sign the articles but they had been reworded in much more succinct form. Walpole and the pensionary were very unhappy; they found the new articles unintelligible, susceptible to an infinity of questions, and very dangerous; further, they contradicted the cardinal's previous promises. Walpole wrote saying they were surprised and mortified at the changes. A further exchange took place during the new few weeks, including a new set of articles written by Chauvelin and forwarded on 2 February.[18]

The English were unhappy but they did not want to abandon the Plan of Accommodation and thus submitted it to the several belligerent powers on 17 February without the French agreement on the articles discussed above. Royal instructions to Waldegrave ordered him to tell the cardinal that his letter of 6 January contradicted his instructions to his envoy and raised questions of the cardinal's sincerity. Try also, said the London instructions, to find out what changed the cardinal's mind: whether he had originally no design to come to a conclusion or whether his good intentions were defeated by the credit and influence of M. Chauvelin.[19]

Waldegrave replied on 9 March that he had been three times to Versailles to confer with French ministers. He thought the cardinal looked a little ashamed. In their conversation he was finally able to bring him away from pleasant general comments but found that the cardinal retreated behind the argument that he must consult with his allies. "I own I had much ado to keep my temper," said Waldegrave, telling the cardinal that if he were determined to support Spain right or wrong, there would be a general war and he would be responsible, and that apparently his actions up to that time were to amuse the king of England who, on the other hand, placed confidence in the cardinal. But he could not move the old man. "His last resource was in Almighty God, whom he said we must all pray to, to avoid a general war." [20]

The cardinal told Waldegrave that Chauvelin was still unaware of the negotiations on 9 March, although Jannel had admitted privately that Chauvelin had been brought in. The cardinal had succeeded in the past by difficult and tortuous negotiations but this time he had fumbled. He had admitted more to Walpole than he admitted to Jannel and was faced with opposition in the council and from Chauvelin and was trying to scramble back to safer ground. Wilson believes that Walpole was duped in the exchange.[21]

But the English did not give up on Fleury. They continued to put pressure on him while the Spanish, Austrians, and Sardinians considered the plan. Walpole himself came to Paris on 29 March and after a meeting reported that he was sure Chauvelin was behind the cardinal's change of direction. "It is as dangerous to negotiate directly with M. Chauvelin, for fear of being cheated, or betrayed, as it is to negotiate directly with the cardinal for fear of being disappointed by the intrigues of Chauvelin." [22]

In the meantime the Plan of Accommodation was rejected by the "three crowns." The emperor's refusal, according to Arneth, was because of the influence of the Spanish party at the Viennese court and because of reports of sickness in the French army.[23] Eugene had hoped the emperor would accept and on 6 April wrote to Philip Kinsky, "There is no other solution in the position in which we find ourselves than that of accepting purely and simply the plan; it is only to be feared that Spain and France will not accept it." [24] Another explanation for the emperor's refusal could have been the belief that a strong rejection would bring the maritime powers to some realization of their responsibilities to him.[25] This, of course, did not happen.

The English continued to negotiate with the French but with meager results. Waldegrave thought that the French had now begun to reveal their true objective. "Your Lordship I fancy will be of opinion from this account that France has an eye upon Lorraine, and that it is her principal aim thô the ministers have hitherto had modesty enough not to mention it directly as being diametrically opposite to their repeated declaration in public and private that France would have nothing for herself."[26]

In a long letter to Eugene written 28 May 1735 the emperor reviewed the matters that had taken place since Eugene had gone to take command of the army on the Rhine once again. He noted that the most recent efforts had been to achieve some sort of armistice rather than a peace treaty. One of his enclosures was a proposal from France and her allies in the form of an armistice. In general the emperor was discouraged. "Now from all that remains Your Grace sees that there is little hope of arriving at a bearable or consequently even a precarious peace through the good offices of the two sea powers." The emperor goes on to discuss the military situation, which he admits is very bad.[27]

There had already been in the first part of 1735 a great number of efforts by various mediators to bring Versailles and Vienna together for negotiations. Some mediators were working on their own initiative; others had the blessing of the emperor or Cardinal Fleury. But the two courts were suspicious of one another. One curious episode came from an ostensible effort of the cardinal to draw out the emperor at the end of 1734. The cardinal had sent a season's greeting note to the emperor in December. Such a formal communication was normal even in wartime. But the cardinal added a handwritten note that invited a response. After due consideration among his advisers the emperor responded with a careful note in his own hand, which passed to Fleury via the papal nuncio in Brussels. Word came back eventually from the nuncio that the cardinal in opening the packet had accidentally dropped the emperor's note in the fire.[28] This particular exchange went no further.

But in April 1735 there began a complex passing of messages and visits among a half-dozen persons, and this finally established the definitive channel for peace negotiations. It centered in the small German principality of Neuwied in the Rhineland, where the sovereign count of Wied employed a Swedish Baron Nierodt as his councilor. Nierodt had dealt with the French in contribution matters and in March 1735 had an audience with Cardinal

Fleury in Paris. He returned to Neuwied with authorization to make contact with the emperor and the count sent his son to Vienna at the end of April to convey certain proposals to the court. The son returned with a cautious response from Count Sinzendorff, and Nierodt took this to the cardinal.[29]

The cardinal accepted this barely proffered hand by a letter to the emperor dated 16 July. He drew up a set of negotiating instructions and had a man on the road to Vienna before the first of August. The road to Vienna in this case lay through Neuwied, and Nierodt would accompany the negotiator, M. de La Baune, who traveled under the name of St. Jean. In his instructions the cardinal admitted that he did not know the situation in Vienna, but since the contact was made in the name of Count Sinzendorff, the envoy should attempt to negotiate with him. Absolute secrecy was imperative. "No one must know that we have a man in Vienna. Better to do nothing than to be found out."

Sinzendorff will start directly or indirectly with the English plan, said the cardinal in his instructions, and you will call attention to the fact that we and our allies have rejected it and that other more equitable principles are needed. If you are pressed for conditions, use the following: 1) reestablishment of the king of Poland or at least an agreed satisfaction; 2) an acceptable share (*partage convenable*) for Don Carlos; 3) a reasonable share for the king of Sardinia in the Milanese; 4) justice for the house of Guastalla if obliged to cede Mantua.

These will let the count know more advantageous terms are needed for our allies. And above all you must disabuse him of the idea that I have gone over to the English, added the cardinal.[30]

But while the cardinal's right hand wrote this letter in answer to the contact through Baron Nierodt, his left hand had already caused the opening of another channel of communication with Austria. On the day of the cardinal's letter to the emperor, 16 July, Count Friedrich Harrach, the emperor's representative in the Austrian Netherlands, wrote to his father, the elder Count Harrach, who was then a member of the Privy Council in Vienna.

An approach has just been made to me desiring to know if I can seek authorization to negotiate a treaty between the emperor and France independent of the British court. The channel by which this proposal has come is the Count de La Marc, who commands the French armies on the frontiers and who has been in conversation on three occasions with the papal nuncio from here who was taking the waters at Saint Amand. I feel that there is a danger that the French are setting a trap in order to sacrifice us later to the English, but I think I have found the means to appear to listen and sacrifice them later to the English in turn.[31]

Harrach the Younger then continued the contact through the nuncio and Count de La Marc, who is also referred to as Count Marek.

At some point the cardinal must have seen that the negotiations were proliferating unduly and getting out of hand and would soon involve him in unexplainable contradictions. He then wrote directly to the emperor once again, sending his letter through Count Marek and through the suspicious Count Harrach in Brussels.[32] The cardinal's letter, dated 28 August, is a masterpiece and cleared the air.

Sire:

It is from duty and from the honesty that I owe to Your Majesty that I have the honor to inform him about that which was taking place for more than a month at Brussels without my knowledge, and of which I have just learned in detail. The nuncio of Flanders and Count Marek, lieutenant general of the armies of the king, having met some time ago at the spa of Saint Amand, the conversation turned, as it naturally would, to the present war, and the count assures us that the nuncio made some approaches to see if he could not find a way to arrive at a peace. They have mèt twice since then, and the last time the nuncio told him that Count Harrach, because of the several conferences that had been held, gave an accounting to Your Majesty, which by no means departed from the reasonable conditions which should be offered to you to arrive at a peace. I omit all that took place regarding this since Your Majesty has been amply informed. Count Marek adds that the matter has gone so far that if we should wish to send a man in complete secrecy to Brussels with full powers to negotiate with Count Harrach, there would be hope for a happy result.

This same count adds further that Your Majesty had some doubts as to our intentions because having already undertaken two negotiations with us, one through the Pretender, and the other through the Count of

Wied, who was traveling in France, there has been no result except to have prevented Your Majesty from making other arrangements which might have suited you. It seems by this that Your Majesty suspects me of having used artifice and bad faith, and nothing touches me more at heart than to remove such a suspicion from your mind. Here is literally the story of the two negotiations, which I swear to be true.

It is true that the Pretender contacted me through an agent he has in Paris, the first time in general terms, and the second time in more specific terms, giving even the name of the person through whom the matter had come, but with the condition that we did not dare yet to speak of it to Your Majesty. My reply has always been that the king will never draw away from a solid and honorable peace and would enter with pleasure into all the means which might lead to it, but that the proposal for us to send a man to Rome to treat there on this important matter seemed to me subject to many inconveniences. Moreover, O'Brien, the agent for the Pretender, offered himself to go to Vienna for us.

I confess frankly to Your Majesty that this triangular negotiation of Rome, Vienna, and Paris seemed to me subject to long delays and, although I was not in any way disheartened, I did not expect of it any significant result, the more so since I saw no positive assurance on the part of Your Majesty. It was at this point that the Swedish Baron Nierodt brought me a letter of the count of Wied with the two pieces which I have the honor of sending you. . . .

However, the character and birth of the Count of Wied, and all the particulars which the Baron Nierodt told me of his trip to Vienna, left no doubt of the facts he alleged, and I did not hesitate to inform the king, who found it well that I follow up this matter. Your Majesty knows the rest so that I will say no more about it. I have heard nothing from de La Baune and I await news with great impatience.[33]

The cardinal concluded by offering to use any of the channels mentioned above, but the result of the letter was to eliminate all but the direct negotiation carried out by La Baune.

The British ambassador Robinson was feeling a coolness in the Viennese court at this time. He reported a conversation with Sinzendorff in which he was asked if his king still would do nothing. "Did England have any proposal to make?" I said no. "What," he said, "no proposal, no assistance, no hope, not one mark of the king's friendship?"[34]

It was strong language. Meanwhile the negotiations were finding a single channel between France and Austria.

La Baune had traveled with the count of Wied and arrived on 13 August in Vienna. On the sixteenth he reported to the cardinal that he had had a three-hour conference in the Convent of the Trinitarians at the edge of the city. He had taken a place at a long table in the library of the convent with Sinzendorff and Bartenstein opposite him, the former doing most of the talking.[35] Things did not start off well. On the first point, that of finding a satisfaction for Stanislas, Sinzendorff tried to equate Stanislas's position with that of James II of England. La Baune began to use stronger language. Sinzendorff said they could make him king of Hungary, but La Baune did not take this seriously. When the two imperial negotiators at length said they had nothing more to propose on this point, La Baune said that his voyage was useless and made a gesture to leave. Sinzendorff and Bartenstein held a fifteen-minute conference and all three sat down again.[36]

Now the matter of actually ceding Lorraine was brought up. The throne will be vacant, said La Baune, and the king of France cannot have the emperor in possession of an area in the middle of France. The matter was resolved in the following manner. Stanislas would become the sovereign of Lorraine and Bar, and the duke of Lorraine would be given Tuscany, to take possession when the reigning Medici duke died. In the meantime Spain would be required to pay the duke of Lorraine revenues equivalent to those he would receive from Tuscany when he came into possession. At the death of Stanislas the province of Lorraine would revert to his daughter, the queen of France, thus becoming a part of France.[37] All this was agreed upon only after prolonged and bitter talks, with a last minute threat by La Baune to leave Vienna.[38]

Before agreement was reached, La Baune's presence became known, and this further urged both parties to come to agreement. The English ministry in London was aware early of a secret French envoy, even his name, and asked Robinson to verify. But Robinson replied rather loftily that there was no trace of secret negotiations and was skeptical of the report. A few days later he discovered his mistake. La Baune, wearing false hair, was passing as an Englishman in the company of Baron Nierodt. Robinson demanded an explanation from the imperial ministers who gave him half-hearted assurances that no treaty had been signed. This was true, but it was late September and agreement was very close.[39]

The preliminaries to what would be called the Third Treaty of Vienna were signed on 3 October 1735. Except for the article on Lorraine they were very close to what had been offered in the Plan of Accommodation which came out in February. Don Carlos was given the kingdoms of Naples and Sicily, the king of Sardinia was given two territories in the Milanese, and the emperor was given back Parma and Piacenza and the fortresses in the Rhineland taken by the French. The French guaranteed the Pragmatic Sanction.[40] These articles had been agreed upon in a few weeks, although England and France had bargained for over a year without success. Both sides were ready. Chauvelin knew this when he told La Baune: "Don't worry about your stay in Vienna in any case; it can only be extremely short."[41]

The sudden signing of the preliminaries between France and Austria left three areas of uncertainty.

First, the Spanish army in Italy found itself deserted by its ally and facing the emperor's superior army. Both sides were ready to find a solution, however, and no serious fighting occurred.

Second, La Baune signed the preliminaries with a reservation. He could not get clear agreement for immediate possession of Lorraine by Stanislas and the matter was tied to the indemnification for the duke of Lorraine. The French ministry refused the offer of an "expedient" to circumvent this problem, and La Baune said he was not authorized to sign without a reservation. Nevertheless the cardinal approved the ratification of the preliminaries and thereafter the Austrians used this to drag out more than a year of painful negotiations over the legal possession of Lorraine by Stanislas.[42]

The third area of uncertainty is historical. The acquisition of Lorraine was of such importance that France actually was the country which acquired the most from the war. Was the cardinal such a wily statesman that he could work for this result for nearly three years of diplomacy and war without acknowledging his objective until the very last? Wilson believes he could and did. On the other hand, was it possible that the cession of Lorraine was a last-minute device that had suddenly occurred to the French? It hardly seems likely. It was no secret that the French had had their eyes on Lorraine for a great many decades. Lord Henry's memoirs suggest that the cession of Lorraine was a silent part of the agreement when the Plan of Accommodation came out in February.[43] But none of the remarks made by the British ministers give this impression. What seems more likely is that the French were willing to stand by their protestations of a no-aggrandizement policy until they were surer of the outcome of the fighting and until the device of giving the duke of Lorraine compensation in Tuscany was discovered. After all, if Lorraine were kept out of the hands of the Habsburg family, France could have waited for an appropriate moment to acquire this already surrounded island of territory.

The war and its negotiations were essentially at an end. The final treaty would not change the preliminaries. The war had followed the old pattern of the victorious power taking his advantages in Italian property; the dignities of hereditary sovereigns, even the defeated ones, were preserved; and the side that was getting the worst of the military action was allowed to cut its losses and withdraw. Both victor and vanquished knew that another round might be played in a few years and the forces and alliances might be reversed, as well as the fortunes of war. The reverence for hereditary rights mingled with playacting here. Stanislas is still king (momentarily), the honor of Louis XV is saved, the old cardinal's position at Versailles is secure, the emperor has his Pragmatic Sanction, Count Sinzendorff maintains his dignity, the army commanders on both sides are dining together amicably as they work out details. We are reminded of the final lines of Thackeray's great novel: "Come children, let us shut up the box and the puppets, for our play is played out."

☩

# NOTES

## ABBREVIATIONS

AAE    Archives des Affaires Etrangères, Paris
AG    Archives du Ministère de la Guerre, Paris
BA    Bibliothèque de l'Arsénal, Paris
FE    *Feldzüge des Prinzen Eugen von Savoyen* (Vienna, 1876)
KA    Kriegsarchiv, Vienna
PRO    Public Records Office, London
RIO    Russian Historical Society (Russkoe istoricheskoe obshchestvo), *The Diplomatic Correspondence of British Ministers to the Russian Court at St. Petersburg, 1704–1776* (St. Petersburg, 1897–1916)
SA    Staatsarchiv, Vienna

## CHAPTER ONE

1. V. Gere, *Borba za Polskii Prestol v 1733 Godu* (Moscow, 1862), Prilozhenie (Supplement), p. 47.

2. Waldegrave to Delafaye, 10 June 1733, State Papers, France, 78 204, PRO.

3. E. J. F. Barbier, *Journal historique du Règne de Louis XV* (Paris, 1849), p. 7; *Journal de Mathieu Marais, 1715–1737*, ed. de Lescure, 4 vols. (Paris, 1863–68), 4:519–20.

4. Pierre Boyé, *Stanislas Leszczynski et la troisième traité de Vienne* (Paris, 1898), pp. 138–43. Similar information is given in M. P. Massuet, *Histoire de la Guerre présente* (Amsterdam, 1735), pp. 15–23. There are other variations on the Stanislas journey in the *Cambridge History of Poland*, ed. W. F. Reddaway et al. (New York, 1971), p. 26. According to a recent biographer of Stanislas, there is no detailed account of the trip across Europe. Maurice Garçot, *Stanislas Leszczynski* (Paris, 1953), p. 93.

5. From Versailles, 22 Mar., 25 May, 9 June, 10 July, 1 and 4 Aug. 1733, MS 6622, vol. 9, BA. See also Boyé, *Stanislas Leszczynski*, p. 127.

6. Chauvelin to Monti, 22 Aug. 1733, Mem. & Doc. (Mémoires et Documents), Pologne, 16:125, AAE. Also quoted in Boyé, *Stanislas Leszczynski*, p. 143.

7. There seems to be no doubt that the embarkation of a false Stanislas in the person of Commander Thianges actually was carried out. The French ambassador in Copenhagen wrote to the ministry on 22 September 1733 that it was ridiculous to keep up the farce any longer since Monti reported the king of Poland in Warsaw. All the squadron was fooled, he added. Plélo to Minister, 22 Sept. 1733, Cor. Pol. (Correspondance Politique), Danemark, jan-août 1733, AAE.

8. Hans Delbrück, *Geschichte der Kriegskunst im Rahmen der politischen Geschichte*, 7 vols. (Berlin, 1920), 4:347. In the War of the Polish Succession, he tells us, tensions were slight and did not require important decisions, and he has no more to say about it. In Lynn Montross's *War through the Ages* (New York, 1946), p. 374, this war is given a single paragraph and characterized as "trivial operations concerning only the various diplomats and professional armies." As a possible example of how significant this war may seem to commanders in recent times one notes that, although he includes a chapter on eighteenth-century warfare, Field Marshal Sir Bernard Montgomery does not have a word to say about this particular war in his *A History of Warfare* (New York, 1968).

9. Lee Kennett, *The French Armies in the Seven Years' War*, (Durham, N.C., 1967), p. 141. Kennett also stresses a limiting factor in the monarch's use of his army, one which acted in most of the armies of Europe at that time. A commander, he tells us, must remember that "though he led the 'king's army,' in a very real sense that army was not royal property but the possession of the proprietary colonels and captains who trained, equipped, and led their own men" (p. 35).

### CHAPTER TWO

1. Ellinor v. Puttkamer, *Frankreich, Russland, und der polnischen Thron, 1733* (Berlin, 1937), p. 1.

2. *Feldzüge des Prinzen Eugen von Savoyen*, 21 vols. (Vienna, 1876), 20:245. This work (hereafter cited as *FE*) by the historical branch of the Austro-Hungarian general staff blames the Spanish party in Vienna for Austrian mistakes in the eighteenth century.

3. Puttkamer, *Frankreich, Russland, und der polnischen Thron*, p. 2.

4. Fleury never took the title of first minister although there was no doubt of his precedence. The *Conseil d'Etat du Roi* (not to be confused with the present-day *Conseil d'Etat*) was the body in which the secretary

of state for foreign affairs was the principal reporter. He read the dispatches from the ambassadors and the answers to be made to them. From what is known of the council meetings, however, many important questions were not considered here. A recent work asserts that in important matters the council under Louis XV was a fiction. Michel Antoine, *Le Conseil du Roi sous le règne de Louis XV* (Paris, 1970), p. x.

5. See *Mémoires du Maréchal Villars*, ed. de Vogüe, 5 vols. (Paris, 1892), 5 : 386–89; Petitot, ed., *Collection des Mémoires relatifs à l'histoire de France* (Paris, 1828), vol. 71, *Mémoires du Maréchal Villars*, pp. 98–100.

6. Villars, *Mémoires*, ed. de Vogüe, 5 : 310, 407.

7. *Journal et Mémoires du Marquis d'Argenson*, ed. E. J. B. Rathery, 4 vols. (Paris, 1859), 4 : 157–58. These remarks were made in his journal entries for 15–16 March 1733.

8. Argenson, *Journal et Mémoires*, 1 : 227.

9. E. Driault, "Chauvelin, 1733–1737," in *Revue d'histoire diplomatique* (Paris, 1893), pp. 38, 69; *Mémoires du Comte de Maurepas*, 2d ed., 2 vols. (Paris, 1792), 2 : 76–77; *Memoirs of Horatio Lord Walpole*, ed. William Coxe, 3d ed. (London, 1820), 2 : 292. An interesting and possibly accurate account of the relationship between Chauvelin and Fleury is in an anonymous volume published in England, perhaps written by Horatio Walpole, *Memoirs of the Life and Administration of the Late Andrew-Hercules de Fleury, by an Impartial Hand* (London, 1743).

10. Maurepas, *Mémoires*, 2 : 9, 28.

11. Pierre Boyé, *Stanislas Leszczynski et la troisième traité de Vienne* (Paris, 1898), p. 200.

12. See Driault, "Chauvelin," p. 36; Manstein, *Memoirs of Russia from 1727 to 1744* (London, 1770), p. 66.

13. In his first message to Monti following news of the death of Augustus II, Chauvelin noted that it was a *situation forcée* and posed a long list of questions on how to go about supporting a Stanislas candidacy. Mem. et Doc., Pologne, vol. 14, p. 18, AAE. Also see Alfred Baudrillart, *Philip V et la cour de France*, 5 vols. (Paris, 1901), 4 : 156.

14. See Paul Vaucher, *Robert Walpole et la politique de Fleury* (Paris, 1924), p. 4. Vaucher states that Fleury tried to find Chauvelin's papers after the latter's disgrace in 1737 but in vain. Vaucher also sought these papers among various branches of the family of Chauvelin's descendants, likewise in vain.

15. Argenson, *Journal et Mémoires*, 1 : 72–80, 119; Driault, "Chauvelin," p. 39.

16. See, for example, Arthur M. Wilson, *French Foreign Policy during the Administration of Cardinal Fleury, 1726–1743* (Cambridge, Mass.,

1936), pp. 176–89. Wilson argues that Fleury was always in command and Chauvelin his subordinate, often working a game that left the cardinal to smooth over the brusqueries of Chauvelin, as though the subordinate had gone too far.

17. Chavigny to Chauvelin, 8 Jan 1733, Cor. Pol., Angleterre, vol. 379, AAE.

18. Chauvelin to Chavigny, 28 Jan. 1733, ibid.

19. Chauvelin to Chavigny, 12 Feb. 1733, ibid.

20. Chavigny to Chauvelin, 24 Feb. 1733, ibid. William Stanhope, Baron (later earl of) Harrington, was the English secretary of state in charge of the northern region. The duke of Newcastle was in charge of the southern region. The dominant voice at this time was that of Robert Walpole, acting as prime minister, if not yet bearing that title. His brother Horatio, or Horace, Walpole may be considered the real minister of foreign affairs; at least the most important negotiations were carried on by him. In the message noted above, Chavigny reported a conversation with the duke of Newcastle who, he said "doubtless had already had his lesson from Horace Walpole."

21. Chavigny to Chauvelin, 19 Mar. 1733, ibid.

22. Chauvelin to Chavigny, 2 Apr. 1733, ibid; Vaucher, *Robert Walpole*, pp. 69–70. Vaucher also points out that the aggressive phrase used by Chavigny had actually originated with Chauvelin.

23. Chavigny to Chauvelin, 10 Apr. 1733, Cor. Pol., Angleterre, vol. 380, AAE.

24. Waldegrave to Newcastle, 23 Feb., 11 Mar., 10 June 1733, State Papers, France, 78 204, PRO.

25. Chauvelin to Chavigny, 24 June 1733, Cor. Pol., Angleterre, vol. 380, AAE; Chavigny to Chauvelin, 6 July 1733, ibid. vol. 381.

26. Chauvelin to Chavigny, 20 July 1733, ibid., vol. 381.

27. Waldegrave to Delafaye, 12 Aug. 1733, State Papers, France, 78 204, PRO.

28. Cor. Pol., Autriche, vol. 176, doc. 93, AAE. The French made frequent use of memoirs to study a problem. These memoirs probably would be called studies today although they were, at least by today's standards, rather brief. As a rule one does not know who wrote them and they are seldom, if ever, approved by formal signatures on the document. But even though they indicate decisions only indirectly, they are an excellent source of information about the factors under consideration when decisions were required. According to Wilson (*French Foreign Policy*, p. 188) the extensive use at this time of memorials and summaries by the French was a method unknown to British diplomacy.

29. Robinson to Harrington, 25 Apr., 6 May 1733, State Papers, Austria, 80 95, PRO.

30. Cor. Pol., Espagne, vol. 405, doc. 80, AAE.

31. Vaulgrenant to Minister, 4 June 1733, Cor. Pol., Sardaigne, vol. 163, AAE.

32. Rottembourg to Minister, 9 and 13 Mar. 1733, Cor. Pol., Espagne, vol. 404, AAE. The duke of Liria, a Spanish noble and Spanish general officer, was the son of Marshal Berwick, duke of Fritzjames, who was a natural son of the exiled James II of England. Berwick as a Marshal of France would command armies in the Rhineland in the fall of 1733. Liria acquired his Spanish titles from his father who received them from Philip V for military services in the War of the Spanish Succession.

33. Vaulgrenant from Minister, undated, Cor. Pol., Sardaigne, vol. 163, AAE; Chauvelin to Vaulgrenant, 6 July 1733, ibid.

34. Vaulgrenant to Minister, 16 July 1733, ibid.

35. Villars, *Mémoires*, ed. de Vogüe, 5:421.

36. Chauvelin to Vaulgrenant, 3 Aug. 1733, Cor. Pol., Sardaigne, vol. 163, AAE.

37. Vaulgrenant to Minister, 8 Aug. 1733, ibid.

38. Villars, *Mémoires*, ed. de Vogüe, 5:415.

39. Vaulgrenant to Minister, 15 Aug. 1733. Cor. Pol., Sardaigne, vol. 163, AAE.

40. Vaulgrenant to Minister, 30 Sept. 1733, ibid., vol. 164.

41. See Vaucher, *Robert Walpole*, p. 74; Wilson, *French Foreign Policy*, p. 244.

42. Quoted in Baudrillart, *Philip V*, 4:137.

43. Rottembourg to Minister, 6 Mar. 1733, Cor. Pol., Espagne, vol. 404, AAE.

44. King of Spain to King of France, 31 May 1733, ibid. The new French-Spanish understanding was marked by a family compact as well, signed later in the year. This was the Treaty of El Escorial, known as the First Family Pact, 7 Nov. 1733. In Hargreaves-Mawdsley, ed., *Spain under the Bourbons, 1700–1833* (Columbia, S.C., 1973), p. 97.

45. Villars, *Mémoires*, ed. de Vogüe, 5:415.

46. Driault, "Chauvelin," p. 69.

## CHAPTER THREE

1. P. Muret, *La prépondérance anglaise, 1715–1763* (Paris, 1951), p. 193.

2. Ibid., p. 196. See also "Histoire des négociations de la France pour le rétablissement du Roy Stanislas sur le Trone de Pologne," Mem. & Doc., Pologne, vol. 14, p. 4, AAE. Memoirs 14, 15, 16, and 17 have the above title and represent an effort in 1737 by the foreign affairs secretary, Le Dran, to put together in chronological order the French diplomatic correspondence pertaining to the election.

3. *FE*, 19:9.

4. Bussy to Minister, 7 Feb. 1733, Cor. Pol., Autriche, vol. 175, AAE.

5. Arneth, the nineteenth-century chronicler of the Habsburg court, states that for twenty years almost all state papers of the Austrian government came from his pen. Alfred Arneth, *Prinz Eugen von Savoyen*, 3 vols. (Vienna, 1858), 3:215. This remark may be taken quite literally, for it is evident that the signature block at the end of many briefings is in the same hand as the preceding pages of text.

6. Reichskanzlei, "Vorträge an den Kaiser, 1733," Karton 37, 5 Feb. 1733, SA.

7. *FE*, 19:7–9.

8. Robinson to Harrington, 7 Feb. 1733, State Papers, Austria, 80 93, PRO.

9. Bussy to Minister, 11 Feb., 14 Feb. 1733, Cor. Pol., Autriche, vol. 175, AAE.

10. Reichskanzlei, "Vorträge an den Kaiser, 1733," Karton 37, 23 Feb. 1733, SA.

11. Harrington to Robinson, 20 Mar. 1733, State Papers, Austria, 80 94, PRO. Harrington's message was actually dated 9 March since England was still using the Old Style calendar. Dates in this work have been revised where necessary to the new calendar which was eleven days ahead of the old.

12. James Stuart, the Old Pretender, was married to a Sobieski and possibly would have had active papal support as a candidate. He was reported to be in Poland at the time.

13. Cor. Pol., Austriche, vol. 175. doc. 120, AAE. See also Cor. Pol., Danemark, jan-août, 1733, doc. 28, AAE.

14. For the text of the emperor's reply see Rousset de Missy, *Recueil historique d'actes, mémoires, et traités* (The Hague, 1728–1755), 9:185–86. Also in A1 2697, doc. 1, AG, where the texts of both messages may be found.

15. V. Gere, *Borba za Polskii Prestol v 1733 Godu* (Moscow, 1862), p. 62.

16. Reichskanzlei, "Vorträge an den Kaiser, 1733," Karton 37, SA.

17. *FE*, 19:11; Arneth, *Prinz Eugen*, 3:366.

18. Reichskanzlei, "Vorträge an den Kaiser, 1733," Karton 37, SA.

19. Bussy to Minister, 1 Apr. 1733, Autriche, vol. 174, AAE; Bussy to Minister, 1 Apr. 1733, ibid., vol. 175.

20. Arthur M. Wilson suggests that Fleury always had his eye on Lorraine and that the failure of the Stanislas kingship was necessary to the success of his policy. *French Foreign Policy during the Administration of Cardinal Fleury, 1726–1743* (Cambridge, Mass., 1936), p. 248.

21. Bussy to Minister, 8 Aug. 1733, Cor. Pol., Autriche, vol. 176, AAE.

22. Edward Armstrong observed that Fleury's methods differed from those of Walpole: "The English minister relied upon abstention, the French upon intricate negotiations." *Elisabeth Farnese* (London, 1892), p. 366.

23. Kinsky to Eugene, 14 Apr. 1733, Gr. Kor. (Grosse Korrespondenz), 94b, SA; Kinsky to Eugene, 17 Apr. 1733, ibid.

24. Harrington to Robinson, 10 July 1733, State Papers, Austria, 80 96, PRO.

25. In case of hostilities between France and the emperor over Poland the king reserved the right to act as the case would require. This was the English interpretation of the George II-Chavigny conversation as relayed to the English minister in Saint Petersburg. RIO, 67:97.

26. Robinson to Harrington, 27 July 1733, State Papers, Austria, 80 96, PRO. The emperor's resolve to move these troops out of Silesia was basically to put himself in a better defensive position toward the French.

27. Bussy to Minister, 6 May 1733, Cor. Pol., Autriche, vol. 175, AAE.

28. Reichskanzlei, "Vorträge an den Kaiser, 1733," Karton 37, SA.

29. Cor. Pol. Autriche, vol. 174, doc. 372, AAE.

30. The text of the treaty appears in Gere, *Borba za Polskii Prestol Prilozhenie*, p. 162.

31. Reichskanzlei, "Vorträge an den Kaiser, 1733," Karton 37, SA.

32. The king of Prussia let it be known through his minister in Vienna as early as 13 July 1733 that in case of war with France he would contribute not just the 10,000 men required by the treaty of 1728, but an army of 40,000. This only embarrassed the emperor at that time; he wrote to Seckendorff on 26 August that it would not be helpful but would make matters more difficult, and "would incur the general hatred of the Catholic and Protestant estates of the Empire and separate us from the maritime powers." *FE*, 19:130; 19:13.

33. *FE*, 19:129.

34. *Memoirs of Horatio, Lord Walpole*, ed. William Coxe, 3d ed. (London, 1820), 1:32. This information comes from a document known as the "Apology" which was written by Walpole during the latter part of his life but covered the events from 1715 to 1739.

35. Mem & Doc., Hollande, vol. 60, doc. 164, AAE.

36. Ibid., doc. 165; Ministry to Fénelon, 17 Sept. 1733, ibid., vol. 397.

37. Ibid. This is in a long 1 September message in the French files signed by Grumbkow, having to do with the Dutch seeking neutrality.

38. Bussy to Minister, 7 Mar., 1 Apr. 1733, Cor. Pol., Autriche, vol. 175, AAE. How Bussy managed to be aware of the contents of so many messages to the Austrians he does not explain, but reading the secret dispatches of other governments is an ancient game. Braubach notes that in the handwritten correspondence of the emperor with Prince Eugene there is frequent mention of intercepted diplomatic messages. Max Braubach, *Prinz Eugen von Savoyen*, 5 vols. (Munich, 1963–65), 4:253.

39. Wilczek to Eugene, 27 Mar. 1733, Dipl. Cor. Pr. Eugene (Diplomatic Correspondence of Prince Eugene), fasc. 345, KA.

40. Gere, *Borba za Polskii Prestol*, Prilozhenie, p. 45. Also see C. P. V. Pajol, *Les Guerres sous Louis XV*, 7 vols. (Paris, 1881), 1:172, for the statement that the French government intercepted the instructions sent by Vienna to the resident at Saint Petersburg, and that the publication of the documents opened the eyes of the British.

41. Reichskanzlei, "Vorträge an den Kaiser, 1733," Karton 38, 3 June 1733, SA; Messages 10 and 11 on 18 July, and messages on 22 and 25 July 1733, Cor. Pol., Autriche, vol. 176, AAE.

42. Braubach, *Prinz Eugen*, 5:261.

43. Elector Philip Karl to Emperor, 10 Aug. 1733. Quoted in *FE*, 19:17.

44. Quoted in *FE*, 19:12.

### CHAPTER FOUR

1. V. Gere, *Borba za Polskii Prestol v 1733 Godu* (Moscow, 1862), Prilozhenie, p. 18.

2. Ibid., p. 38. This Count Löwenwolde, active as chargé, is a younger brother of the Count Löwenwolde who was the Russian ambassador in Warsaw but who was at this time in Saint Petersburg.

3. *Recueil des traitez, manifestes, et autres pièces curieuses, concernant l'élection au Royaume de Pologne et la présente guerre* (Geneva, 1736), "Re-

25. Bussy to Minister, 14 Feb. 1733, Cor. Pol., Autriche, vol. 175, AAE; Bussy to Minister, 11 July 1733, ibid., vol. 176.

26. Bussy to Minister, 19 and 30 Sept. 1733, ibid., vol. 176.

27. Alfred Arneth, *Prinz Eugen von Savoyen*, 3 vols. (Vienna, 1858), 3:398–99.

28. Bussy to Minister, 21 Oct., 7 Nov. 1733, Cor. Pol., Autriche, vol. 176, AAE.

29. Bussy to Minister, 9 Sept. 1733, ibid.

30. Gere, *Borba za Polskii Prestol*, Prilozhenie, p. 28.

31. Reichskanzlei, "Vorträge an den Kaiser, 1733," Karton 38, 18 Sept. 1733, SA.

32. Chauvelin to Monti, 14 Mar. 1733, Mem. & Doc., Pologne, 14:161, AAE.

33. Monti to King, 15 May 1733, ibid., 15:42; Monti to Chauvelin, 5 June 1733, ibid., p. 134; Chauvelin to Chavigny, 28 June 1733, ibid., p. 241.

34. Stanislas to Du Bourg, 7 Feb., 5 Mar., 11 Mar. 1733, MS 6615, BA; Pierre Boyé, *Stanislas Leszczynski et la troisième traité de Vienne* (Paris, 1898), pp. 132–34; Monti to Chauvelin, 15 May 1733, Mem. & Doc., Pologne, 15:64, AAE.

35. Boyé, *Stanislas Leszczynski*, pp. 136–37.

36. Ibid., p. 139.

37. Details of the election by acclamation are from the messages of Monti to Chauvelin, 19 Sept. 1733, Mem. & Doc., Pologne, 16:321, AAE, and from Boyé, *Stanislas Leszczynski*, p. 144. Woodward, the British representative, agrees generally with this description although noting that many protested loudly against Stanislas and that groups known to be anti-Stanislas were placed away from the primate, who could not hear their protests (Woodward to Harrington, 14 Sept. 1733, State Papers, Poland, 88 42, PRO). But a private letter of Monti to a Cardinal Corsini indicates that the primate and Monti were well aware of the protests. "It was decided to name Stanislas king in spite of a notable schism and a considerable body who retired to Prag with a solemn protest several days before the election." The number opposed he believed to be six or seven thousand nobles. "In my modest opinion the election could not be more doubtful, having been against the specific protests of many of the nobility, and in a definite division during which it was not permitted the primate to name another person king, as he had repeatedly promised to do" (Monti to Cardinal Corsini, 12 Sept. 1733, Mem. & Doc., Pologne, 16:321 AAE).

38. Rousset de Missy, *Recueil historique*, 9:214.

sultat du conseil des Senateurs de Pologne, tenu à Varsovie 6, 7 févriei 1733," 1 : 3. Also see Gere, *Borba za Polskii Prestol*, Prilozhenie, p. 19.

4. Reichskanzlei, "Vorträge an den Kaiser, 1733," Karton 37, 27 Feb. 1733, SA; Gere, *Borba za Polskii Prestol*, Prilozhenie, p. 19.

5. L. Farges, ed. *Recueil des instructions données aux ambassadeurs et ministres de France, Pologne* (Paris, 1888), 5 : 2–20.

6. Mem. & Doc., Pologne, no. 14, p. 11, AAE.

7. Woodward to Harrington, 7, 14, 21 Feb. 1733, State Papers, Poland, 88 41, PRO; Harrington to Woodward, 13, 20 Mar. 1733, ibid.

8. RIO, 66 : 271.

9. Ibid., 66 : 186, 557; 67 : 16.

10. Ibid., 66 : 156. Under the later regime of Tsarina Elisabeth, Osterman was tried and condemned to be broken on the wheel and then beheaded. Muennich was to lose his hands first and then his head. Both were reprieved at the place of execution and were banished to the provinces, where they died. See R. Nisbet Bain, *The Daughter of Peter the Great* (New York, 1900), p. 62.

11. Magnan to Minister, 28 Feb. 1733, Cor. Pol., Russie, vol. 27, AAE.

12. Wilczek to Eugene, 27 Mar. 1733, Dipl. Cor. Pr. Eugene, fasc. 345, KA.

13. *Recueil des traitez*, 2 : 15. See also Cor. Pol., Autriche, vol. 174, doc. 366, AAE.

14. *Recueil des traitez*, 1 : 211, 18.

15. Rousset de Missy, ed., *Recueil historique*, 21 vols. (The Hague, 1728–55), 9 : 212–13.

16. *Recueil des traitez*, 2 : 43.

17. Ibid., p. 65.

18. Ibid., p. 67.

19. Ibid., p. 75.

20. Ibid., p. 100.

21. Villars, in Petitot, ed., *Collection des Mémoires rélatifs à l'histoire de France* (Paris, 1828), vol. 71, *Mémoires du Maréchal Villars*, p. 102; Cor. Pol., Autriche, vol. 175, doc. 137, AAE; Villars, *Mémoires*, ed. Petitot, 71 : 107.

22. Mem. & Doc., Russie, vol. 3, AAE. The memoir is not dated but since it contained instructions to Magnan, who returned in July 1733, it was presumably written before that time.

23. Gere, *Borba za Polskii Prestol*, Prilozhenie, pp. 1, 23.

24. Magnan to Minister, 11 Apr. 1733, Cor. Pol., Russie, vol. 27, AAE.

39. Reichskanzlei, "Vorträge an den Kaiser, 1733," Karton 38, 18 Sept. 1733, SA.

40. Gere, *Borba za Polskii Prestol*, Prilozhenie, p. 146.

41. Reichskanzlei, "Vorträge an den Kaiser, 1733," 18 Sept. 1733, SA.

42. Ibid., 25 Sept. 1733 briefing; St. Petersburg to Eugene, 3 October 1733, fasc. 345, KA.

43. Magnan to Minister, 10 Feb. 1733, Ministry to Magnan, 2 March 1733, Cor. Pol., Russie, vol. 27, AAE.

44. Magnan to Minister, 21 Mar., 28 Mar., 15 Apr., 21 Apr. 1733, ibid.

45. Magnan to Minister, 2 June 1733, ibid.

46. Magnan to Minister, 9, 20, 30 June 1733; Villardeau to Minister, 18 July, 29 Aug. 1733, all ibid.

47. Rousset de Missy, *Recueil historique*, 9:215; Rondeau to Harrington, 4 July 1733, RIO, 67:12.

48. Villardeau to Minister, 8 Aug. 1733, Cor. Pol., Russie, vol. 27, AAE. Villardeau notes that he is not being informed of the meetings between Rudomina and the Russian ministers. A few days later he wrote that he could act only as a consul and that he would relay whatever he was told by Rudomina. Villardeau to Monti, 27 Aug. 1733, ibid.

49. RIO, 67:53, 72.

50. Albert Vandal, *Une Ambassade française en Orient pour Louis XV: La Mission du Marquis de Villeneuve, 1728–1741* (Paris, 1887), p. 184. See also Arthur Hassal, *The Balance of Power, 1715–1739* (New York, 1903), pp. 95–98, for an assessment of the Turkish significance in the War of the Polish Succession.

51. Vandal, *Ambassade française*, pp. 200–213.

52. Gere, *Borba za Polskii Prestol*, Prilozhenie, pp. 59–61.

53. Villardeau to Minister, 3 Oct. 1733, Cor. Pol., Russie, vol. 27, AAE.

54. Villardeau to Monti, 14 July 1733, ibid.

55. Woodward to Harrington, 6 Oct. 1733, State Papers, Poland, 88 42, PRO.

56. M. P. Massuet, *Histoire de la Guerre présente* (Amsterdam, 1735), pp. 26–27; Gere, *Borba za Polskii Prestol*, Prilozhenie, p. 153.

57. The conditions are described in Massuet, *Histoire*, p. 24. Woodward's dispatches reflect the same conditions.

58. *FE*, 19:19.

59. Monti to King, 22 Sept. 1733, Mem. & Doc., Pologne, vol. 16, AAE.

60. Massuet, *Histoire*, p. 28.

61. Wilczek to Eugene, 2 Nov. 1733, Römisches Reich, fasc. 345, KA.

62. Wilczek to Eugene, 12 and 15 Nov. 1733, ibid.

63. King to Monti, Oct. 1733, Mem. & Doc., Pologne, 16:42, AAE.

CHAPTER FIVE

1. Michel Antoine, *Le Conseil du Roi sous le Règne de Louis XV* (Paris, 1970), p. 124. In a foreword on sources the author points out that no records show how council decisions were made. The files of the chancelier de France might have provided some of this information but they were destroyed during the Revolution.

2. Lee Kennett, *The French Armies during the Seven Years' War* (Durham, N.C., 1967), p. 4.

3. *Mémoires du Maréchal Villars*, ed. de Vogüe, 5 vols. (Paris, 1892), 5:407–20.

4. A1 2697, doc. 69, AG.

5. Villars, *Mémoires*, ed. de Vogüe, 5:426–27.

6. Belle Isle to Dangervilliers, 25 Aug. 1733, A1 2697, AG. The count of Belle Isle, later to become marshal duke of Belle Isle, was a grandson of the flamboyant minister of Louis XIV, Nicholas Fouquet. Belle Isle, at this time a lieutenant general, was well on his way to a spectacular career which would reach its zenith, and nadir, in the War of the Austrian Succession. Already we see evidence of his separate reporting to the ministry and other attempts to find favor for his projects at court.

7. Dangervilliers to Belle Isle, 1 Sept. 1733; Dangervilliers to Berwick, 10 Sept. 1733, both ibid.

8. Berwick to Dangervilliers, 28 Aug. 1733, ibid.

9. Berwick to Dangervilliers, 24 Sept. 1733; Dangervilliers to Berwick, 26 Sept. 1733, both ibid.

10. Berwick to Dangervilliers, 21 Aug. 1733, doc. 1 bis; Belle Isle to Dangervilliers, 22 Aug. 1733, both ibid.

11. *FE*, vol. 19, Suppl., p. 12.

12. Ibid., p. 39.

13. Ibid.

14. Ibid.

15. Ibid., pp. 45–46.

16. Ibid., pp. 40, 41.

17. Ibid., p. 43. Four reigning monarchs of states outside the Holy

Roman Empire were also sovereigns of states within the Empire—the kings of England, Sweden, Denmark, and Prussia.

18. Ibid.

19. Villars, *Mémoires,* ed. de Vogüe, 5:415.

20. Villars, *Mémoires,* ed. Petitot, 71:128–38.

21. A1 2697, doc. 181 bis, AG.

22. Ibid., doc. 68.

23. Ibid., doc. 78.

24. Dangervilliers to Berwick, 10 Sept. 1733; Berwick to Minister, 14 Sept. 1733, both ibid.

25. Dangervilliers to Belle Isle, 21 Sept. 1733, ibid; Berwick to Minister, 10 Oct. 1733, A1 2698, AG.

26. A1 2697, docs. 72, 116, 116 bis; Berwick to Minister, 20 Sept. 1733, A1 2697; Berwick to King, 8 Oct. 1733, A1 2698; A1 2699, doc. 23, all AG.

27. A1 2696, doc. 68, AG. Arneth, in *Prinz Eugen von Savoyen,* 3 vols. (Vienna, 1864), 3:383, states that election of the elector of Saxony as king of Poland was the signal for the war to begin.

28. A1 2696, docs. 68, 116; A1 2698, doc. 101, AG.

29. Berwick to Minister, 17 Oct. 1733, A1 2698, AG.

30. *FE,* 19:44–45. Pajol states flatly that in 1733 no contributions were levied, that the French paid for all taken. C. P. V. Pajol, *Les Guerres sous Louis XV,* 7 vols. (Paris, 1881), 1:184.

31. A1 2698, doc. 160, AG. The army intendant in Italy, in a detailed report of strengths, gave 685 as the establishment strength of most battalions and 160 as the number of riders per squadron. But total figures in numbers of men are notoriously difficult to establish and are usually suspect since organizations often fall far below normal strength for reasons that are not easily determined. Even the number of battalions before Kehl is somewhat in question since the detailed Austrian study gives 49 battalions and 71 squadrons as the French force with a total of 25,000 infantry and 8,000 riders, also an entirely reasonable figure. *FE,* 19:43.

32. Fürstenberg to Eugene, 13, 15 Oct. 1733, Dipl. Cor. Pr. Eugene, fasc. 345, KA.

33. Dangervilliers to Berwick, 28 Oct. 1733, A1 2696, AG. Fort Louis was about 30 kilometers downstream from Strasbourg with the principal defense works on an island in the Rhine. The site is no longer on the river.

34. Berwick to Minister from the Camp at Kehl, 20 Oct. 1733, A1 2696, AG.

35. Ibid., docs. 160, 162. According to the Austrian staff study, local people were forced to do the digging for the parallels around the fortress during the siege. After the French were in possession of the fortress and were themselves working to make it defensible again, the local German authorities at Baden-Durlach and Speyer were required to pay five sous daily for each Frenchman working. *FE*, 19:33, 52.

36. A1 2699, docs. 3, 6, AG.

37. Ibid., doc. 109, 29 Oct. 1733.

38. *FE*, 19:46–51.

39. "Journal de M. le Comte de Bavière pour la Campagne 1733," KA. This is a manuscript unpaginated diary. The author was the natural son of the elector of Bavaria. He had been legitimized and commanded Bavarian troops until 1713. Naturalized French in 1715, he had risen to the rank of brigadier in 1733. He was killed in the Battle of Laufeld in 1747.

40. A1 2699, doc. 129, AG.

41. Ibid., Berwick to King, 29 Oct. 1733; Du Bourg to Eugene, Dipl. Cor. Pr. Eugene, fasc. 345, KA.

42. From Berwick, 7 Sept. 1733, A1 2697, AG.

43. Belle Isle to Minister, 14 Oct. 1733, A1 2698. Also docs. 103, 113, and A1 2699, doc. 21, all AG.

44. A1 2699, docs. 66, 88, 157; A1 2700, doc. 3, all AG.

45. Lutteaux to Minister, 2 Jan. 1734, A1 2723, AG; *FE*, 19:42.

46. Ibid., pp. 14–15, 37.

47. *FE*, vol. 19, Suppl., p. 24. Eugene to Prince Friedrich von Württemberg, 7 Oct. 1733. Most of the messages from Eugene in this period are in German and obviously drafted by his staff. Letters he wrote with his own hand are usually in French. Arneth states that he never found so much as a single sentence in German among the thousands of written pages he left behind. Arneth, *Prinz Eugen*, 3:494.

48. *FE*, 19:27–28.

49. *FE*, vol. 19, Suppl., p. 25. French chargé Bussy in Vienna had been indignant at the attitude of the Austrian court during September. He found them "insolently happy" in that they felt they had dethroned Stanislas and at the same time protected the emperor from French attack by the use of Russian troops. Now, in later October, he reports that since the news of the siege of Kehl and the French-Sardinian alliance, the court has been unable to believe that France wants to make war, and that the king of Sardinia would dare to make a treaty against the emperor, and even to believe that Spain is against the emperor. Cor. Pol.,

Autriche, vol. 176, doc. 56, 30 Oct. 1733, doc. 74 bis, 21 Oct. 1733, AAE. Another court may also have misjudged the situation. The minister of the duke of Lorraine in Vienna was under the impression in August that the French had declared that they would not act against the emperor on the Rhine or anywhere else so long as his troops did not enter Poland. Jacquemin to the Duke, 15 Aug. 1733, Lothringischen Hausarchiv, doc. 178, SA.

50. Ibid., p. 25.

51. Ibid., p. 35; Berwick to Minister, 9 Nov. 1733, A1 2700, AG.

52. Cor. Pol., Bavière, doc. 84, 9 May 1733; doc. 100, Treaty Draft; doc. 107, Draft of Secret Articles, 8 Aug. 1733; doc. 169, Statement of Signature, 15 Nov. 1733, AAE. The French-Bavarian Treaty also appears in *FE*, 20:273.

53. Ibid., doc. 197.

54. Römisches Reich, fasc. 367, KA.

55. Arneth, *Prinz Eugen*, 3:397.

56. Fürstenberg to Eugene, 27 Nov. 1733, Gr. Kor. (Grosse Korrespondenz), 86a, SA.

57. *FE*, 19:100–103. See also vol. 19, Suppl., pp. 25–34; Arneth, *Prinz Eugen*, 3:388. The three accounts do not agree in all details notably in totals.

58. Fritz Redlich, *The German Military Enterpriser and His Work Force*, 2 vols. (Wiesbaden, 1964), 2:18.

59. Gunther Rothenberg. *The Austrian Military Border in Croatia, 1522–1747* (Urbana, Ill., 1960), pp. 110–11.

60. *FE*, vol. 19, Suppl., p. 43.

61. Ibid.

## CHAPTER SIX

1. *Mémoires du Maréchal Villars*, ed. de Vogüe, 5 vols. (Paris, 1892), 5:411.

2. Ministry to Fontanieu, 1 Sept. 1733, A1 2704, AG.

3. Docs. 16, 23, 24, ibid.

4. Ministry to Maillebois, 16 Oct. 1733; Maillebois in Grenoble to Ministry, 19 Oct. 1733, both ibid.

5. Memoir, doc. 48, 21 Oct. 1733, ibid.

6. D'Asfeld to Minister, 28 Oct. 1733; de Pezé to Minister, 30 Oct. 1733, both ibid.

7. D'Asfeld to Minister, 4 Nov. 1733, ibid. "Je suis bien mortifié,

Monseigneur, d'être obligé de vous rompre la tête," he began his tale of trouble.

8. From de Pezé at Turin, 17 Oct. 1733, ibid.

9. D'Asfeld to Minister, 31 Oct. 1733, ibid.; C. P. V. Pajol, *Les Guerres sous Louis XV,* 7 vols. (Paris, 1887), 1 : 337, quotes a letter of 12 Nov. 1733 from Dangervilliers to de Pezé: "The abandonment of Pavia, which you report, with its fortifications, abundant munitions of war, and three-battalion garrison, is an astonishing thing. It is still more surprising that they left the artillery in working order." According to the Austrian version of this there were 62 cannon left in Pavia and they were spiked. *FE,* 19 : 59.

10. Villars to King, 13 Nov. 1733, A1 2704, AG.

11. Fontanieu to Minister, 11 Nov. 1733, ibid.

12. Villars, *Mémoires,* ed. de Vogüe, 6 : 120.

13. *FE,* 19 : 63; Villars to King, 27 Nov. 1733, A1 2704, AG.

14. Quoted in Pajol, *Guerres,* 1 : 334. As to how much military detail fell under the cardinal's eye, there is an example from the period just after the suspension of hostilities in 1735. Dangervilliers wrote to Belle Isle as follows: "I read your two letters to the cardinal. He approved that Kaiserslautern and its dependencies remain under one command and under the department of Metz. You may regard this as definitely decided." 11 Nov. 1735, A1 2805, AG.

15. Quoted in *FE,* 19 : 63–64.

16. Ibid., pp. 63–73; Villars to King, 1 Dec. 1733, A1 2705, AG.

17. Quoted in Pajol, *Guerres,* 1 : 352.

18. Ibid., p. 346.

19. Villars, *Mémoires,* ed. de Vogüe, 6 : 122.

20. *FE,* 19 : 77.

21. Quoted in Pajol, *Guerres,* 1 : 353. Also see *FE,* 19 : 78.

22. Villars, *Mémoires,* ed. de Vogüe, 6 : 127.

23. FE, 19 : 78.

24. Vaulgrenant to Chauvelin, 4 Dec. 1733, A1 2705, AG.

25. Dangervilliers to Fontanieu, 29 Dec. 1733, ibid.

26. Pajol, *Guerres,* 1 : 336.

27. Message of the Marquis de l'Isle, 16 Dec. 1733, A1 2705, AG; Pajol, *Guerres,* 1 : 355.

28. Villars to Minister, 15 Dec. 1733, A1 2705, AG; letter to Louis quoted in Pajol, *Guerres,* 1 : 359.

29. Fontanieu to Minister, 16 Dec. 1733, A1 2705, AG ("The trenches were opened yesterday"); Marchant to Minister of War, 16 Dec. 1733, ibid.

30. *FE*, 19:80–83.

31. *FE*, 19:55–56.

32. Ibid., p. 57.

33. Quoted in Arneth, *Prinz Eugen*, 3:595.

34. Ibid., p. 389. "I have to this no more to add save to praise Your Lordship's careful zeal, your love for my service, and your steadfastness. Your Lordship carries on so that I and my house are always indebted, as I will always recognize. With your ideas, with which my own opinion is in complete agreement, we must go forward and Your Lordship must keep me constantly informed how things are progressing, where a delay occurs, and how it is to be removed."

35. *FE*, vol. 19, Suppl., p. 43; ibid., p. 52.

36. Ibid., p. 53. The discussion in the imperial staff regarding a possible attack on France from the Moselle or Meuse Valley may have leaked. Villars wrote to his king on 20 February 1734 that an informant thought that Eugene intended action on the Meuse. The minister of war answered this report a few days later with the observation that he did not think it very probable since a large number of French troops would be in the area by April. Villars to King, 20 Feb. 1734, A1 2752, AG; Minister to Villars, 27 Feb. 1734, ibid.

37. Reichskanzlei, "Vorträge an den Kaiser, 1733," Karton 39, 29 Dec. 1733, Protocoll dated 30 Dec. 1733, SA.

38. Paris (unsigned) to Eugene, 13 Nov. 1733, Dipl. Cor. Pr. Eugene, fasc. 345, KA.

39. Pajol, *Guerres*, 1:379.

40. Ibid., pp. 370–71.

41. Villars, *Mémoires*, ed. de Vogüe, 6:136–38.

42. Villars to King, 1, 2 Feb. 1734, A1 2752, AG.

43. Villars to Montemar, 1 Feb. 1734; Broglie to Minister, 2 Feb. 1734, both ibid.

44. Villars, *Mémoires*, ed. de Vogüe, 6:142; King to Villars, 15 Feb. 1734, A1 2752, AG.

45. Villars, *Mémoires*, ed. de Vogüe, 6:144; King to Villars, 23 Feb. 1734, A1 2752, AG.

46. Villars to Ministry, 4 Feb. 1734, A1 2752, AG; Villars to King, 9 Feb. 1734, ibid.

47. Fontanieu to Ministry, 26 Feb. 1734, ibid.

48. *FE*, 19:297–98.

49. Villars to King, 26 Feb. 1734, A1 2752, AG; King to Villars, 23 Feb. 1734, ibid.

50. Dangervilliers to Villars, 27 Feb. 1734. ibid.

51. Pajol, *Guerres,* 1:382.
52. Letters quoted ibid., p. 392.
53. Ibid., pp. 388–94, 397, 395.
54. Ibid., pp. 409, 410.
55. Ibid., p. 421.
56. *FE,* vol. 19, Suppl., p. 94. According to Arneth, attacks that rendered Mercy unfit for duty had twice occurred in earlier campaigns. *Prinz Eugen,* 3:442.
57. *FE,* vol. 19, Suppl., p. 99. Ludwig was one of three brothers, sons of the duke of Württemberg, who were active in the war. He had replaced his brother Friedrich as second-in-command in the Italian theater. He is considered to have been the most competent soldier of the three.
58. Ibid., p. 102.
59. "Nos sentinelles et celles de l'ennemi s'entretiennent, et même les officiers généraux, avec la plus grande politesse. Je compte bien les entretenir aussi." Coigny to Minister, 26 Apr. 1734, quoted in Pajol, *Guerres,* 1:432.
60. Ibid., pp. 435, 434.
61. *FE,* 19:315–17; Pajol, *Guerres,* 1:439.
62. Dipl. Cor. Pr. Eugene, fasc. 345, 21 Apr., 5 May 1734, KA.
63. Claude C. Sturgill, *Marshal Villars and the War of the Spanish Succession* (Lexington, Ky., 1965), pp. 10, 127–38.
64. Quoted in Pajol, *Guerres,* 1:442; Villars to Minister, 5 June 1734, A1 2755, AG.

CHAPTER SEVEN

1. E. J. B. Rathery, *Le Comte de Plélo* (Paris, 1876). This volume contains material on the early life of Plélo as well as on his subsequent public career.
2. Rathery, *Plélo,* p. 64.
3. Ibid., pp. 84, 129. Duguay-Trouin was a brilliant French naval-commander who had some notable victories over the English in the War of the Spanish Succession.
4. A. Geffroy, ed., *Recueil des instructions données aux ambassadeurs et ministres de France* (Paris, 1895), vol. 13, *Danemark,* pp. 129–43; Plélo to Monti, 24 Feb. 1733, Cor. Pol., Danemark, jan-août, 1733, AAE; Minister to Plélo, 19 Mar. 1733, ibid.
5. Plélo to King, 19 May 1733, Cor. Pol., Danemark, jan-août, 1733,

AAE (see also Ministry to Plélo, 22 Mar.; Plélo to Ministry, 31 Mar.; Plélo to King, 14, 21 Apr., 12 May); Plélo to King, 12 May, 1733, ibid.

6. King to Plélo, 12 May 1733, ibid.

7. 13 July 1733, Danish document signed by Schulin, ibid.

8. Rathery, *Plélo*, p. 198.

9. Plélo to Minister, 18 Aug. 1733, Cor. Pol., Danemark, vol. 95, AAE.

10. Minister to Plélo, 27 Aug., 3 Sept. 1733; Plélo to Minister, 8 Sept. 1733, all ibid.

11. Plélo to Minister, 19, 22 Sept. 1733; Plélo to King, 29 Sept. 1733, all ibid.

12. Plélo to Minister, 29 Sept. 1733; Plélo to Minister, 8 Oct.; Plélo to Monti, 9 Oct. 1733, all ibid.

13. Plélo to King, 13 Oct. 1733; Plélo to Minister, 13 Oct. 1733; Plélo to King, undated, all ibid.

14. Minister to Plélo, 8 Nov. 1733; Plélo to Monti, 24 Oct. 1733, both ibid.

15. RIO, vol. 67, Forbes to Harrington, 28 July 1733; ibid., Harrington to Forbes, 11 Sept., 19 Oct. 1733.

16. Plélo to Minister, doc. 160, late Oct. 1733, Cor. Pol., Danemark, vol. 95, AAE; Plélo to Minister, 3 Nov. 1733, ibid.

17. Memoir, 10 Nov. 1733, ibid.

18. Minister to Plélo, 3 Dec. 1733, ibid.

19. Rathery, *Plélo*, pp. 212–13; Plélo to Minister, 24 Nov. 1733, Cor. Pol., Danemark, vol. 95, AAE.

20. Minister to Plélo, 16 Dec. 1733, ibid.

21. Casteja to Minister, 9 Dec. 1733, ibid.

22. Plélo to Minister, 9 Dec. 1733, Cor. Pol., Danemark, vol. 102, AAE. Also see Rathery, *Plélo*, p. 224.

23. Quoted in Pierre Boyé, *Stanislas Leszczynski et la troisième traité de Vienne* (Paris, 1898), pp. 166–67.

24. Ibid., pp. 166–77.

25. Ibid., pp. 91–93.

26. Cited in ibid., p. 184.

27. Ibid., pp. 199–200; 15 Dec. message quoted in C. P. V. Pajol, *Les Guerres sous Louis XV*, 7 vols. (Paris, 1881), 1 : 173.

28. Boyé, *Stanislas Leszczynski*, p. 208.

29. RIO, vol. 67, Forbes to Harrington, 6 Feb. 1734.

30. C. H. Manstein, *Memoirs of Russia from 1727 to 1744* (London, 1770), p. 71. These memoirs are probably accurate. Manstein believed

that Lacy had only 12,000 troops. But Manstein was then in the service of the king of Prussia and did not join the Russian army until 1736; he was thus probably not a firsthand witness for the Danzig actions.

31. Quoted in Boyé, *Stanislas Leszczynski,* p. 214.

32. Ibid., p. 214. Also see M. P. Massuet, *Histoire de la Guerre présente* (Amsterdam, 1735), pp. 152–63. British resident Kenworthy reported from Danzig that on 20 March the Russians lost 400 men but were thereafter masters of the suburbs and all land approaches to the city. State Papers, Poland, 88 43, 24 Mar. 1734, PRO.

33. The king of Prussia was already defending his diplomatic position with the French in a note of 10 January 1734. His reasoning was that he preserved an exact neutrality by according a right of passage to both parties. Thus, the troops of Stanislas might use Prussian territory as the Russians had done. Cor. Pol., Prusse, vol. 97, 1734, AAE.

34. RIO, vol. 67, Forbes to Harrington, 24 Apr. 1734. Kenworthy in Danzig reported that the bombardment as of 24 April was not very effective, having killed 4 or 5 people and breaking many roof tiles. He was grateful that Marshal Muennich was "generous to leave our trade [presumably English] unmolested," and said that if he knew where "our houses" were he would avoid bombarding them. State Papers, Poland, 88 43, 24 Apr. 1734, PRO.

35. Massuet, *Guerre présente,* p. 143; Boyé, *Stanislas Leszczynski,* p. 218.

36. Manstein, *Memoirs,* p. 73; RIO, vol. 67, Forbes to Harrington, 6 Feb. 1734, p. 169; State papers, Poland, 88 43, Woodward to Harrington, 13 Mar. 1734, PRO.

37. André Corvisier, *Armées et sociétés en Europe de 1494 à 1789* (Paris, 1976), pp. 100–101.

38. RIO, vol. 67, Forbes to Harrington, 3 Apr. 1734, p. 187; 1 May 1734, p. 205; 15 May 1734, p. 212.

39. Quoted in Boyé, *Stanislas Leszczynski,* p. 224. Boyé found this document in the archives in Danzig.

40. Plélo to Minister, 27 Mar. 1734, Cor. Pol., Danemark, vol. 102, AAE.; Des Angles to Ministry, 7 Apr. 1734, A1 2745, AG.

41. Segent to Minister, 4 May 1734, ibid. The importance of the position of *commissaire* is reflected in Segent's possession of the letters of credit for the expedition and his acceptance of responsibility for surrendering them to Plélo. Lee Kennett in the *French Armies in the Seven Years' War* (Durham, N.C., 1967), p. 34, speaks of the role of the civil functionaries as creating a system very close to dual command with the military leaders.

42. Jules Chérias, *Histoire du Général La Motte de la Peyrouse* (Gap, 1842), p. 365. Chérias also points out that in 1673, at the age of six, La Motte was made a lieutenant in his father's company, and from 1682 took part in actions. By the age of eighteen he had twelve years of military service and his own company (pp. 7–9). Thus in 1734 he could claim sixty years of military service!

43. Boencourt, *Voyage de Troupes françaises en Pologne*, p. 13. The chevalier de Boencourt was an ensign in the Blaisois regiment and a survivor of the expedition. The edition consulted was printed in Edinburgh in 1831 under the title *A Narrative of the French Expedition to Danzig in 1734.*

44. Fritz Redlich, *The German Military Enterpriser and His Work Force,* 2 vols. (Wiesbaden, 1964), 2:133.

45. Plélo to Minister, 24 Apr. 1734, Cor. Pol., Danemark, vol. 102, AAE.

46. Plélo to Minister, 1 May 1734, ibid.

47. La Motte to Minister, 4 May 1734, A1 2745, AG.

48. Segent later tried to explain away the return to Copenhagen as a move to join with the forces that were following so that a return to Danzig in greater force could be made. Segent to Ministry, 25 May 1734, A1 2745, AG. The council of war is mentioned in Boencourt, *Voyage,* p. 20.

49. Plélo to Minister, 18, 19 May, Plélo to King, 20 May 1734; Plélo to Chauvelin, 20 May 1734, Cor. Pol., Danemark, vol. 102, AAE.

50. Baraillh to Maurepas, 20 May 1734, ibid.

51. La Motte to Minister, 28 May 1734, A1 2745, AG; La Motte to Minister, 25 May 1734, ibid. Chérias (*Général La Motte,* p. 383) adds that La Motte was suspicious of the Swedish commander of the fort, Baron Stackelberg, who had not furnished landing craft or the promised shelter.

52. Many of Monti's letters were found by Boyé only in the Czartoryski Archives in Cracow. Monti's order, which was received by the French on 26 May, is mentioned in Boyé, *Stanislas Leszczynski,* pp. 230–31.

53. La Motte to Ministry, 28 May 1734, A1 2745, AG.

54. Doc. 237, A1 2745, AG; La Motte to Ministry, 28 May 1734, ibid.

55. Ibid. Copy of a letter written by La Luzerne from the fort at the mouth of the Vistula to his brother, 31 May 1734.

56. The marquis d'Argenson, later to become French foreign minister, was a personal friend of Plélo. He believed that Plélo was overex-

cited by the events and may have been killed by his own men to stop the attack. *Journal et Mémoires du Marquis d'Argenson,* ed. Rathery, 4 vols. (Paris, 1859), 1 : 192–95. In a footnote in Boencourt (*Voyage,* p. 27) it is asserted that three Frenchmen whom Plélo had brought with him in spite of La Motte put out that French troops killed Plélo, but the author notes that these "adventurers" were not seen in combat. An account of the battle by Stackelberg, given in a letter by Malbran, Plélo's successor in Copenhagen, states that Plélo's body was pierced by a bayonet and his head by a bullet. But Stackelberg asserts that they were only charging and firing during the attack. Malbran La Noue to Ministry, 8 June 1734, Cor. Pol., Danemark, vol. 102, AAE.

57. At this time the Scottish Jacobite, Admiral Gordon, was in command of the Russian fleet. He told Rondeau in confidence that he was to sail toward Danzig on 26 May, weather permitting, and attack the French fleet if he had any chance of success. There were to be fourteen ships of the line, six frigates, one fireship, and two bomb ketches. But Rondeau wrote, "they are not the best seamen and his officers are but very indifferent." RIO, vol. 67, Rondeau to Harrington, 22 May 1734, p. 215.

58. La Motte to Ministry, 28 May, 1, 3, 11 June 1734, A1 2746, AG.

59. Chauvelin to Plélo, 29 May 1734, Cor. Pol., Danemark, vol. 102, AAE; Ministry to Malbran, 14 June 1734, ibid.

60. Segent to Ministry, 28 May 1734, A1 2745, AG. Rathery asserts that the interlineations are those of Dangervilliers. (*Plélo,* p. 291). I am less certain, since other unquestioned handwriting of Dangervilliers appears different in shape. Moreover, Rathery does not quote the interlined passage precisely.

61. Both Chauvelin and Maurepas wrote to Malbran to caution him not to permit the five transports to pass Copenhagen unless escorted by vessels of war. Maurepas to Malbran, 20 June 1734, Cor. Pol., Danemark, vol. 102, AAE; Chauvelin to Malbran, 20 June 1734, ibid.

62. Malbran to Ministry, 26 June 1734; Maurepas to Malbran, 11 July 1734; both ibid.

63. Monti to La Motte, 10, 18 June 1734, A1 2746, AG; La Motte to Monti, 11, 16 June 1734, ibid. The exchange between Monti and La Motte is also given in Rousset de Missy, *Recueil Historique,* 21 vols. (The Hague, 1728–55), 9 : 495–512.

64. A1 2746, doc. 49, AG; Muennich to La Motte, 19 June 1734, ibid.; Stanislas to La Motte, 20 June 1734, ibid.; doc. 58 bis, response of La Motte, ibid.

65. Doc. 64, 22 June 1734, ibid. is a copy of the *plein pouvoirs* of La

Motte. Doc. 73 contains the requests of the French forces. The details of the last days of the expedition and the story of their imprisonment and eventual return is given in Chérias, *Général La Motte*.

66. See Chérias, *Général La Motte*, 442–52; Boencourt, *Voyage*, pp. 40–78.

67. Gr. Kor., fasc. 91a, SA. According to the document these terms were sent to Muennich. Presumably the document did not originate with the Austrian representative in Berlin, Seckendorff, since it mentions that he had been informed.

68. *FE*, vol. 19, Suppl., p. 107.

69. RIO, vol. 67, p. 207.

70. Dipl. Cor. Pr. Eugene, fasc. 345, doc. 0330–0333, KA. One such letter, accepting the elector of Saxony as king, was signed by Andreas Zaluski, the bishop of Plock; Casimir Czartoryski, Castellan of Vilna; Stanislas Poniatowski, the palatin of Warsaw; and forty others. Wratislaw in Dresden reported to Eugene on 9 July the fall of Danzig and stated that Monti was delivered up by the citizens. Ibid., doc. 0352.

71. Boyé notes several accounts of the escape of Stanislas which appeared in subsequent years. One was edited by Solignac, Stanislas's literary aide, who shared the Danzig siege with him. Boyé, *Stanislas Leszczynski*, pp. 243–44. Another account is in the Bibliothèque de l'Arsénal in Paris as MS 4143, designated as a letter of King Stanislas to one of his friends.

72. RIO, vol. 67, Rondeau to Harrington, 4 Sept. 1734, p. 270.

73. Rousset de Missy, *Recueil Historique*, 9:464–69.

74. Boyé, *Stanislas Leszczynski*, p. 292.

75. Rondeau was kept informed of the events in Poland. He reported the defeat of Tarlo at Lublin and learned that the primate had sent a very submissive letter to the tsarina and had submitted to Augustus III. RIO, vol. 67, Rondeau to Harrington, 30 Apr. 1735, p. 391, 30 July 1735, p. 420.

76. Boyé, *Stanislas Leszczynski*, p. 547.

### CHAPTER EIGHT

1. *Journal du siège de Philippsburg* (The Hague, 1734). See also Pajol, *Guerres*, 1:200) for French consideration of alternative plans in early 1734.

2. A1 2745, docs. 15, 16, AG.

3. Berwick to Belle Isle, 3 Apr. 1734; Chetardie to Belle Isle, 3 Apr. 1734, both ibid.

4. Doc. 39, 12 Apr. 1734, ibid.

5. *Journal du siège.*

6. Berwick to Belle Isle, 15 Apr. 1734, AG; Noailles to Belle Isle, 18 Apr. 1734; Berwick to Belle Isle, 20 Apr. 1734, both ibid.

7. Dangervilliers to Belle Isle, 6 Apr. 1734, ibid.

8. Berwick to Belle Isle, 6 Apr. 1734, ibid.

9. Lee Kennett, *The French Armies in the Seven Years' War* (Durham, N.C., 1967), p. 6.

10. Dangervilliers to Belle Isle, undated, and 18 Apr. 1734, A1 2745, AG; Dangervilliers to Belle Isle, 14 Apr. 1734, ibid.

11. *FE*, 19:167–68; *Journal du siège.*

12. Berwick to Belle Isle, 23 Apr. 1734, A1 2745, AG; Chauvelin to Belle Isle, 6 May 1734; Fleury to Belle Isle, 17 May 1734, both ibid.

13. Berwick to Belle Isle, 6, 11 May, both ibid.

14. Doc. 66, 17 Apr. 1734, ibid; letter from Belle Isle to Botzheim, 29 Apr. 1734, is mentioned in *FE*, 19:169; Belle Isle to elector of Trier, 3 May 1734, A1 2746, AG.

15. Dipl. Cor. Pr. Eugene, fasc. 376, doc. 249, KA. Undated and country unidentified.

16. Römisches Reich, fasc. 363, June 1734, KA.

17. *Journal du siège;* Folard to Belle Isle, 9 May 1734, A1 2745, AG.

18. De Prié to Eugene, 25 Apr. 1734, Dipl. Cor. Pr. Eugene, fasc. 345; *FE*, vol 19, Suppl., p. 117.

19. Noailles to Belle Isle, 23 Apr. 1734, A1 2745, AG; Berwick to Minister, 1 May 1734, ibid.

20. Ibid., doc. 111; Preface to A1 2730, AG; For Eugene's estimate see *FE*, vol 19, Suppl., p. 132.

21. See Josef Fresin, "Kriegerische Operationen an den Ettlinger Linien," in *Ettlingen einst und jetzt* (Ettlingen, 1927), pp. 41–45.

22. Doc. 106, 13 Jan. 1734, A1 2723, AG; *FE*, 19:181.

23. *FE*, vol. 19, Suppl., pp. 103–6.

24. Ibid., p. 179; quotation in *FE*, 19:180, from a 9 May message to the imperial representatives.

25. *FE*, vol. 19, Suppl., pp. 114–17.

26. Ibid., ppl 181, 185.

27. Noailles to Minister, from Graben, 8 May 1734, A1 2745, AG.

28. Doc. 188, "Journal du Premier Mai au 5. 1734," ibid.

29. Dangervilliers to Comte de Saxe, 19 May; Fleury to Comte de Saxe, 22 May 1734, both ibid.

30. Comte de Bavière, "Journal de M. le Comte de Bavière pour la campagne, 1733," KA.

31. *FE*, vol. 19, Suppl., p. 136.

32. Ibid., p. 124.

33. Quoted in *FE*, 19:191.

34. Ibid., Suppl., p. 128.

35. Comte de Bavière, "Journal," KA; d'Asfeld to Minister, 12 May 1734, A1 2728, AG.

36. *FE*, vol. 19, Suppl., p. 160; second letter quoted in Arneth, *Prinz Eugen*, 3:414.

37. Berwick to Belle Isle, 9, 13 May 1734, A1 2745, AG; The Austrian staff study comments (*FE*, 19:205) that the reason why the French did not use their superiority was "a name, a single name, an old man in the imperial camp who had taught them to tremble before him when he stood at the head of an army; even if it was not half so strong as the French, he was still the feared Eugene." Perhaps Berwick was less concerned when he stated to his minister that the enemy troops were in flight with Eugene at their head. Berwick to Minister, 10 May 1734, A1 2728, AG.

38. Berwick to Minister, 5 May, Berwick to King, 12 May 1734, A1 2728, AG; *Mémoires du Duc de Noailles*, vol. 73 in *Collection des mémoires rélatifs a l'histoire de France*, ed. Petitot (Paris, 1878), p. 209; Minister to Berwick, 11 May 1734, A1 2728, AG.

39. *FE*, vol. 19, Suppl., Eugene to Emperor, 1 May 1734.

40. Arneth, *Prinz Eugen*, 3:415, contains a paraphrase of the 27 May message to the emperor.

41. *FE*, 19:213–15.

42. Noailles to Minister, 8 June 1734, A1 2730, AG; Dangervilliers to Berwick, 8 June 1734, ibid.; *FE*, vol. 19, Suppl., p. 186.

43. *FE*, vol. 19, Suppl., p. 205.

44. Berwick to Minister, 9 June 1734, A1 2730, AG.

45. Christopher Duffy, *Fire and Stone: The Science of Fortress Warfare, 1660–1860* (New York, 1975), p. 130.

46. Mörner to Eugene, 14 June 1734, Römisches Reich, fasc. 367, KA. Some idea of the speed of these movements may be derived from the march plan of the Royal Prussian Horse and Foot Regiment from Magdeburg and Halle to Heilbronn, a distance of about 230 miles airline. It was in four columns and took eighteen days, with the four columns coming together in Heilbronn. Römisches Reich, fasc. 366, doc. 13/1560, KA.

47. Noailles to Minister, 7 July 1734, A1 2732, AG.

48. Arneth, *Prinz Eugen*, 3:418; *FE*, 19:149; Pajol, *Guerres*, 1:212.

49. *FE*, 19:189. Quoted in footnote.

50. *FE*, vol. 19, Suppl., p. 187. Seckendorff in a private letter later in the year explained the hesitation and failure at Philippsburg, stressing that the army was not the fighting force of earlier years. "A disorderly crowd of undisciplined farmers' sons and foreign deserters filled the ranks." Quoted in *FE*, 19:238.

51. Alfred Vagts, *A History of Militarism* (New York, 1959), p. 56.

52. Kennett notes that during months of bibliographical work and a year of archival work for his study of French forces in the Seven Years' War he did not find one letter from a common soldier. *French Armies*, p. 86.

53. *FE*, 19:218. During the siege an Austrian officer's servant deserted to the enemy with the officer's horse. A "tambour" was sent to the enemy camp to ask for a return of the horse. Four French prisoners were offered in exchange and this was accepted. "Verteidigung der Festung Philippsburg im Jahre 1734," in *Strefflers Oestreichische Militärische Zeitschrift* (Wien, 1896), pp. 277–310. With regard to the value of soldiers by rank, a treaty in the Austrian files for 1734 dealing with the matter of prisoner exchange puts the following money values by rank, (Römisches Reich, fasc. 367, doc. 13/390, KA): Marshal—25,000 florins; Maréchal de camp—1,500; Colonel of infantry—600; Lieutenant—24; Sergeant—10; Soldier (fusilier)—4.

54. Friedrich Heer, *The Holy Roman Empire* (New York, 1968), p. 242.

55. Quoted in *FE*, 19:237.

56. Römisches Reich, fasc. 363, KA; De Brou to Minister, 1 July 1734 and messages of 2 July 1734, A1 2732, AG.

57. Du Bourg to Minister, 3 July 1734, A1 2732, AG.

58. Ibid., Report from d'Asfeld, 15 July 1734.

59. *FE*, 19:244–48; Comte de Bavière, "Journal."

60. Arneth, *Prinz Eugen*, pp. 428–34.

61. *FE*, vol. 19, Suppl., p. 211.

62. Schmettau Memoir, 23 July 1734, Römisches Reich, fasc. 363, KA. Also see Arneth, Prinz Eugen, 3:235–36.

63. D'Asfeld to Dangervilliers, 27 July 1734, A1 2733, AG.

64. Noailles, *Mémoires*, ed. Petitot, 71:214–18. Noailles continued his criticism in correspondence with Dangervilliers, finally working up to the statement on 9 September that he could not serve under d'Asfeld after this campaign.

65. Dangervilliers to d'Asfeld, 25 July 1734, A1 2733, AG; d'Asfeld to Dangervilliers, 1 Aug. 1734, ibid.

## CHAPTER NINE

1. *FE*, 19:320.
2. Ibid.
3. *FE*, vol. 19, Suppl., p. 93. This decision is also reflected in the message of the Court War Council to the emperor. *FE*, 19:321.
4. Arneth, *Prinz Eugen*, 3:447.
5. W. N. Hargreaves-Mawdsley, ed., *Spain under the Bourbons, 1700–1833* (Columbia, S.C., 1973), p. 100.
6. *FE*, 19:451.
7. Ibid., p. 325; Arneth, *Prinz Eugen*, 3:445.
8. Minister to Villars, 1 June 1734, A1 2755, AG; Minister to Coigny, 1 June 1734; Minister to Broglie, 1 June 1734, both ibid.
9. Coigny to Minister, 2 June 1734, ibid.
10. Coigny to Minister, 5, 7 June; King to Coigny, 5 June, all ibid.
11. Minister to Coigny, 5 June 1734, ibid.
12. Coigny to Minister, 18 June 1734, ibid.
13. Minister to Coigny, 8 June 1734, ibid. Coigny to Minister, 18 June 1734, ibid; Pajol, *Guerres*, 1:474.
14. *FE*, 19:340–41; daily news report from Fontanieu, 1 July 1734, A1 2755, AG. See also Pajol, *Guerres*, 1:479.
15. Coigny to King, 30 June 1734, A1 2755, AG. There are discrepancies in the reporting of the battle. The 30 June report of Coigny is the confident report of a general who has won a battle. He does not mention that there was a midnight council of war to decide what to do but implies that he and Broglie made their own reconnaissance and their own decisions. He says that at midnight on 29 June the imperials admitted their defeat and withdrew in order. But according to a French officer who was present in the action, when the two armies were camped on the battlefield a false round of firing wakened and startled the imperial soldiers who thought an attack was coming. Their flight could not be stopped by their officers, who were forced to abandon camp. Count F. F. d'Espie, *Mémoires de la guerre d'Italie, depuis l'année 1733 jusqu'en 1736* (Paris, 1777), pp. 180–86. I cannot find the message of Coigny prematurely admitting defeat which is noted by Pajol (*Guerres*, 1:479). The Austrian account of the battle is in *FE*, 19:345–55.
16. *FE*, 19:355; Pajol, *Guerres*, 1:479.
17. Fontanieu, the French intendant, in a letter of 29 July discussed whether Mercy was acting in accordance with the emperor's orders at the moment of attack and mentions a report that Mercy had shown a

letter from the emperor to his council of war to force them to agree to an attack. Or was it, Fontanieu suggests, that Mercy, knowing that Königsegg was to relieve him, ordered the attack to avoid sharing the glory with him? Pajol, *Guerres,* 1:492.

18. Coigny to Minister, 5, 13 July 1734, A1 2755, AG. Kennett states that in the Seven Years' War the French scorned the portable field ovens developed by the Prussians and Austrians and continued to build their stationary ovens, which sometimes took two weeks to build, and kept them within a five-day march. *The French Armies in the Seven Years' War* (Durham, N.C., 1967), p. 110.

19. *FE,* 19:356.

20. Ibid., p. 361. See also Minister to Coigny, 21 July 1734, A1 2755, AG. The letter from Cardinal Fleury (quoted in Pajol, *Guerres,* 1:494, 498) is a masterpiece of firmness couched in polite and delicate terms. Coigny reported that the king of Sardinia read the letter in a conference but continued to stall.

21. *FE,* 19:365; Königsegg to Eugene, 4 Aug. 1734, Italien 1734, 358/VIII, KA.

22. *FE,* 19:365.

23. Königsegg to Eugene, 20 Aug. 1734, Italien 1734, 358/VIII, KA.

24. Quoted in Arneth, *Prinz Eugen,* 3:446.

25. Königsegg to Eugene, 10 Sept. 1734, Italien 1734, 358/VIII, KA.

26. Memo from the French ambassador to king of Sardinia, 3 Sept. 1734, A1 2758, AG.

27. Minister to Coigny, 10 Sept., 1734, ibid.

28. Königsegg to Emperor, 15 Sept. 1734, Italien 1734, 358/VIII, KA.

29. Coigny to Minister, 17 Sept. 1734, A1 2758, AG.

30. Coigny to Minister, 19 Sept. 1734, ibid.

31. Minister to Coigny, 28 Sept. 1734, ibid.; Dangervilliers to Broglie, quoted in Pajol, *Guerres,* 1:269, 521.

32. Pajol, *Guerres,* p. 521.

33. 26 Sept. Report of Losses, 30 Sept. Report of Austrian Losses via the French Chargé at Ferrara, A1 2758, AG.

34. Königsegg at Borgoforte to Eugene, 29 Sept. 1734, Italien 1734, 358/VIII, KA.

35. Arneth, *Prinz Eugen,* 3:446; Königsegg to Eugene, 7 Oct. 1734, Italien 1734, 358/VIII, KA. The emperor's comments on this communication are in Arneth, *Prinz Eugen,* 3:605. The 4,000 prisoners

mentioned by Königsegg were not reported by Coigny in the latter's message of the seventeenth. Some were doubtless included in the two Piedmontese battalions Coigny referred to at the end of his report.

Field Marshal Prince Hildburghausen was with the Austrian forces in Italy. The following comments on the battle are from his papers. "The first mistake made on that day, in my opinion, was the lack of foresight and support needed for such an enterprise. The reconnaissance was faulty. The enemy was surprised, but not as he would have been if we had arrived a half-hour earlier, at least before dawn. Dispositions had to be made on the spot; no one had orders what to do. The most unpardonable mistake was that after the whole corps had crossed and the enemy in complete rout and our army approaching Quistello, we did not have M. Waltech cross with his battalions of the second line which were along the Secchia from Quistello to Bocca and with whose cavalry we should have taken all the garrison of Quistello without a cat being able to save himself. It was there that we missed the decisive stroke." Italien 1734, 358/VIII, doc. 20, KA.

36. Königsegg to Eugene, 29 Oct., 23 Nov. 1734, ibid.

37. Quoted in Arneth, *Prinz Eugen*, 3:449.

38. Ibid.

39. Ibid., pp. 453–54.

40. Ibid., pp. 456–59.

41. John (Lord) Henry, *Memoirs of the Reign of George the Second*, 2 vols. (London, 1848), 1:398.

42. *FE*, 20:39.

43. Pajol, *Guerres*, 1:273. This was quite successful, incidentally. The French continued to watch these boats and report on them.

44. *FE*, 20:43–44.

45. Arneth, *Prinz Eugen*, 3:453.

46. *FE*, 20:55.

47. *FE*, vol. 20, Suppl., p. 21.

48. Arneth, *Prinz Eugen*, 3:462.

49. *FE*, vol. 20, Suppl., p. 30.

50. Ibid.

51. Du Bourg to Minister, 2 Apr. 1735, A1 2785, AG.

52. *FE*, vol. 20, Suppl., p. 37.

53. Ibid., p. 43.

54. Pajol, *Guerres*, 1:275, 276.

55. Ibid., pp. 288–90.

56. Königsegg in Vienna commented to Robinson that additional forces in Eugene's army on the Rhine would be useless, since one army

had only to cross the Rhine in order to force the other army which had crossed it to return. Robinson to Harrington, 26 Aug. 1735, State Papers, Austria, 80 118, PRO.

57. Quoted in Arneth, *Prinz Eugen*, 3:464.

58. Ibid., pp. 464–67.

59. There had also been discussions on sending Russian troops to help the emperor in Italy. According to the British ambassador, Osterman had opposed this, telling the tsarina that her troops would perish in Italy where they could not have "black bread, beer or brandy, without which the Russian soldiers cannot live." RIO, vol. 67, Rondeau to Harrington, 21 Sept. 1734, p. 281.

60. *FE*, vol. 20, Suppl., p. 122.

61. The emperor's reasons for discounting the possibility of a Bavarian attack came from an intercepted communication from Bavarian Minister Törring to Grimbergen, French ambassador in Munich, on 9 July 1735. Emperor to Eugene, 25 July 1735, Gr. Kor., 91b, SA.

62. Quoted in Arneth, *Prinz Eugen*, 3:471.

63. Pajol, *Guerres*, 1:301. Pajol says these instructions came on 26 Aug. 1735. Direct French-Austrian negotiations were under way by this time.

64. Ibid., p. 302. Coigny's response was dated 30 August. Something of the excessive number of high-ranking officers in the French army is revealed in his message. There were 27 lieutenant generals, 30 maréchaux de camp, 64 brigadier generals as of 1 September; all of this for an army of roughly 100,000.

65. *FE*, 20:123, 125; ibid., Suppl., p. 221.

66. *F*,. 20:140. The Russians were used on 16 September in an unsuccessful diversionary attack against a redoubt near Worms.

67. Pajol, *Guerres*, 1:303. Although Belle Isle did not move his army toward the Moselle until the first of October, the commander of the imperial forces in Luxembourg had heard for some time that Belle Isle would soon be sent to Trier. Thungen to Eugene, 29 Sept. 1735, Römisches Reich, 345, doc. 0540, KA.

69. Pajol, *Guerres*, 1:309–22; *FE*, 20:152–63.

69. Pajol, *Guerres*, 1:322.

70. Ibid., 1:283, 288.

71. A1 2825, AG, contains letters of complaint from several areas, notably the Palatinate. On 25 July 1735 Cardinal Fleury wrote the Duchesse de Deux Ponts regretting the taking of forage by the French army and promising restitution.

72. *FE*, vol. 20, Suppl., pp. 122, 123, 126.

73. Pajol, *Guerres*, 1 : 549–50.

74. According to the Noailles memoirs, Villars and the king of Sardinia barely avoided a clash, which was described in a letter from Fleury to Noailles on 10 July 1734. *Mémoires du Duc de Noailles*, vol. 73 in *Collection des Mémoires rélatif a l'histoire de France*, ed. Petitot (Paris, 1829), p. 231. The Noailles memoirs were actually written by an Abbé Millot who had access to his papers.

75. Noailles, *Mémoires*, 73 : 218–19, 223–25. On Noailles's problems in Germany see *Journal du siège de Philippsburg* (The Hague, 1734), a 9 September letter from Noailles at the camp of Offenburg. The Marquis d'Argenson, an informed observer and a friend of Noailles, noted in his memoirs that he had learned of the "disgrace of Marshal Noailles, accused of having failed in his duty in the Heilbronn affair. But on his return he justified himself so well that he disgraced M. d'Asfeld." *Journal et Mémoires du Marquis d'Argenson*, ed. E. J. B. Rathery, 4 vols. (Paris, 1859), 1 : 209.

76. Noailles, *Mémoires*, 73 : 229.

77. Pajol, *Guerres*, 1 : 559. Reports of sickness continued throughout the winter.

78. Noailles, *Mémoires*, 73 : 237.

79. Ibid., pp. 238–40.

80. Ibid., p. 234; Pajol, *Guerres*, 1 : 561.

81. Pajol, *Guerres*, 1 : 565, 566.

82. Noailles, *Mémoires*, 71 : 243, 249, 255; Pajol, *Guerres*, 1 : 589, 571.

83. Noailles, *Mémoires*, 71 : 259; Dangervilliers quotation in Pajol, *Guerres*, 1 : 604; Noailles to Minister, 14 Oct. 1735, A1 2817, AG.

### CHAPTER TEN

1. Max Brauback, *Prinz Eugen von Savoyen*, 5 vols. (Munich, 1963–65), 5 : 292.

2. Quoted in Arneth, *Prinz Eugen*, 3 : 606.

3. Davenant to Eugene, 23 Oct. 1733, 9 July 1734, 28 June, 16 Sept. 1735, Gr. Kor., 75b, SA.

4. John (Lord) Henry, *Memoires of the Reign of George the Second*, 2 vols. (London, 1848), 2 : 7.

5. Mem. & Doc., Pologne, vol. 18, AAE. "Sur la négociation liée en 1734 entre le Cardinal de Fleury premier ministre de France et les principeaux ministres des puissances maritimes, dans la vue de terminer la guerre allumée dan l'Europe à l'occasion de la double élection à la cou-

ronne de Pologne," pp. 37–38. Although emphasizing the security of their man-to-man negotiation, Fleury told Walpole that he would not write in his own hand, which was very bad, but assured him that Du Parc, his secretary, was "un homme sûr."

6. Ibid., pp. 40–53.

7. Ibid., pp. 53–59.

8. Mem. & Doc., Hollande, vol. 140, p. 26, AAE.

9. Ibid., p. 30.

10. Ibid., pp. 32–48.

11. Mem. & Doc., Pologne, vol. 18, pp. 60–92, AAE.

12. Ibid., p. 93.

13. Ibid., pp. 94–106.

14. Ibid., pp. 108–13.

15. Ibid., p. 116. The Medici grand duke of Tuscany was without issue.

16. Ibid., p. 150.

17. Waldegrave to Newcastle, 12 Jan. 1735, State Papers, France, 78 207, PRO.

18. Mem. & Doc., Pologne, vol. 18, pp. 156–70, AAE.

19. Ibid., pp. 171–90.

20. King to Waldegrave, 28 Feb. 1735; State Papers, France, 78 207, PRO.

21. Arthur M. Wilson, *French Foreign Policy during the Administration of Cardinal Fleury, 1726–1743* (Cambridge, Mass., 1936), p. 99.

22. Walpole to Newcastle, 2 Apr. 1735, State Papers, France, 78 207, PRO. Walpole went over the whole ground of their negotiations in long private session with the cardinal. He reported: "On the whole, my Lord, I do not flatter myself with the hope of being able to prevail with the cardinal to sign the act I have projected . . . but I do not despair absolutely of being able to obtain some declaration under his hand about procuring an armistice." Eleven articles are given in the British correspondence. The problem of Lorraine is not treated. Walpole on 4 April described the cardinal as "weak and irresolute and so much influenced by the last conversation and insinuations he hears, whether true or false, and has constantly at his elbow one of such dangerous views and principles, and who is so useful and necessary to him in the multiplicity of business with which His Eminence is loaded at his age that it is impossible for me to promise myself certain success in anything," in a letter to Slingelandt, ibid.

23. Arneth, *Prinz Eugen*, 3:457–58.

24. Quoted in ibid., p. 606. Eugene had been advised of the plan

being prepared by Robinson and he had brought it up with the emperor, reporting back to Robinson that the emperor thought the plan would be an acceptable basis for negotiations. (See Braubach, *Prinz Eugen,* 5 : 99) The English had the impression as late as 6 May that the emperor would accept the plan. Newcastle to Waldegrave, 6 May 1735, State Papers, France, 78 207, PRO.

25. Arneth, *Prinz Eugen,* 3 : 457–58.

26. Waldegrave to Harrington, 7 June 1735, State Papers, France, 78 207, PRO.

27. Emperor to Eugene, 28 May 1735, Gr. Kor., 91b, SA.

28. Max Braubach, *Versailles und Wien von Ludwig XIV bis Kaunitz: Die Vorstadien der diplomatischen Revolution im 18. Jahrhundert* (Bonn, 1952), p. 204.

29. Ibid., pp. 211–38. Using the archives of the state of Neuwied, along with the French and Austrian archives, Braubach worked out the details of this extraordinary story.

30. Mem. & Doc., Autriche, vol. 181, July 1735, AAE. Instructions for the as yet unnamed envoy.

31. Harrach to Harrach, 16 July, 1735, Gr. Kor., 91b, SA.

32. Harrach forwarded the cardinal's letter, along with a letter from Count Marek and another from Gonzaga, the papal nuncio in Flanders, and a letter of his own addressed to the emperor. All this he sent directly to his father on 2 September. Ibid.

33. Ibid. What appears to be the original of the cardinal's letter with Fleury's very modest unadorned signature "Le Card. de Fleury," is in the Vienna files. Braubach doubts Fleury's ignorance of Count Marek's approach since Marek had earlier been involved in intimate dealings for both Chauvelin and Fleury. Braubach, *Versailles und Wien,* p. 209.

34. Robinson to Harrington, 5 Aug. 1735, State Papers, Austria, 80 117, PRO.

35. La Baune to Fleury, 16 Aug. 1735, Mem. & Doc., Autriche, vol. 181, AAE.

36. Mem. & Doc., Hollande, vol. 140, pp. 23–27, AAE. La Baune found the "hauteur" of the Viennese court, and in particular that of Count Sinzendorff, most extraordinary. Sinzendorff could not permit himself to be flexible on the slightest matter. Bartenstein would make a necessary concession when Sinzendorff was out of the room and Sinzendorff would never afterward allude to the point.

37. Ibid., p. 3. See also Römisches Reich, Friedenshandlung 1735, Italien, fasc. 382, doc. 2, KA, a copy of the agreement of the duke of Lorraine to the preliminaries in which he agrees to surrender Lorraine

and Bar for Tuscany and be indemnified for the revenues of the latter until he takes possession at the death of the last Medici grand duke.

38. The details of the negotiations are outlined in Braubach, *Versailles und Wien*, pp. 238–60.

39. Harrington in Hanover to Robinson, 9 Sept. 1735, State Papers, Austria, 80 118, PRO; Robinson to Harrington, 21, 24, 28 Sept. 1735, ibid.

40. The text of the preliminaries is doc. 3 in Römisches Reich, Friedenshandlung, 1735, Italien, fasc. 382, KA.

41. Chauvelin to La Baune, 10 Sept. 1735, Mem. & Doc., vol. 181, AAE.

42. Römisches Reich, Friedenshandlung, 1735, Italien, fasc. 382, doc. 10, KA. "Die Abtrennung des Herzogtums Lothringen." Driault ("Chauvelin, 1733–1737") lays the difficulty at the door of the cardinal who, he says, then turned the problem over to Chauvelin to find a solution. Wilson (*French Foreign Policy*, p. 263) calls La Baune an "indifferent negotiator."

43. Lord Henry, *Memoirs*, 2 : 3. Henry states that the cession of Lorraine, agreed to by England and Holland, could not be put in the original draft since the duke of Lorraine was not a participant in the war.

✝

# BIBLIOGRAPHICAL NOTE

The most complete published account of military activity in the War of the Polish Succession is in the *Feldzüge des Prinzen Eugen von Savoyen,* 21 vols. (Vienna, 1876), referred to in this work as *FE*. A product of the historical section of the general staff of the Austro-Hungarian monarchy, it gives considerable detail on military dispositions and strengths, particularly of the Austrian forces. The information is principally from the Kriegsarchiv in Vienna. Many of the messages of Prince Eugene, which for this period exist in documentary form only as virtually illegible drafts, are reproduced in print in a supplement to each volume. The work of Alfred Arneth, *Prinz Eugen von Savoyen,* 3 vols. (Vienna, 1858), is based ostensibly on a complete freedom to search through the Habsburg archives and describes mainly the diplomatic and higher-level governmental aspects of the war touching the Austrian side. The more recent biography of Eugene, *Prinz Eugen von Savoyen,* 5 vols. (Munich, 1963–65), by Max Braubach, also covers mainly the diplomatic side of the war and the relations among the leaders in the imperial ruling group. It is more critical than the Arneth work and is based on the Staatsarchiv. *Les Guerres sous Louis XV,* 7 vols. (Paris, 1881), by C. P. V. Pajol, is based principally on the Archives du Ministère de la Guerre and reproduces many important messages. It is mainly concerned with military strategy, army strengths and dispositions, and battle outcomes for this and later French wars. The work of Pierre Boyé, *Stanislas Leszczynski et la troisième traité de Vienne* (Paris, 1898), describes a large segment of the diplomatic activity during the war period and represents a very wide search for French documentation throughout France and even in some archives in Poland. V. Gere's *Borba za Polskii Prestol v 1733 godu* (Moscow, 1862) is not an annotated work and is concerned only with events leading up to the election of Stanislas. But a number of Russian diplomatic messages are printed here in an annex. Two of the finest works covering the period are studies of the foreign policy of Fleury; Arthur M. Wilson's *French Foreign Policy during the Administration of Cardinal Fleury, 1726–1743* (Cambridge, Mass., 1936), and Paul Vaucher's *Robert Walpole et la Politique de Fleury* (Paris, 1924).

# INDEX

Anna, tsarina of Russia, 13, 40, 46, 48, 57
Argenson, René-Louis de Voyer, marquis d', 13, 15, 16
Asfeld, Claude-François Bidal, marquis d', 73, 90
Atrocities, 154–56
Augustus II, elector of Saxony and king of Poland, 3, 5, 6, 10, 15, 27, 30, 43, 113
Augustus III, elector of Saxony and king of Poland: requests assistance of emperor, 33–34; election, 132–33
Austria: chronic lack of funds, 5, 50–51; decision to oppose Stanislas, 29–31; lack of support from German princes, 41, 85; inadequacy of Rhine defenses, 69–72; misplacement of forces, 80–81; efforts to mobilize forces, 85–86; collapse of positions in Italy, 100–103; defeat on the Rhine, 146–50; attack on French at Parma and Guastalla, 168–69, 172–73; emperor insists on continuing war in 1735, 176–78; negotiation of preliminaries, 203–9
Austrian Netherlands, 11; barrier fortresses, 39–40, 66, 67, 204
Austria-Saxony treaty of 1733, 36–38, 41

Balance of power, 3–4, 26
Bartenstein, Johann Christoph von, 29–33, 52, 55, 102, 103, 207
Bavaria, Maximilien-Emmanuel-François-Joseph, count of, 78, 153
Bavaria, 41; Eugene fears attack by, 82, 181; French treaty, 84

Belle Isle, Charles-Louis-Auguste Fouquet, 66, 68; strategic proposals, 73–74, 79, 112; enters Trier, 139; siege of Trarbach, 140–41, 185
Berwick, James Fitzjames, 15, 18, 61, 66–68, 72–75, 87; relations with Belle Isle, 139–42; attacks across Rhine, 144; approves siege of Philippsburg, 150; siege and death, 152–54
Biron, Ernst Johann, 46, 47, 50, 58
Braunschweig-Bevern, Ferdinand Albrecht, duke of, 80–84
Breisach, fortified city, 19, 64, 65, 69
Broglie, François-Marie, 90, 100, 169, 173
Bussy, François de, 28, 34, 40, 41, 49, 50

Chambord, chateau of, 1, 2, 53
Charles VI, emperor of Holy Roman Empire, 5, 11, 14, 28–33, 36, 40, 41, 176–78, 202–9
Charles XII, king of Sweden, 11, 112
Charles Emmanuel, king of Sardinia, 65, 81, 99, 163
Chauvelin, Germain-Louis de, 2, 3; character of, 14–15; negotiations with England, 17–18, 23, 52, 53, 58, 64, 68, 72; guidance to ambassador in Copenhagen, 119–20, 121, 201; hated by English, 202
Chavigny, Théodore Chévignard de, 16, 18, 36, 52
Coigny, François: quarrels with king of Sardinia, 166–67; at battle of Parma, 168–69; at battle of Guastalla, 173; in command on